LANDSCAPES
OF THE NIGHT

LANDSCAPES
OF THE NIGHT

CHRISTOPHER EVANS

WASHINGTON SQUARE PRESS
PUBLISHED BY POCKET BOOKS NEW YORK

A Washington Square Press Publication of
POCKET BOOKS, a division of Simon & Schuster, Inc.
1230 Avenue of the Americas, New York, N.Y. 10020

Published by arrangement with Viking Penguin, Inc.
Library of Congress Catalog Card Number: 83-40476

ISBN: 0-671-55190-6

First Washington Square Press printing September, 1985

10 9 8 7 6 5 4 3 2 1

WASHINGTON SQUARE PRESS, WSP and colophon are
registered trademarks of Simon & Schuster, Inc.

Printed in the U.S.A.

CONTENTS

LANDSCAPES OF THE NIGHT

Prologue

ENCOUNTER ON THE BEACH

IN THE AUTUMN of 1963 Britain enjoyed an unusually pleasant Indian summer. Mild, misty mornings gave way to balmy, cloudless days and for some weeks the high-pressure system which was generating all this held its own against the procession of Atlantic lows which normally dominate British weather. From my point of view the timing could hardly have been better; I had just reached a state of terminal struggle with my Ph.D thesis, and while there still remained the formidable task of writing up the material, the basic research was over and done. At the same time I had just accepted a job as a junior research scientist at the National Physical Laboratory in Teddington, and was therefore about to make the momentous break from student life and enter the rough-and-tumble world of practical science. In comparison with the minuscule research grant I had been surviving on for the past three years, the monthly pay cheque I could anticipate looked like a small fortune. My wife, whose job as a research pharmacologist was still contributing the bulk of our income, had some vacation in hand, and to mark my own expected shift from economic parasite to potential breadwinner we decided to embark on a motoring holiday in Wales.

Our plans were simple: we drove through the day, exploring deserted beauty spots with the aid of ordnance survey maps, and when we found one to our liking, preferably within a walk or short drive of a pub, we established camp. On our very first afternoon we found what we wanted. At the end of a bumpy, degenerating farm track lay a long beach of sand and boulders, cliffs and coves and rocky promontories, lapped by the waters of Cardigan Bay. It was a spot of glorious solitude, a perfect transitional zone between one phase of life and another. Our first night, spent sleeping in the car, was extremely uncomfortable, but ambling around on the deserted beach the next morning, as the sun rose over the coastal hills, I felt clouds evaporating rapidly from my mind. By mid-morning it was unusually warm and, leaving my wife dozing on a comfortable rock, I set out to explore the less immediate surroundings. The tide was going out and slowly revealing a flat promontory of rocks which stretched far out to sea. Though weedy and uneven the rocks lured me on, and before long I found myself some hundred yards away from the shore line with at least another hundred yards to go if I wished. The scene was one of almost total stillness. The sweep of Cardigan Bay continued to the south, and to the north, beyond a low line of hills, rose the peak of Snowdon. Apart from myself and the distant figure of my wife, immobile on her rock, the world seemed devoid of any evidence of man.

It was while I was wondering whether to push on or return that my eye caught sight of something standing on one of the most seaward rocks. For a brief period of time I had the eerie sensation that another human being was standing out there and had been silently watching my progress, but after a moment's hiatus for adjustment, my brain accepted that the scale was wrong and that the figure must be much smaller than any man or woman. Nevertheless there was something unmistakably biological about its outline which, despite its total lack of motion, singled it out from any outgrowth of rock or piece of driftwood. Picking my way carefully across wide pools and weedy surfaces, I made my way towards it. As I drew closer, the silhouette, which had initially seemed to be very like that of a cowled human figure, began to generate fine detail, and by the time I had got within twenty feet of it I could see that it was a large black bird of some kind. Even at this distance it seemed quite oblivious of my presence and, as I got closer, it became obvious why. The bird was fast asleep, and its peculiar posture—standing stiffly on one leg with its head tucked beneath a wing—explained why at a distance it looked vaguely human. It was clear that here was a rare opportunity to observe at close quarters a largish bird asleep in the wild, and I determined to get as near as I could without disturbing it.

The bird (which I am now fairly certain was a cormorant) was perched rather precariously on its single leg (the other being tucked away somewhere), and I noticed with great interest that from time to time it swayed as though about to overbalance, only to correct its posture apparently automatically. It was breathing regularly and fairly slowly and remained totally unaware of me even as I seated myself on the rock beside it. I was now so close that I could hear its breath and could examine its black, rather small feathers and claw-like foot. It would have been the easiest thing in the world for me to grasp it, capture it and, if I had wanted to, kill it. I even briefly wondered whether it would make any kind of acceptable meal, but in the end I contented myself with staring. After a while, not being able to think of anything better to do, I reached over, touched it on the shoulder and said "Hallo." Until that moment, I had never seen a bird, or for that matter any animal, look surprised. Perhaps "surprised" is too mild a word to describe the cormorant's rapidly changing set of postures and facial expressions, amazingly reminiscent of the exaggerated facial expressions of a *Tom and Jerry* cartoon. Feet splayed apart, feathers eccentrically ruffled, neck stretched out to its fullest, beak wide open and eyes round and wide, the bird was catapulted out of its sleep state into an awareness of its monstrously dangerous position. Its eyes met mine and for a brief moment we gazed at each other. Then with a hopping shuffle and wildly flapping wings it took off out to sea.

I set off back to the beach, eager to tell my wife about the strange encounter. I walked across towards the boulder where she was soaking up the uncharacteristically generous October sun: she was sound asleep, her arms hanging loosely at her sides, and supremely indifferent to my presence. The parallel with the earlier encounter on the rocks was impossible to avoid, but it presented itself to me in a somewhat oblique form. "How odd," I thought to myself, "that within such a short space of time I should have come across two sleeping creatures and have been able to get close enough to touch them before they became aware of my presence!" When I later spoke to my wife about the cormorant she merely remarked that she could not recall having ever seen a wild bird asleep before and we left it at that. But another signal rocket was coming my way.

On our third and final night at this camp site, after beer and sandwiches at the local pub, we fell asleep in the car with glorious ease. What specific sound woke me is hard to say, but wake me it did. I swam up into consciousness rapidly, and, untangling my feet from the steering wheel, looked round in surprise. It was a dark, moonless night and as my eyes came into focus I saw, with a wild thump of the heart, that the car was surrounded by dark, slowly moving objects. I had barely time to entertain the possibility that we were about to be the victims of some assault when the realization dawned on me that the figures were cows. There seemed little point in shooing the creatures away and awakening my wife, so, with the passing thought that it was astonishing that one could find oneself surrounded by a herd of large animals in the night and remain asleep for most of the time, I gathered the pillows and blankets together and drifted off to sleep.

It was only the next morning, when we were bowling along a main road in search of the three-star hotel which would provide us with hot baths, giant meals and general revelry, that the three encounters came together in my mind to complete a very tiny jigsaw. A sleeping animal, it suddenly occurred to me, was a defenceless one, at the total mercy of its environment and its predators. In biological terms sleep was an immensely dangerous exercise—perhaps the most dangerous single thing an animal could do—and yet all animals indulged in it. What fundamental process could it possibly serve? This was the question that percolated through my mind as I drove on the deserted autumnal roads. And this book represents an attempt to answer it.

PART ONE

Traditional Theories of Sleep and Dreams

Chapter 1

LIFE ON A DANGEROUS PLANET

IMAGINE THAT AN alien is observing earth from a spaceship in geo-stationary orbit equipped with high-power telescopes capable of giving detailed close-ups of any point on the planetary surface. Try to imagine also that the alien is from another universe and is therefore totally un-acquainted with the principles of biological life on this planet, with no preconceptions about what living things are or how they should behave. Now, as the alien gazes down on the surface of the third planet from the sun, what does it see?

The first thing it notices is that the surface of the planet, including a bit of the subsoil, the oceans, and a thin mantle of atmosphere, is teem-ing with activity. This activity consists of immense numbers of different-shaped "living things" walking about all over the place eating each other. Further inspection reveals that one whole class of living things tends to consist of relatively immobile structures, incapable of chasing or run-ning away, and with no apparent objection to being eaten. Indeed most of them—their local name is plants—turn the fact of their being eaten to their advantage in one way or another and use it to ensure the widespread dissemination and propagation of their offspring. All the re-maining living things—animals—clearly resent being eaten and make strenuous, sometimes frenzied, efforts to avoid this fate, though few are able to do so in the long run. By now the alien will have decided that the surface of this planet is hideously dangerous and will have deter-mined to complete its inspection from the safety of its orbiting spacecraft. Returning to its examination, however, it detects certain fundamental similarities in shape between many of the animals, which make it suspect that they have common origins. After a while it guesses that they have all been changing their shape and characteristics subtly over an immense period of time, and they possibly all spring from a common, structurally very simple creature in the remote past. There now come the critical questions as to how and *why* this endless process of change has been occurring.

The first question turns out to be relatively easy to answer. The beings, not having eternal life, begin reproducing themselves as soon as they can in their life cycle, this reproduction being effected by a process in which miniature copies of the parent organism are constructed within it using a kind of blueprint known to the more intelligent inhabitants of the planet as the "genetic code." These miniatures grow rapidly to their maximum size and set about reproducing themselves, after which, sooner or later, they die. This process might be expected to continue *ad infinitum* were it not for an interesting quirk of nature. The planet is under constant bombardment from a stream of high-energy particles emanating from its sun and other regions of space, and when they strike (as they frequently do) the various beings' genetic blueprints, these are often damaged or altered in some way. This leads to interference with the copying process with the result that inexact miniatures of the creatures are made. The vast majority of these imprecise copies seem not to survive to copy themselves again, but very, very rarely one of them *will* do so, and a minor variant of the original creature will start roaming around and generating identical versions of itself.

At this point the alien has discovered the mechanism by which biological creatures on this bizarre planet have assumed their wide variety of different forms. But it is still unable to answer the subsidiary question as to why some of the altered copies survive, while others—the great majority—die out in the first generation. In due course it realizes that a rare minority of the mutations have, by chance, some feature which makes them better able to compete with other creatures in the constant quest for food and other essentials and will thus tend to survive and reproduce their own variations, while the majority of mutations come with a disadvantage of some kind and therefore tend to be eliminated.

Now the whole pattern becomes clear. The variations in the biological systems are all to do with successful competitions in a terrifying planetary game of life and death, where danger is omnipresent and only the most vigorous, adaptable and ruthless survive. An inspection of the physical make-up of most of the animals, particularly the more elaborately constructed ones, makes this doubly clear. Most of the creatures, for example, come equipped with elaborate sensing mechanisms capable of detecting potential danger or prey at some distance from themselves. There are fantastically efficient light detectors, sound and vibration sensors, chemical sensors and the like, all geared to perceiving other creatures long before they come into close physical proximity. Some of the creatures—those predominantly concerned with catching and eating other animals—have terrifyingly efficient destructive mechanisms in the form of claws and teeth, and in certain cases special-purpose weapons, like

the anteater's tongue or the kingfisher's beak, which allow them to concentrate with great efficiency on a single species of prey. Others—those
mainly concerned with eating plants, and which tend to be on the receiving end of the predators' attention—come with specialized equipment
to allow them to detect and escape from danger before it descends on
them: super-efficient hearing; magnificently responsive musculature;
aerodynamically-optimized body shapes. Others attempt to deter any ag-
gressor from attacking them by heavy armour, vast strength or such
special-purpose defences as the porcupine's quills and the skunk's odour.
And all these animals, whatever their place on the biological carousel,
come equipped with an elaborate brain and central nervous system to
integrate the vast array of information fed through their senses and make
the most rational and rapid use of it.

This terrible vista, with its bewildering array of life forms endlessly
chasing or escaping from each other, is what would present itself to the
alien through its telescope. But repelled though it might be at the
mindless cruelty of it all, it would have to admit that it all made a kind
of logically horrible sense. Given any planet where self-reproducing
animals exist in a suitably supportive biosphere, and where the
mechanisms of morphological change can be effected through genetic
mutations, this kind of deathly rough-and-tumble between millions of
competing life forms must *inevitably* arise.

Here would be the cue for the alien to hasten back to its own universe,
but the chances are that, before departing, it would have observed
something glaringly at odds with everything it had previously observed.
From time to time, often at noticeably regular intervals, almost all the
animals on this planet would engage in a most peculiar exercise: they
would relax their magnificent musculature, normally tuned to an incredible state of responsiveness; they would switch off their distance receptors, normally hunting endlessly for signs of other animals; they would
settle themselves in one place—admittedly one of maximum security
—and, most incredible of all, they would damp down their biological
computers and descend into a state of torpor and quiescence. The sum
total of millions of years of competitive evolution on a fearsome planet,
the numerous survival aids so painfully acquired over such immense
stretches of time, the vast heritage of a million successful mutations and
a quintillion unsuccessful ones would all be cast to the winds. Faced
with this bizarre paradox, the alien would be forced to the only possible
conclusion: dangerous though the surface of the planet might be, and
important though it was that the animals inhabiting it should protect

themselves from each other, one motive force—the need for sleep—was sufficiently strong to cause all these risks to be ignored. Thus, whatever function sleep served must be of enormous importance, possibly the most important single function of an animal's life.

I have spelled all this out rather deliberately because before one can begin to appreciate the very real nature of the mystery of sleep (and its attendant phenomena such as dreams) one has to get at least a glimmering of comprehension as to how extraordinary and apparently paradoxical the habit is. No unbiased observer could ever predict that anything so risky and dangerous would be seen where the rules of Darwinian-style natural selection applied. Where it did occur—as it does on earth—the only possible way of accepting its existence without assuming an essential illogicality in the universe would be to assign to it some function of transcending importance, comparable at least to the functions of eating, drinking and mating—the prime requirements for survival. But note that while eating, drinking and mating are behaviour patterns fraught with some risk—an animal preoccupied with one or other of these activities is to some degree at risk from predatory attack —they *can* be interrupted if danger threatens, and, perhaps more important, the animal's sensory mechanisms remain in operation at all times. But the behaviour patterns involved in sleep are glaringly, almost insanely, at odds with common sense.

First of all, what is sleep? Sleep can be defined as a state of inertia and loss of consciousness of a temporary nature and from which the sleeping being can be relatively easily aroused. While finer definitions are possible, this is one which is more or less internationally accepted by physiologists and psychologists. In particular, note the use of the word "temporary" to describe the unconsciousness, and the reference to the relative ease of arousal from the state. This clearly separates sleep from such other states as coma, anaesthetic or drug-induced unconsciousness, the stupor of hibernation and so on, which present the same external appearance to the observer but which reflect very different internal states. That there is something both supremely odd and supremely important about sleep has been obvious for the past few thousand years, and a number of attempts have been made, at best with only partial success, to explain the phenomenon. At first glance there seems to be a multitude of them, but on closer inspection they break down into essentially three groups, or types, of theory. In the following chapters I shall be looking at these to see how effectively they tackle the problem and what their main strengths and weaknesses are. The first class of theory is predominantly concerned with sleep *per se* and has relatively little to say about dreams. The second is predominantly concerned with dreams, while the third treats sleep and dreams with roughly equivalent emphasis. Without delving more deeply into them at the moment, it is just necessary to comment that all three approaches—in reality they are amalgams of virtually hundreds of mildly differing sub-theories—tend to concentrate on the function of sleep (or dreams), but fail to take into account the need for the creature to lapse into unconsciousness in order to perform the function. But as I hope I have made clear, this is an aspect of the problem which cannot be ignored, and any really satisfactory theory of sleep *must* include a convincing explanation of why its mechanisms, whatever they are, cannot reasonably be performed while the animal is awake and responsive to its environment. In Part Three of this book I shall be proposing a theory which, uniquely I believe, does tackle this problem.

There are some other features of sleep that cannot be ignored. A brief look is all that is necessary now, for we shall be picking up the points in detail in due course, but they will serve to set the stage for the main argument of this book.

1 *The widespread occurrence of the phenomenon in the animal kingdom.* All the higher animals need sleep (we will discuss more precisely what we mean by "higher animals" in due course) and some need very large amounts of it. Under this heading one can place the subsidiary problem as to why some animals need more sleep than others.

2 *The fact that sleep is not universally present in biological systems.* It might be easier to pull together a theory of sleep if it were something present in *all* living systems, like the need to ingest food or to reproduce. Then one could assume it was a property of life itself and steer one's thinking that way. But, disobligingly, things are not that simple. Sleep, in terms of the way we shall define it, is not present at all in the plant kingdom (an enormous component of the biological world), nor is it present in most of the simpler living organisms. Any sound theory, therefore, will have to take this differential into account.

3 *The catastrophic effects of sleep deprivation.* Just as catastrophic changes occur in any animal deprived of food or drink, so depriving an animal of sleep causes serious problems, ranging from disorientation and erratic

behaviour to death. No theory of sleep carries much conviction unless it can explain why loss of sleep produces these changes.

4 *The fact that sleep requirements alter with the age of the animal.* Allowing for inter-species differences, which are considerable and which also need to be explained, there are very striking divergences between the sleep needs of a young and an old animal. This is a consistent phenomenon within the animal kingdom which needs a sensible explanation.

5 *The fact that there appear to be at least two distinct types of sleep.* As we shall see later, the electrical activity of the cortex of the brain and various behavioural changes which occur in most, if not all, animals indicate that sleep is not a single, homogeneous phenomenon.

6 *The so-called "rebound phenomenon."* An animal selectively deprived of one particular type of sleep for several nights apparently attempts to make up the deficit by devoting a greater proportion of any recovery nights to this type of sleep.

7 *The psychological phenomenon of dreams.* A very striking concomitant of sleep in humans (and possibly in some animals) is the presence of structured thought patterns, some bizarre, others with a strong narrative form, known popularly as dreams. Add to this the fact that dreams appear to be commonly associated with the critical phase of sleep described under heading 6 above, and whose deprivation is followed by the rebound effect, and one is faced with yet another mystery which must be solved.

There are a great number of other minor puzzles about the sleep/dream processes which need to be solved, but the seven points listed cover the main territory. With the possible exception of the last (one *might* attempt to dismiss dreams themselves as being totally insignificant and therefore not worth having a theory about!) each point must be taken into account in formulating a comprehensive theory about sleep and dreams. A close examination of those theories that have been formulated suggests that they can all be grouped, with a bit of artistic and scientific latitude, under three main headings: the *physical*, the *psychical*, and the *psychological*.

Chapter 2

PHYSICAL THEORIES: THE BODY

THE DIVIDING line between the physical and the psychological is not an absolute one, and any theory of sleep and dreams must draw from both camps. It is not even all that easy to give an absolutely clear-cut definition of the word "physical," but for the purposes of this discussion I define a physical theory as one which views the phenomena in terms of basic physical, bodily mechanisms, and which explains the need for sleep in terms of some physiological need or requirement. Most "physical" theories of sleep are very similar in their main themes. The first explicit one I can trace was put forward by Aristotle who, two-and-a-quarter millennia ago, attempted to develop a nutritional/digestive model based on the vague contemporary knowledge of the physiology of digestion. He assumed that after eating and drinking, a certain amount of "internal evaporation" took place (this evaporation representing the difference between the quantity of food eaten and that ultimately excreted). Because evaporated substances, being warm, were carried upwards, they would end up in the top part of the body—the head or the brain. "This explains," he remarked, "why fits of drowsiness are especially apt to come on after meals; for the matter, both the liquid and the corporeal, which is born upwards in a mass, is then of considerable quantity." This produces a literal heavy-headedness and tendency to nod off to sleep. Fatigue, as opposed to eating, had the same effect because hard work acts like a solvent, breaking down body tissues, causing them to evaporate and move upwards to the head. Aristotle even had a stab at explaining a child's need for extra sleep in the same terms—hyperactivity led to vast quantities of "evaporated matter" moving up to the head, and this also explained the fact that a child's head is disproportionately large in relation to the lower parts of its body.

Over the gulf of 2300 years, Aristotle's ideas, while naive, impress one because of their logical consistency and their attempt to provide a sensible (within the limitations of contemporary knowledge) explanation of sleep which also fitted certain common observations, such as the tendency to become drowsy after a big meal. His theories do not add up to much today, but here nevertheless is an excellent example of a simple physical model: Sleep is caused by a concentration of evaporated matter in the head or brain which in turn is produced by either (a) eating and drinking or (b) physical exercise leading to fatigue. After a period the evaporated substances cool and descend to lower parts of the body, making the head lighter again, and the human or animal wakes up. In this sense sleep is restorative in some way, a period when an imbalance of some kind in the body is "put right" so that the organism can resume its normal state.

The vast majority of modern physical theories in fact follow similar lines, though taking into account, of course, the enormous advances in our understanding of anatomy, physiology, and brain function which have occurred since Aristotle's day. Essentially they all suggest that sleep has a restorative function of some kind, and that its cyclical nature reflects the body's need to have regular periods of "time off" to recover some lost function. Superficially the notion that sleep is a period of inactivity which allows us to "rest" is a magnetically tempting one. It seems to fit so closely with the observed behavioural evidence and with one's own powerful subjective impressions that it makes one wonder how any other explanation could be contemplated. All these animals and humans rush around throughout the day, and what is more reasonable than that they should sooner or later need to come to a stop, cease activity of every kind, and restore their depleted reserves of energy? And what is more reasonable than that the night hours, when normal activity is hampered by lack of light, should be the period chosen for regular recuperation?

Put that way, the theory seems almost inarguable. It is bolstered by one's own feelings and experiences: one runs around for most of the day, generally feeling fine, but after twelve hours or so, one begins to feel less well able to cope, less motivated to tackle new tasks. Later this matures into a very definite disinclination to do anything at all, which in turn is followed by a definite, but not unpleasant, desire to lose consciousness, which sooner or later becomes quite overwhelming. In the end one *does* lose consciousness, for several hours, after which one "wakes up" with the feeling of "fatigue" gone away and all set to launch into another extended session of activity. How unreasonable it would seem to be to ignore the chain of events Activity/Fatigue/Sleep/Loss of Fatigue/Activity etc. and not to assume that the sleep period had something to do with the elimination of the fatigue.

Perhaps a slight quibble might be made by debating what is meant by fatigue. Why should one not be able to go on in a state of activity indefinitely without having to come to an inconvenient stop from time to time? If one exercises a muscle vigorously for a period—say, repeatedly flexing one's arm—a feeling of strain followed by something approaching pain builds up which ultimately forces one to stop. There is a perfectly straightforward physiological explanation for this: skeletal muscles—those involved in arm and leg movements—need energy to power them and this is largely provided by the breakdown of a substance known as adenosine triphosphate (ATP). ATP is pretty readily available to the muscles and in the healthy person there is enough to allow more or less continuous muscle activity. Unfortunately, in the breakdown of ATP a waste product is formed, a lactate which is pulled out of the muscle and sent to the liver where it is converted into glucose, thus providing a fresh supply of energy. Now, the removal of the lactate from the muscle is a much slower business than its build-up, and after a while its accumulation reduces efficiency and causes cramp. This and various similar consequences of unremitting exercise have been understood for many years now, and provide an adequate explanation of why periodic rest periods are needed by any animals equipped with a skeletal muscle system—which also happens to mean the great majority of those who need sleep. So why does that not close the issue? Sleep is a period of enforced inactivity when active animals allow their bodies to eliminate dangerous waste products (lactates need not be the only ones). The theory has the incomparable merit of being simple. There is a rule of science known as Occam's Razor, after its author the medieval philosopher Bishop William of Occam, which says that given a choice of rival theories one should always pick the *simplest one which is in accord with all the facts*. But the qualifying phrase is an important one, and the trouble with the rest/fatigue theory of sleep is that, however simple, it is not in accord with all the facts.

In the first place, lactate reduction and the subsequent regeneration of muscle power can be achieved simply by ceasing muscular activity for a few minutes, and there is no necessity to sleep in order for the restorative process to get under way. Even when a whole host of muscles in different parts of the body are used, and for quite a long period, the same rule applies. After a vigorous game of tennis you flop down in a deckchair with a cold, sugary drink, and after a few minutes feel fit for another game. What you do not do is find a bed and lapse into unconsciousness. In the second place there are muscles in the body which can pound away more or less indefinitely without the need for "rest" —the heart muscles are a classic example, as are those which control respiration. These operate at a rhythmic pace, rarely speeding up for more than very brief periods and waste products within them are eliminated more quickly than they are built up. But the main point is that there is a considerable component of the body's muscular system which does not need cyclic periods of "rest." Thirdly, the sleeping person is simply not a totally immobile being undergoing a period of enforced inactivity. The best evidence for this comes from studies of sleeping people using time-lapse photography. A few years ago, I conducted a series of experiments on the effects of different kinds of drinks (water, beer, warm milk, Horlicks, etc.) taken before going to bed. What I was interested in was how sleep was affected by the various drinks, and in particular whether any of them promoted "sounder sleep"—whatever that might be. In the end I decided to measure the total amount of body movement occurring in the night, assuming (arguably) that the more movement there was, the more "restless" the sleeper would have been, and the "poorer" the night's sleep accordingly. There are various ways, most of them highly restrictive to the sleeper, by which one can measure body movement, but the time-lapse camera does it most painlessly. The subjects slept in a dimly lit room kept at a warmish temperature to allow them to do without bedcovers. Over the bed a discreetly muffled camera took one photograph every fifteen seconds or so throughout the night, and therefore "sampled" the body position at regular intervals. The developed film was run through at regular movie speed and one saw a compressed version of the night's activity which one could infer was reasonably representative. The total number of body movements made by the sleeper (or more precisely the total number of movements being made while the camera was in action) could be counted, and these compared with some other subject or some other experimental condition.

Watching these time-lapse movies run through at normal speed and seeing the whole of a night's sleep compressed, as it were, into a couple of minutes' viewing, is a strange experience. The hands on the wall clock whizz round, but most impressive of all is the frenetic tossing, turning and general leaping about which even the most subdued sleeper displays. There are brief periods of quiescence, rarely more than four or five minutes in length, after which there will be a burst of rolling over, arm and leg thrashing, followed again by a period of quiet. This continues throughout the night, the least activity (and even that is fairly intensive) occurring in the small hours, until a storm of activity heralds the morning awakening. Nor is this simply a function of the unsettling conditions of the laboratory environment; the restless behaviour continues, essentially unchanged, even after several nights have been spent in the laboratory, by which time the subjects could be expected to have grown used to their surroundings. Similar time-lapse studies performed on people in their own homes reveal the same pattern of behaviour.

What are all these movements about? Quite a number of them turn out to be associated with dreams of various kinds, but most appear to be postural shifts, accompanied by muscle stretching, which come into action automatically after a period of relative immobility. The body is basically a dynamic system, thriving on movement, abhorring total inactivity. Regular readjustments of posture are necessary both to prevent muscles and joints from "seizing up," and to allow the free circulation of blood in limbs. All this contradicts the naive assumption that sleep is a process of enforced *in*activity to allow muscles to recuperate, and clearly demands an alternative explanation.

That the "sleep-is-to-rest" hypothesis—surely one of the most widely held of all views, and certainly the one which appeals to common sense—is not really supported by the facts is depressing for those who like the simplest possible explanation for things. But the idea is so tempting that many people have insisted that it really *must* be true, and while accepting the inadequacy of the muscle-recovery argument, have proposed that there must be some general fatigue product which builds up in the body throughout the day, and which is somehow eliminated from the system during "restful" sleep. In an effort to make it sound convincing they even invented a name for this substance—hypnotoxin (meaning "sleep poison")—and a fair bit of research has gone into trying to identify it in the bloodstream. Unfortunately, nothing remotely comparable to a hypnotoxin has ever been found, and the majority of scientists working in this area now feel that it is most unlikely to exist. But there are even more cogent arguments against the hypnotoxin theories. For example, at the most mundane level they fail to take into account the considerable variability that is present in the time we go to sleep. If we were being switched on and off by a trigger which itself was activated when a certain level of "ingredient X" was present in the blood, we would tend to fall asleep, whether we liked it or not, as soon as that trigger was pressed. Equally we would not wake up until the reverse trigger, so to speak, had been operated. In fact, with only minimal effort we can manage to stay awake until it is convenient for us to go to sleep, even for very trivial reasons like wanting to read a book or watch a late-night TV programme. But there are also somewhat less homely reasons why the "ingredient X" hypothesis will not do.

Once in a while a human or an animal will be born in a mutated state where two heads share a single body. These parabiotic "monsters," as they are known in the medical literature, are extremely rare these days thanks to effective early-warning tests which allow gross mutations to be detected at a very early stage of pregnancy. However, they do reach full term from time to time even today, and occasionally result in a healthy, though malformed, infant. Siamese twins fall into roughly the same category. Now, a feature of these unfortunate infants—particularly the two-headed variety—is that they have a single circulatory system. The body is common to both heads, and so is the blood supply. One of the first systematic observations of a two-headed infant, made by Geoffrey Saint-Hilaire in 1836, showed that the heads appeared to lead relatively independent lives, and that it was quite common for one to be awake and active while the other slept. Saint-Hilaire even noticed on a number of occasions that while one head was feeding vigorously, the other would be fast asleep. Similar observations were made of the famous Siamese twins exhibited by Barnum and Bailey's circus at the turn of the century and it was obvious that, though sharing a common blood supply, the twins could have widely independent sleep/wakefulness cycles. To clinch the matter, experiments have been performed in Russian laboratories in recent years, where the heads of puppies have been transplanted on to the necks of adult dogs. Some of the creatures would survive for as long as a month, and in all cases independent sleep behaviour was noticed. The transplanted head would often react "briskly to its surroundings, show an intelligent expression and eagerly lap up milk and water." Tempting though the notion of a hypnotoxin circulating in the blood might be, the evidence, including that provided by two-headed creatures, virtually rules it out.

Before closing the topic altogether, however, some findings which originally stemmed from work conducted over seventy years ago need to be mentioned. Two French physiologists, Legendre and Pieron, deprived dogs of sleep for ten days by making them trot endlessly in a treadmill, after which they extracted from the wretched creatures' brains some cerebro-spinal fluid (CSF), a nutrient and protective liquid in which the brain and spinal cord are bathed. They then injected this fluid into normal waking dogs, which promptly became drowsy or fell asleep. CSF from *non*-sleepy dogs similarly injected produced no soporific results. Legendre and Pieron took this as being striking evidence of the "hypnotoxin" idea to which they were very partial, and one has to agree that it seems a reasonable interpretation of the experimental findings. Something was evidently present in the CSF of the desperately sleepy dogs which could induce sleep in the normal group, so why should it not be the mystery fatigue factor? For various reasons most physiologists remained sceptical of the Legendre/Pieron findings, mainly because other workers did not find it at all easy to repeat the experiment. More recently, in the 1970s a team in Basle, Switzerland, led by H. Monnier isolated a protein made up of nine amino acids present in the blood of sleeping animals which, when injected into waking animals of the same species, promptly sent them off to sleep. At about the same time the Harvard physiologist John Pappenheimer isolated a peptide from the cerebro-spinal fluid of sleeping animals which again has a hypnotic effect when transferred into another waking brain. Although this seems to establish the very clear biochemical presence of some sleep factor, there is no evidence to suggest that this is hypnotizing in the sense that the early investigators accepted. All the signs are that the biochemical substances, whether they are proteins, peptides or whatever, are part of the communication system by which the brain commands or induces other parts of the central nervous system to change from the waking to the sleeping state.

Thus, however convenient and "obvious" the "sleep-is-to-rest" theory might be, it does not accord with the facts and we are forced to consider some alternative view, even if it ends up being more complex and less in accord with common sense. But before discarding it altogether, let us consider an alternative, possibly less naive, variant which puts the emphasis not on resting the body, but on resting the brain.

Chapter 3

THE RESTING BRAIN?

LOOKING AT SLEEP from this direction one suddenly gets a totally new perspective. The brain is the most complex and, in one sense, the most important single organ in the body, a compressed mass of billions of nerve cells, all capable of independent activity, and all beavering away hour after hour, assisting with the functions of vision, hearing, touch, speech, thinking, walking, calculating, picking up objects and so on. It is mind-boggling to contemplate the sum total of activity occurring in the brain at any one time in the day. Ought not this super-complex dynamo of sensation, thought and emotion crave a period of rest and general inactivity? We have already seen that individual muscles need brief static periods, so ought not the same rules to apply to the brain?

What would be the symptoms or the observed signs of a brain at rest? If a resting brain behaves like a resting muscle and shows a temporary loss of function, then the symptomatology would be fairly predictable. There would be little doubt, for example, that in addition to a general damping down of internal activity (however that might be measured), one would not expect consciousness and self-awareness to be present. Secondly, one would expect sensory input to be blocked or ignored. Thirdly, one would expect little, if any, information-processing to go on—information storage, learning and all kinds of thought processes would not occur. There would also be no awareness of the passage of time and, of course, a marked reduction in bodily mobility as the brain's psychomotor centres were inactive. This is not only a fair picture of what might be expected to be the manifestations of a resting brain, but it also offers a very compelling image of what can be observed in a sleeping animal. Once again the temptation to accept this view—that sleep is a state of quiescence in the central nervous system to allow it to recover from the day's exertions—is almost overwhelming, particularly as it offers again a "simple" theory which fits William of Occam's requirements so nicely. The most powerful feature of the argument is, of course, that it offers a convincing and down-to-earth explanation of the critical problem of unconsciousness which we highlighted earlier. Dangerous sleep might be, but if it were an *inevitable* concomitant of a resting brain, then one would expect to find it present throughout the animal kingdom despite the attendant risks to the sleeping creature. But having set up this promising argument, which seems so reasonable and so much in tune with the facts, it is now unfortunately necessary to demolish it. To understand why, we must dwell a little on an important technique used in the study of the brain known as electroencephalography.

Until the 1920s or thereabouts practically nothing was known about what kind of activity actually took place inside the living brain. It was known, through anatomical studies, that the organ as a whole was made up of a series of interlinked structures serving different (and not fully understood) functions. Broadly speaking these structures, such as the hypothalamus, the cerebellum and the reticular formation mounted close to the spinal cord, were believed to serve basic bodily functions such as the control of cardiac activity, respiration, and so on. The "higher structures" of the brain, on the other hand, known collectively as the cerebral cortex—the parts lying next to the inside of the cranium—were associated with sensory experience, with language, thought processes and the like. The picture was one of an "old" brain serving basic housekeeping and instinctive functions, which made up the core of the system, and a "new" brain wrapped around the latter, which tended to be present only in the evolutionary "higher animals."

Examined under a microscope, the brain is seen to be made up of a tangled mass of neurones, the specialized cells which carry electrical signals from point to point within the body and which serve as its primary communication channels. Once upon a time it was fashionable to liken them to telephone wires, and while that tends to liken the brain to a telephone exchange (a grossly oversimplified, and therefore misleading, model) the analogy is not totally inappropriate. The neurone or nerve cell is a remarkable device, found in enormous numbers in the body, though nowhere as commonly as in the brain. Basically it is a cell like any other cell in the body, but with two exceptions. Firstly, and most obviously, it is enormously elongated: the cell body has two thin appendages stretching out in opposite directions and which, in the case of certain motor neurones, can be up to a metre in length. Secondly, the neurones propagate electrical impulses along their stems. The propagation is not quite the same as a current running along a wire, but is more a shift in electrical potential along the membrane or cell surface. The electrical properties of neurones were first discovered in the nineteenth century when it was immediately realized that they were communication cells. It was also obvious, since the brain, and especially the cortex, was made up of enormous numbers of neurones, that the incomparably elaborate structure sealed up in the protective armour of the skull would have to be a seething mass of electrical activity. How nice it would be, neurophysiologists mused, if there was some way in which one could somehow study and analyse all this electrical activity within the living, active brain. It was not until the late 1920s that a way was found.

Credit for the discovery is almost always assigned to the German Ralph Berger, though parallel work was proceeding quite independently under the brilliant Englishman E.D. Adrian (later Lord Adrian) at Cambridge. Berger, deciding to put the infant science of electronics to work on the problem, glued electrodes to the scalp, hooking these up through a crude but effective amplifier and thence to a pen recorder which drew up the amplified signals on a moving chart of paper. The device, which in its present refined form is well known as the electroencephalograph, or EEG, was really only a gross kind of sounding board, for the recording electrodes were striving to detect electrical activity occurring on the other side of the thick bony wall of the cranium—which itself was coated with a carpet of hair follicles, sebaceous secretions, dandruff and suchlike. What Berger imagined he would detect through all this is a bit of a puzzle, but despite the Heath Robinson electronics of the time he found to his delight that relatively powerful electrical signals were being picked up by the device. Initially the signals were swamped by electronic noise of one kind or another, but Berger was able to cut back much of this by using finer electrodes and by a regime of cleaning the scalp and coating it with an electrolytic jelly. A minimum of two electrodes were needed at any one time, but if one wanted to record simultaneously from various parts of the brain as many as a dozen, even more, could be used.

The biggest surprise of all came in the pattern of signals emanating from the surface of the brain. This consisted of distinct rhythms, cyclic waves of extremely low voltage with a frequency varying from about one per second to about twenty per second. The waves, which made no particular sense in terms of contemporary knowledge of electrophysiology, nevertheless showed certain common features, and Berger soon realized that he had discovered something very much more than a random electrical phenomenon. In the meantime, Adrian in Cambridge had started a whole series of studies of his own, and was coming up with findings which supported and strengthened the other's pioneering study.

There were two salient findings. The first was that different rhythms occurred depending upon which part of the skull the electrodes were placed. The second was that these rhythms were to be found emanating from most people's brains, but not everybody's. From time to time, people would turn up with much feebler rhythms or with markedly different patterns of rhythms, and once in a very long while with hardly any rhythms at all. With the much finer methods now employed brain waves are detectable in everybody, and there are a few people who produce rhythms unlike anybody else's. These exceptions aside, it was obvious that Berger and Adrian had discovered some regular, possibly highly significant, features of the electrophysiology of the brain. But the big questions remained: What did it all mean? And what did the different rhythms signify?

In the first place there was no question of the waves representing the activity of any *single* neurone or nerve cell. The frequency of firing was quite unlike single-cell activity, and in any case the electrodes were so huge in relation to individual neurones that the minimum number of cells they could be sampling would have to be numbered in the thousands, perhaps tens of thousands. The only reasonable explanation seemed to be that entire segments of the brain were populated by neurones which for some reason were synchronized, all switching on and off together in some mysterious cerebral harmony. Presumably that, in turn, reflected some kind of co-ordinated driving activity, perhaps coming from deeper in the brain—but beyond this speculation it was not really possible to go. Then came a finding which sent a jolt of excitement and anticipation through the world of brain physiology.

In an effort to establish whether the brain waves, as they became popularly known, were in some way related to the operation of the senses, Adrian fastened electrodes to the occipital region of the scalp—the bulges on each side at the back of the head, roughly above the shoulder blades. At first he detected only an irregular, rather flattened rhythm, but when he asked his subjects to close their eyes a powerful rhythm, cycling about ten or fourteen times per second, emerged. This, the first electro-cortical signal to show dependence on outside influence, he called the alpha rhythm.

The first and natural assumption was this had something to do with the receipt of visual information by the brain—the occipital regions being the areas where visual signals are processed—but it was soon discovered that the alpha rhythm could also be picked up from other "non-visual" areas of the cortex. Later still, it was discovered that it was not really the presence or absence of visual input but rather whether the subject was "concentrating" or "attending" to something that produced the effect. When concentrating on some mental process such as doing mental arithmetic, the alpha rhythm would disappear, but when the subject relaxed and let his or her mind go blank, the rhythm would surge back in its full glory. The implication seemed inescapable. Adrian had discovered an electrophysiological index of whether a person was "attending" or "concentrating" or perhaps, to be more precise, when he was studiously *not* attending but just sitting back and relaxing. The jubilation in the world of brain physiology is very evident if one thumbs through the scientific journals of the period, for hardly had this new technique been developed than it had already yielded information on some fundamental aspect of the brain's electrical activity. No doubt other even more important and significant rhythms would quickly turn up.

Other rhythms did indeed turn up, but none was ever found with the beautiful symmetry and reliability of the alpha rhythm—nor, for that matter, any which could so obviously be linked to some easily describable internal psychological state. Ironically, when Lord Adrian died a few years ago after a distinguished and productive career in brain physiology, not much more was known about the alpha rhythm than he and his colleagues had turned up with their primitive apparatus forty years previously. The device's greatest value has turned out to be in the field of clinical medicine: other EEG traces were subsequently identified which could help diagnose brain tumours at an early stage, locate the focal point of an epileptic seizure and other useful features. Little, if anything, has been discovered about the basic mechanisms of psychophysiology as Berger, Adrian and the other pioneers had so ardently (and so reasonably) hoped. But in one respect the electroencephalograph has made a useful contribution, and that is in sleep research.

Among the first measurements electroencephalographers decided to make were of the brains of normal human beings, wide awake, dozing and drifting off into deep sleep. The patterns yielded by recordings of this kind are uniquely interesting and (allowing for inevitable person-to-person variations) enormously reliable in their occurrence. The progression into the sleep state is marked by a number of characteristic electrical signposts which are so readily identifiable that if one examines the EEG of a sleeper one can, without seeing the person himself, immediately say whether he is asleep, and also what level of sleep he has attained. One can also, with a bit of training in interpreting the EEG's squiggles, indicate when he is dreaming.

The tapestry of electrical patterns that appear and replace each other as the brain moves from wakefulness into sleep is an interesting one. The waking "unrelaxed" EEG consists of some rather fast but irregular waves with occasional peaks or spikes coming at unpredictable intervals. It is this kind of haphazard picture which is normally traced out when subjects first settle down in the laboratory after they have gone through the minor indignity of having electrodes fixed to their scalp. After a brief period during which the subject relaxes and, in due course, closes his eyes, the first bursts of alpha appear, and these become more and more common as relaxation proceeds. Later the height of the alpha waves becomes slightly less, the first sign to the watching expert that the subject is on the edge of drowsiness. As this becomes better established so the drowsy state in turn gives way to the first, transitional, stage of sleep. On the evidence of the EEG, researchers have identified four levels or stages of sleep, each of which is characterized by a distinct and fairly universal pattern of brain rhythms. The classification is quite arbitrary in that there might be a million levels of sleep as far as the brain's interior operation is concerned, but only four give off discrete sets of signals which show up on the EEG. Furthermore, there is no guarantee that the four levels which *do* show are the most important from the point of view of understanding the nature of sleep. Nevertheless, for studying the living, normal human brain, the EEG is all we have at the moment, and fortunately it does seem to offer some useful clues.

In Stage One sleep the brain waves speed up markedly, but at the same time become more irregular with a tendency to high peaks and low troughs. Once in a while alpha rhythms will still burst through, but at decreasing intervals. A subject disturbed during this phase of sleep and asked to report his impressions will generally say that he was drifting on the edge of consciousness and perhaps experiencing fantasies and a few visual images. After a few minutes, the brain shifts gently into Stage Two, the onset of which is signalled on the EEG trace by the appearance of short bursts of rapid, high-peaking waves. These build up from the base level in a series of gradually increasing peaks, and then fall off rather symmetrically to the base again, producing a spindle-shaped pattern on the graph. These spindles are wholly characteristic of Stage Two, and they tell the experimenter that the subject is now well below the stage of light sleep, and will not be aroused by light sounds or minor disturbances. A few minutes of spindle sleep, and Stage Three is about to commence. Now another new feature of the EEG appears—large, slow waves of about a second in duration and peaking high on the graph—perhaps four or even five times as high as the classic alpha rhythm. These slow waves are infrequent, but their occasional presence on the graph is unmistakable evidence of Stage Three sleep. By now the sleeper will be difficult to arouse—a good shake or his name spoken loudly two or three times are the minimal stimuli—and his respiration and pulse will have slowed, his temperature dropped and his muscles will be flaccid and relaxed. Once again a few minutes will pass without much change. Then persistently the number of large, slow waves will gradually build up until they occupy almost the entire EEG record. This is Stage Four, the so-called "deepest" level of sleep. The huge, even waves which dominate the Stage Four record are generally known as delta rhythms, and they are extremely resistant to outside interference. Introduce regular, disruptive stimuli during Level Three and we see the EEG pattern going into reverse as slow waves give way to spindles, spindles to low-peaking alpha, low-peaking alpha to full alpha and so on as the subject ascends into wakefulness. Do the same in Stage Four, however, and the steady march of the delta waves will hardly falter. Only with vigorous shaking or very loud noises will the normal sleeper wake up into irritable consciousness. Once at this level the average sleeper will remain in it for a longish period of time, sometimes for hours, until the normal process of awakening takes place.

This is the classic picture of the progress of sleep as revealed by the electroencephalogram, a picture which remained more or less unchanged from the work with the crude apparatus of the '30s, right up to the far more sophisticated technology of the postwar era. Interestingly enough —with one crucial exception which we shall discuss in a moment—the picture was intuitively in line with classic assumptions about sleep, including the notion of different "levels" reached at different times in the night, the "deeper" levels being those in which the sleeper was harder to arouse, and so on. One of the findings, that Stage Four or delta sleep was more likely to occur in the early part of the night, even seemed to fit in with the Old Wives' Tale that the most important and "restful" time of sleep did tend to come before midnight. But these homely similarities were more than outweighed by a single, crucial finding. It was this: although the EEG tracings clearly showed a change in the *nature* of the brain's electrical activity during sleep, there was absolutely no hint that there was any reduction in the *amount* of activity going on. Indeed the orderly shift from one stage of sleep to another, each with its definable, characteristic wave forms, was much more suggestive of a set of dynamic functions succeeding each other in some kind of predetermined order. Assuming that such clearly-defined repetitive rhythms were indicative of co-ordinated activity within the cerebral cortex, then the evidence suggested that there was *no reduction in activity during sleep*. Indeed, on certain occasions regularly occurring throughout the night, the brain seemed to be the seat of sustained periods of very vigorous activity, more urgent, in a curious way, than anything recorded in the waking state! The most striking example of this activity, and, as it has turned out, probably the most significant, was discovered quite early on in the history of the topic, though for a long period it was not identified as being a particularly fruitful matter.

Up to the present I have given the impression that the descent into a deep sleep followed by the process of arousal was a simple sequential process, Level One giving way to Two, to Three, to Four with the sequence later going into reverse—Four, Three, Two, One—Wake up! In fact, right back in the 1930s important deviations from this cycle were noted but were treated (one can easily understand why) as irrelevant. For example, after a period of somewhere between one and a half and two hours' sleep, most of it spent in Stage Four, the EEG would almost invariably begin to trace out a steady shift up the ladder to Stage One. But at this point, instead of the subject moving on into the no-man's-land of drowsy wakefulness, the EEG would suddenly begin to generate long bursts of extremely rapid wave forms, rather irregular in their overall shape, but nevertheless characteristically describable. Although now ostensibly in Stage One sleep, the subject would turn out to be unexpectedly *difficult* to arouse, his muscles as relaxed as a rag doll's; it was almost as though the brain was temporarily disconnected from the body. Coupled with the peculiar bodily signs there would be a sustained and violent form of electrical activity taking place in the brain.

From the time this very peculiar variant of Stage One sleep was observed, researchers made the not unreasonable assumption that what they were observing was the activity of a brain on the threshold of awakening, and that the vigorous bursts of activity were signs of the system striving to come to life. The peculiarly reduced muscle tones and the great resistance to awakening were either ignored or dismissed as irrelevant, in the way that things tend to be when they complicate a simple and reasonable idea. We now know that these mystery episodes are in fact periods when dreaming (or at least a particular type of dreaming) takes place, a discovery whose history and implications we shall look at in detail in Chapter 13. But all I shall say for the moment is that the EEG sounded the death knell of the hypothesis that the sleep period is one of cerebral quiescence and rest. Something very different is certainly going on during sleep, but there is no suggestion that anything *less* is happening than when we are awake.

Chapter 4

KLEITMAN: FURTHER PHYSICAL THEORIES

SLEEP AS A recuperative phase is bound to be the most attractive theme to explore for it seems to fit so well with common sense observations, but there are other less obvious and in some ways more penetrating approaches which need to be considered.

Nathaniel Kleitman, at the time of writing an actively retired Professor Emeritus at the University of California, has been conducting research into sleep, and to a lesser extent into dreams, since the 1920s. In his early days he studied the effects of prolonged sleep deprivation —a topic which we shall pick up in detail in Chapter 11. He was particularly interested in the effects on the sleep process of disturbing natural biological rhythms—by confining subjects in caves for a month or so, for example, or observing the sleep/wakefulness cycle of submarine crews. His book *Sleep and Wakefulness* lists 4,337 scientific references to articles and papers published on sleep research up to the mid-60s alone. Interestingly enough, after devoting four or five decades to sleep research, after publishing about a hundred papers himself and after (presumably) having read at least 4,237 other papers, Kleitman himself holds to a view of sleep that is diametrically opposed to almost everybody else's. In his view one has to look upon sleep as the physiologically natural state and wakefulness as a special kind of deviation from the norm. The central nervous system, he believes, is basically a dormant, unsensing, non-learning, disinterested device which gets slammed into periodic activity by physical pressures of one kind or another, such as the need to feed, mate, find a protective den and so on. Once these have been achieved the brain sinks gratefully back into its vegetative oblivion. To be fair, it should be pointed out that Kleitman is not arguing that the least important phase of existence is wakefulness, but simply that sleep is the natural, basic state rather than the other way round, as everybody else assumes. Consequently, what one should really be looking for are theories of wakefulness instead of theories of sleep.

After getting over the initial surprise at the radical nature of his view, one can concede that it has some tempting points in its favour. The most important is that it is far easier to find physiological mechanisms which deal with waking or arousing the brain than those which promote sleep or damp-down activity. The most interesting and convincing of these arose out of the work of the Belgian physiologist, Bremer, who performed certain surgical experiments on the brains of living cats. The cat, by the way, has been much used by sleep researchers, with some very remarkable results, even if some of these experiments have been of an aesthetically objectionable nature.

Bremer's experiments led him to sever the connections between "higher" parts of the brain and "lower" centres at a number of points. In the first instance he made a cut close to the base of the cerebral cortex, which, it will be recalled, is the evolutionary "newer" segment of the total nervous system, particularly well developed in mammals. This preparation he called the *cerveau isolé*, or isolated brain. Roughly speaking, the cut divided the parts of the brain concerned with seeing, hearing, perceiving, learning—and, in humans, thinking and reasoning—from the evolutionary older and deeper structures which look after the housekeeping operations such as cardiac activity and respiration. Now, although the cut divided one part of the brain from another, it did not sever the cortex completely from the body, and a blood supply was still available through the normal channels. Under these conditions the cortex continued to live for a while, but, intriguingly, when EEG recodings were taken from it, it showed nothing but those which are characteristic of sleep. No attempts at prodding the animal or stimulating it in any way would have any effect on the cerebral cortex. Perhaps all this might not seem too surprising. Why should a sensorily deprived cortex not do the "sensible" thing and drop off to sleep?

But a more remarkable finding came when Bremer made his cut far lower down the nervous system, severing the brain as a whole (including the old housekeeping structures) from the spinal cord. In these animals the normal sleep/wakefulness cycle was observed on the EEG, even when the creature was kept in total darkness and deprived of sensory input. Now, what this seemed to imply was that somewhere in between the cuts, in the brain stem and lower centres, there must lie an organ or structure which controlled the sleep/wakefulness cycle. A few years after Bremer's studies, an Italian, Giuseppe Moruzzi, and an American, H.W. Magoun, tracked down the centre. When they inserted fine wires into the central core of the brain stem and passed a small electric current into it, the cerebral cortex (if it had been sleeping) would pass instantly into wakefulness; furthermore, if they stimulated the awake brain in this way, it would show signs of extreme activity and alertness. In due course this critical spot came to be called the arousal centre, and it has become a very important component of modern theories of brain function. The present view is that all sensory input results in the signal being sent to the arousal centre, and that this then pumps "wake up" or "stay alert" signals to the cortex to ensure that the creature is competent to meet the challenge of the outside world. It is clear that these studies provide a perfectly good physiological model of how the sleep state can be converted into a waking one, and it has to be said that nothing so convincing has been found for the reverse process. There are parts of the brain which when stimulated promote sleep but there is a strong suspicion that this sleep is caused more by the interruption of signals from the waking centre than because any sleep centre as such has been discovered.

On the face of it all this fits Kleitman's overall view fairly well, but to accept that sleep is the norm and wakefulness a state of abnormality does not actually help us to understand the fundamental mechanisms of either any better. Furthermore one gets the very powerful feeling that Kleitman's ideas are more relevant to the state of knowledge as it was in the '30s,'40s and early '50s—in other words before it had become absolutely clear that even the sleeping brain was exhibiting constant, and sometimes very vigorous, activity.

A few other theoretical approaches are worth summarizing if only to show how they have, at best, only limited explanatory value. One of the earliest, and for a while most fashionable, theories of sleep was put forward by the great Russian neurophysiologist Ivan Pavlov, whose work and ideas dominated Soviet psychology for nearly fifty years and who was also behind the hard-core behaviourist school which plagued Western psychology in the '30s, '40s and '50s. Pavlov was, of course, the discoverer of the principle of the conditioned reflex. A dog will salivate automatically when a tempting plate of food is put before it, and if the food is preceded on occasions by the sound of a bell, then in due course the poor mutt will begin salivating at the sound of the bell alone. A lot of people have had a lot of fun pointing out that it took Pavlov ten years and hundreds of dogs to demonstrate something which every pet owner knows, but this rather flippantly underestimates his contribution —which was to establish the principles of associative learning, and also to suggest a simple physiological mechanism which might underlie them.

Pavlov, as it happens, also had very clear-cut ideas about sleep. He had noticed that an animal in an experimental apparatus with nothing of interest happening around it would nod off to sleep. The central nervous system, he believed, operated on the dual principles of excitation and inhibition, the former being rather akin to Moruzzi's and Magoun's concept of arousal. Inhibition was just the opposite, a general damping down of activity from some undiscovered centre in the brain. Sleep, then, was due to "waves of inhibition" passing through the cerebral cortex, the cause of which was somehow tied up with reduced sensory input. Presumably a battle was always being waged between the forces of excitation which were at their high-water mark when the animal was in a complex, active environment, and those of inhibition, which reduced the creature to the static state of sleep whenever sensory input was low. This does sound rather like the arousal theory, and thus it fits moderately well with more recent physiological findings. Once again, however, it falls apart when faced with the fact that the sleeping, and supposedly inhibited, brain is in fact pulsing with activity, even if of a different kind from that occurring in the waking state.

Another interesting theory of a predominantly "physical" kind—the boundary between the physical and the psychological is at best blurred, and is in any case arbitrary, since all psychological phenomena must ultimately have some physiological correlative—comes from the American psychologist Frederick Snyder. He takes the line that sleep is a strategy which serves to conserve energy simply because a sleeping animal uses up less energy than a waking one. Animals only stay awake, therefore, for long enough to provide themselves with the bare minimum of food and to perform the various activities connected with reproducing and caring for their young, after which they drop off to sleep at the first reasonable opportunity. If they were awake, he argues, they would inevitably use up energy and need to do more food hunting which would cut down on environmental resources markedly. The theory has its attractive side, but there are one or two points which can be brought up against it. There is, for example, a kind of enforced immobility over long periods of time practised by certain animals to preserve energy which is known as hibernation. But hibernation and sleep have very different characteristics: the former is a state of torpor in which pulse, respiration and body temperature fall to near death conditions, and from which the animal is almost impossible to arouse; the latter is an easily reversible process in which body functions barely differ from the norm. More important, perhaps, is the fact that the EEG of the hibernating animal shows a flat, distinctly *in*active picture—much more in line with what one would expect was characteristic of a "resting" or "switched off" brain. Furthermore, one could reasonably argue that if sleep were an evolutionary device designed principally to conserve food and energy, then one ought to be able to train animals, by a gradual process, to be able to do without it, particularly if food and warmth were always around in profligate amounts.

This latter point would be difficult to support if it were established that sleep was not just a habit but an instinct, and one has to admit that by all our current understandings of what constitutes an instinct, sleep would certainly seem to fall into that category. It is worth devoting a little time to defining the term which is very widely misused outside the biological sciences. In biology an instinct is defined as a pattern of behaviour observed in an animal which (1) is present at birth and in all members of the species and (2) is virtually ineradicable through training or counter-learning. If the behaviour pattern is not universally present within a species and if it can be removed through a training or learning process, then it is *not* an instinct. The concept is of particular interest to the British psychologist Ray Meddis, whose book entitled *The Sleep Instinct* was published in the mid '70s. Meddis's ideas follow rather closely on Snyder's, except that he is less concerned with energy conservation and more with the notion of risk. Life, he points out, is a constantly dangerous exercise and creatures will do well to avoid engaging in its interactions whenever they can. Hence, once all feeding and mating requirements have been satisfied the animal is overwhelmed with the urge to sleep, which, once a suitable bolthole has been found, tends to keep it out of danger. Having advanced this idea, Meddis takes a bold step and suggests that it really ought to be possible to train people or animals out of the habit when it is no longer appropriate for survival, and points to the wide variation in human sleep requirements. Very occasionally, for example, one finds a human being who can apparently get by on as few as three, possibly even two, hours' sleep a night—which suggests that healthy brains *can* get by on a lot less sleep than is normally assumed.

His theory touches on a sensitive and tempting idea which has excited people for a long time—the idea that one might ultimately be able to do without sleep altogether and put all that wasted time to good use. Unfortunately, as we shall see when we come to discuss sleep deprivation experiments in Chapter 11, while there is a good deal of variation in the sleep requirements of adults (the measurable average is between six and nine hours), sustained efforts at reducing that requirement always meet with failure and occasionally with quite serious consequences. The more one tampers with the sleep instinct, the more force and urgency it turns out to have; and the more vital one suspects its function to be.

The main, and in my view the dominating, weakness of Meddis's theory—and indeed of all the physical theories of sleep—is that none of them explains the need to *lose consciousness* which, as we have kept pointing out, has terrifying attendant risks. A mechanism for keeping an animal quiet and subdued in non-food-catching periods might make sense, but this would best be served by an instinct which made it lie still for periods in a comfortable spot, much the way that physical exercise brings on an urge for a period of recuperative quiescence. And all this ought to occur without it surrendering its protective mechanisms, damping down its vitally important sensory and co-ordinating functions. However much one argued that any sleep instinct would force an animal to seek out a place of safety before it lost consciousness, it remains inarguable that a sleeping animal is far—even desperately—less secure than one in the full command of its senses. In other words, unless one includes in one's theory some specific reason why consciousness and sensory functioning should be lost, one is stuck with the weird paradox that the sleep habit seems to fly in the face of the facts of the dangerous world we and all other animals inhabit.

All this, of course, does not imply that restorative or even energy-conserving functions do not take place during the sleep period. One of the world's most experienced sleep researchers, Ian Oswald of Edinburgh University, has produced evidence which seems to show that during sleep protein synthesis takes place in the brain, and suggests that this could be related to the consolidation of memory traces and to other vital neural functions. But once again there is no conceivable reason why such functions should require the effective disconnection of the animal's brain from its environment, and we are left with the inescapable view that protein synthesis, or any other demonstrable neurological activity, is a secondary function of the sleep process and not its prime purpose. And, to emphasize it again, this must be a function which requires loss of consciousness and almost totally reduced sensory input with all its attendant risks. Later in the book I shall propose a theory which does accommodate this striking peculiarity of sleep, but it is enough for the present to underline that none of the physical theories referred to here, or their numerous variants in the academic literature, meets that requirement.

Before closing this chapter and moving on to consider a totally different approach to the topic, it should perhaps be remembered that this book is not only about sleep, but also—indeed primarily—about dreams. How well, then, do the physical theories which we have been discussing cope with the topic of dreams? And, if they do cope with them, how do they set about it? The question is not difficult to answer, for in the main the physical theories of sleep tend to consider dreams to be, at worst, a kind of cerebral mistake or set of circumstances which detract from the efficacy of the sleep process. At best they treat them as peripheral phenomena, occurring in some inescapable way as an adjunct of the sleep process, but of relatively little significance or importance to the individual.

Perhaps the best example of this dismissive view has been propounded by the respected figure of Kleitman, who holds that dreams are so unimportant that it is barely worth trying to work out a theory to explain them. A good parallel, he argues, would be the phenomena associated with "drunken thought." Peculiar mental processes do occur in the brain when an individual has had too much alcohol or is under the influence of some drug, but no one would devote much time to theorizing about them. Why should one feel any different about dreams? The answer is that this view flies in the face of the latest data on dream research. It also does so little justice to the powerful narrative flow of so many dreams, and to their undoubted relevance to our own personal psychology, that one cannot rate it at all highly. In much the same way one can hardly take seriously the suggestion that dreams are nothing more than the background "noise" of a partially active neurological system, rather like the crackles and hum on a radio set tuned to a station which has gone off the air for the night. For both Snyder and Meddis dreams themselves appear to be of very little interest, though Snyder does argue that the high level of cortical activity which occurs during the dream state is a periodic arousing mechanism which serves to keep the sleeping animal partially alert and prevent it from drifting off into a hibernative state. There are numerous variations on these themes, all of which say much the same thing: Sleep is a state which occurs at regular intervals and which serves vital physical or bodily functions, either directly, in terms of some recuperative process, or in order to keep the animal quiet in a period when wakefulness is not required. Dreams, on the whole, are all a big mistake, something to be avoided by the animal or human if what is described as a "good night's sleep" is to be had.

Chapter 5

PSYCHICAL THEORIES: BEGINNINGS

IN THE PREVIOUS chapters we learned that the simplest, most common sense view of sleep was that it was tied up with the need to rest tired muscles or a hard-worked brain. In a poll I conducted in a popular magazine several years ago through a specially designed questionnaire, I found that well over ninety per cent of those readers who responded to the poll took this or a rather similar position, and one can see why the view is so popular. Its beauty (provided that one looks no further than skin deep) is that it really does offer what seems to be a sensible explanation for sleep, even if it has very little to say about dreams. But dreams are not merely an immensely fascinating topic, even more so than sleep, but they are also universally experienced by human beings and are almost invariably associated with sleep. Thus any theory which explains sleep but does not explain dreams must have only a limited purchasing power.

In this chapter we shall look at theoretical approaches which concentrate almost exclusively on the dream and which fall into a category which, to contrast with the physical, I term the *psychical*. In fact, widely held though the "sleep is to rest" view may be, its popularity is negligible when compared with that of psychical theories of dreams. Not only are these almost universally held in some shape or form, but they are also probably the most ancient, going back, one suspects, to the time of our caveman ancestors and the beginnings of language.

Imagine a cave in the time of Cro-Magnon Man, between fifty and a hundred thousand years ago. A woman watches her mate asleep by the dying embers of the fire; he stirs, mumbles, starts in his sleep, and then awakes with a cry. For a brief moment he looks around as though in surprise and then, recognizing his surroundings, he relaxes and squats on his haunches by the fire. The woman questions him about why he had awakened. Hesitantly he explains. It seemed that he and his colleagues had been hunting in territory some distance from their caves, and that they had cornered a large bear in a thicket. Between them they had severely wounded the creature but it had struck back, killing one of the team, an old man who lived in a neighbouring cave. At that point, with the bear making further aggressive moves, this time towards him, he suddenly found himself transported back from the scene of the fight to the home cave. "But you were here all the time," remarks his mate, "from the time you went to sleep after supper." The man shrugs, or whatever is the contemporary equivalent. "But I was also there fighting the bear," he adds, "and saw old so-and-so killed. It would have killed me too had I not suddenly come back home." Both ponder the significance and meaning of the experience, as well they might. Today, many thousand years later, people still puzzle over essentially the same problem, and understand it no better.

On inspection this problem is revealed as being many-layered. The first layer concerns the reality of the dream experience. Primitive peoples, children and some psychotics have great difficulty in differentiating between "inner" experiences such as dreams and "outer" ones which are shared with others and are clearly located in the external world. Today there is a tendency to declare that the shared experience is the *only* reality, and that the personal one, whatever its form, is essentially *un*real. But this is philosophically very naive. Any individual's objective experiences—that is those aspects of the universe which he can share with other humans, and whose existence they can confirm—are themselves only experienced by him because they have been converted from physical stimuli (light, sound waves and so on) into neurological impulses which end up in the form of some kind of electrical activity in his brain. Equally all *personal* experiences, dreams, fantasies or whatever, are in the end no more than bursts of electrical activity somewhere in the brain. No doubt the central nervous system has a pretty good rule of thumb for determining which of the two types of stimuli comes from outside and which from inside, but as both are reduced in the end to the same neural mishmash, how can one be described more real than the other? To the caveman who actually had the experience, and to the cavewoman who in the past had had analogous experiences of her own, there would have been no disputing the reality of the adventure. The fact that next morning old so-and-so was still alive would not affect their belief. No doubt the event, including his death, would occur in due course, so the experience taking place in the dreams was some kind of warning from the gods. And if it did not occur after many months had passed, well, that would be because a glimpse of the future had allowed magic of various kinds to come into play, forestalling the fatal hunt.

It is important to emphasize again that the notion of dreams and even fantasy states as being "unreal" and belonging only to the individual's private world represents a fairly sophisticated level of analysis of such experiences. Young children, as Piaget and others have shown, completely fail to differentiate between inner and outer experiences, and only learn to do so after a long period of indoctrination. People with severe mental deficiencies never seem to learn, and there is some suggestion that many psychotics and others suffering from delusional illnesses slip back into the primitive mode where inner and external realities blend and merge. That the distinction has also only recently become widely realized can be appreciated if one looks at attitudes to dreams in primitive societies and traces the evolution of ideas about dreams through history. As one might expect, these take a wide variety of forms, but they can all be grouped under one catholic assumption: human beings spend their waking lives in one world where they share common experiences with other human beings. When they sleep, however, they enter another world. Here their minds, souls or spirits can have experiences in parts of the waking world separated in space or time from the one they normally inhabit. Quite elaborate theories are occasionally erected to explain the nature of this separation, but in the main the dichotomy is simply accepted as being there, rather in the way that we accept the presence of both the European continent and the Americas without puzzling too much about how they came into being, or how astonishing it is that we can move from one to the other more or less at will.

The assumptions about the dream life of our cave-dwelling ancestors are of course nothing more than that—assumptions. There is no suggestion in any of the cave paintings and other examples of prehistoric art of any scenes which could reasonably be interpreted as depicting dreams. Even so, it is reasonable to assume that *homo sapiens* (or *homo neanderthalensis*) has been aware of having a dream life for roughly the amount of time he has had a spoken language to describe his experiences, to his family and friends and also to himself in the form of introspective musings.

Certainly the first clear evidence of a society's interest in dreams comes from one of the earliest to have developed a written language, which implies a complex spoken language preceding it. This was the Assyrian Empire of the fifth or sixth millennium BC, from which some valuable records have been preserved in the form of clay tablets. Translation of these cuneiform scripts shows that they were "dream books," or guides to dream interpretation, and their importance to the culture is attested by the fact that they were carefully preserved in the library of the Assyrian King Asurnasipal at Nineveh. Most interesting of all, the dreams recorded are very typical of the kinds of dreams that people report today and which also deeply absorb the attention of the psychoanalyst. In other words they included the familiar rigmarole of bizarre sexual incidents, teeth and hair falling out, finding oneself naked in a public place and so on. The cause of the dreams, pleasant or unpleasant, was ascribed by the Assyrians (and the Babylonians for that matter, who had very similar ideas) to evil spirits, including those of dead people with whom direct contact was made during sleep.

The Egyptians took a happier line on dreams, maintaining (on the whole) that they were messages from the gods serving a triple function: urging the dreamer to repent for some moral offence, warning of some danger to come, and in certain cases supplying answers to questions which the dreamer had previously put to them. The peculiar and often enigmatic nature of dreams was explained by the fact—a universally agreed rule which has held right up to the present day—that interaction with the world of the supernatural is never quite what it seems and always fraught with risk. The information conveyed in a dream, therefore, would rarely be entirely straightforward, and one had to read between the lines to get the true message. As a result the profession of dream interpreter became an admired and honourable one, and practitioners set up their offices in association with the numerous temples which were erected to Serapis, the Egyptian god of dreams. The most famous of these was found at Memphis, the capital of Ancient Egypt, and during the excavations in the nineteenth century a dream interpreter's office was discovered bearing over the door the legend: "I interpret dreams, having the gods' mandate to do so. Good luck to you if you enter here."

Egyptian ideas about dreams became embedded in Greek culture in the centuries immediately preceding the birth of Christ. These included the practice which came to be known as incubation. To take advantage of the fact that the gods would, through the dream, answer questions suitably posed, people in trouble or with mysteries to unravel would sleep, perhaps for several nights on end, in one of the Serapea either until something happened or until it became obvious that the gods were simply not bothered with their case. The more important you were the more likely they were to be bothered, and while the hoi polloi might hang around a Serapeum more or less indefinitely without much happening, a member of the royal family would be more or less guaranteed a dream on the first night. Perhaps it was felt that if a certain amount of information was to be passed to mankind through dreams it was more sensible that this should go to royalty, whose problems and difficulties would affect a greater number of people. Great attention was therefore attached to the dreams of kings, and between the paws of the Sphinx there can still be found a portentous dream that Thutmos the Fourth had on one otherwise forgotten night all of 3500 years ago.

The Greeks picked up the idea of incubation with great enthusiasm, but reascribed responsibility to the god Aesculapius who was also their god of healing. In doing so they shifted the principle of incubation from general-purpose advice to medical matters and problems. Aesculapian temples sprang up all over the place and at the height of the cult there were literally hundreds in the Graeco-Roman empire, many of which have survived to this day. The procedure for anyone wishing to incubate a dream varied from region to region. In some areas you first had to be invited by a supernatural being (in a dream) to visit one of the temples, and without a convincing story about such an encounter you would be unlikely to be admitted by the temple custodians. In most cases, however, it was generally sufficient to go through some pre-incubation ritual which would involve abstaining from sex, alcohol, particular foods and so on. There would also normally be a bathing requirement, and sacrificial offerings or gifts. The night's work would generally begin with a ceremony outside the temple, after which the would-be dreamers, suitably robed, would enter its sacred interior. No doubt the atmosphere was relaxing and deliberately hypnotic, though the presence of large numbers of long white snakes which would become active on the dowsing of the lights must have been disconcerting. The snakes, which were of a harmless Mediterranean species, were looked on as the servants of the god Aesculapius (hence the serpent wound round the staff, which is now the international emblem of the medical practitioner) and were allowed to come and go as they pleased. In the morning the fortunate would have had their dream, hopefully replete with useful medical advice, while the unlucky remainder would prepare themselves for another night's stay. If they could afford it.

The link between dream content and the medical condition of the dreamer became very firmly established in the Graeco-Roman civilization, with Hippocrates looked upon as the father of medicine and Plato writing extensively on these matters. Of the influential thinkers of the time only Aristotle, who was Plato's pupil, took a non-supernatural line, proposing, as we have heard, one of the first genuinely *physical* theories of sleep and dreams. His rejection of dreams as having a psychical or a divine origin was based on the interesting observation that animals, as well as humans, lead an apparently active dream-life—a fact which has only been established scientifically in the last few decades.

It was not just the Mediterranean civilizations that produced these dynamic attitudes to dreaming. The Vedas, the Indian sacred books of wisdom which were written in the second millennium before Christ, devoted fair amounts of space to dream interpretations and again it is interesting to note that the dreams recorded included the bizarre kind of incidents familiar to us today. Early Chinese dream books are less well preserved, though much more recent in origin, but it is clear that they also saw the dream as offering valuable information culled from another world. In fact, the Chinese believed that during sleep the soul, or *hun*, became literally emancipated from the shackles of the physical body (as it did on death) and was temporarily free to roam around the world of ghosts and spirits. The main difference between sleep and death was that in the former case the *hun* returned to the body. The process was not without its risks, hence their belief—one that is still found widely in contemporary primitive societies—that disturbing the sleeper by a violent awakening can block the spirit's re-entry, and lead to the death of that particular body.

The important point to grasp is not so much the similarities or dissimilarities in the way in which the various cultures approached the subject, but rather the universal, unquestioning belief that dreams reflect "real" experiences, either in the form of interactions with gods or devils, with travels in some alternative spiritual world, or even with excursions made by the free-roaming soul in this particular world. The anthropologist Levy-Bruhl, for example, reports the case of an equatorial African chief who dreamed one night that he had travelled to England. To him there was no doubt that the trip had really been made, and in the morning he accordingly dressed up in European clothes and was congratulated heartily by all his friends on his good fortune in having visited the heart of the Empire. Similarly, in numerous African societies to dream that one had committed an offence such as theft or adultery was enough to ensure (provided that you admitted it, of course) that you got fined or appropriately punished.

During the Middle Ages in Europe the significance of the dream became a demonic one again, and with the religious obsessions that built up at around the time of the Reformation, this notion of the inherent evil of dreams continued to grow. Some dreams, it was true, consisted of messages from the saints or even from God himself, but most people were highly suspicious of them, for the devil was known to have enormously developed powers of deception and could infiltrate one's dream life without any difficulty and plant evil ideas dressed up in subtle disguises. Martin Luther, who no doubt had to undergo long and profound battles with his unconscious, became plagued with ambiguous dreams and prayed desperately to be spared any messages from God in case they were confused with demoniacal ones. With the slow dawn of the Age of Reason, and with the increasing interest in the anatomy of the body and brain, physical theories of sleep began to replace psychical ones. By the seventeenth century the philosopher Thomas Hobbes was able to declare that dreams were due to a distemper of the "inward parts," and the stage was set for the far more provocative theorizing of the nineteenth century, up to and including the work of Sigmund Freud.

Ostensibly it might seem as if the physical approach to dreams was a product of pre-scientific thinking, arising from a relatively unsophisticated view of the world which failed to distinguish between subjective and objective reality. If so, one might reasonably have expected the idea that during sleep the mind or soul could step through into a supernatural world or acquire supernatural powers to have gently slipped away as it became replaced by new understanding of the nature of the human brain and mind. Unfortunately, or fortunately (depending upon which way you like to look at the universe), the psychical view of dreams failed to disappear conveniently with the advance of science and technology. One can even go so far as to say that this class of theories remains extremely widely supported against the backdrop of computers, laser weapons, robot spaceships on the surface of the planet Mars and the various technological triumphs which one might mistakenly assume are the true symbols of the late twentieth century. One could indeed argue that the psychical view of dreams is still the most ardently held in many parts of the world today, including the technologically sophisticated West.

A statement of this kind, made at the start of the 1980s, would have bitterly dismayed the nineteenth-century rationalists and people such as H.G. Wells, who believed so profoundly in the imminent triumph of science over superstition. If it is to be accepted, it requires substantial support. How easy is it to find this support? Not difficult at all, as the tale of Mr X and his Uncle Harry will demonstrate.

Chapter 6

DREAMING OF UNCLE HARRY

MR X IS SLEEPING comfortably in his bed one night, his wife tucked in beside him, when he has a strange and vivid dream. He seems to see the door of his room open, and the figure of his Uncle Harry walk in. Now Uncle Harry is a close and dear relative who travels the world quite a bit. His appearance in the dream (which Mr X has not yet identified as a dream, of course) is not at first a cause for surprise for he does have the habit of dropping in from time to time. Then suddenly Mr X recalls that only a week or so ago Uncle Harry had announced that he was off on a sea voyage to Australia and wouldn't be seeing them for several months. "What are you doing here, Uncle Harry?" he asks. "I thought you were on your way to Australia!" His surprise is compounded by the fact that the figure of his uncle merely stares at him impassively. Then with a shock Mr X realizes that his uncle's clothes are dripping wet, and that he is holding a bloodstained handkerchief in his hand which he slowly raises and points to the clock of the bedroom wall. At this point the dream shows every sign of changing into a nightmare and Mr X's autonomic nervous system pulls him awake with palms sweating and heart pounding. There is of course no sign of his Uncle Harry, and there are no puddles on the floor to testify to his presence. And the bedroom clock shows the time to be 2.30 in the morning. Mr X now wakes his wife up and tells her about it, turns over and goes back to sleep. The next morning they are woken by the telephone: it is the trans-Pacific steamship company. "Mr X? I'm very sorry to have to tell you that your uncle was lost with all hands when the *Neasden Castle* was sunk in a typhoon last night." Mr X asks one question: "At what time did the ship founder?" "At half-past two GMT, sir."

Needless to say, my story of Uncle Harry and Mr X is a fabrication, but most readers will agree that, with the exception of one or two points of detail, it might quite easily have been true. Indeed, on hearing the story it is hard to avoid the feeling that one has heard it before. This is because it is highly characteristic of a type of anecdote which is widely told in one form or another in just about every part of the world. In fact, there will not be a single person reading this book who has not had a story of this kind told to him or her in all solemnity *as fact*, or who has not read an account of a story of this kind in a serious book or magazine where it has been offered up *as fact*. Far from fading away gracefully in the face of rational science, belief in at least the possibility of a major psychic component in dreams remains exceedingly high, almost to the point of being universal. It may be at odds with good sense, it may be at odds with scientific knowledge, it may even be at odds with our overall understanding of the universe, but if it is supported by such a widespread system of belief, can we reject if for these reasons alone?

The question really boils down to asking what kind of world, or what kind of universe, we really live in. This is the issue that science has been attempting to tackle in a systematized way for several hundred years, making significant but still only partial progress. Simplifying things rather heftily, the pre-scientific view of the universe was totally fashioned by the great religions of the time. We were seen as living in a world which contained physical things—human bodies, houses, rocks, flowers, oceans and mountains—which also interacted with a non-physical world containing the spirits or ghosts of the departed, angels and demons, magical forces, heaven, hell and God or gods. The former domain was mortal and transient, the latter was perpetual and in the most important sense the *real* world. This view of things was not only totally compatible with all man's observations on the universe as he knew it, but also offered reasonable explanations of phenomena which would otherwise be totally puzzling. These varied from the whimsical play of fate, the caprices of sickness and good health, the awesome and apparently uncontrollable forces of nature, and of course stories (with variations according to the contemporary scene) of the Uncle Harry variety. As a working model, it was extremely satisfactory until science slowly but inexorably began to knock away the props that supported it. Finally, after a battle which stretched over centuries and which in the early days led to many scholars meeting fiery deaths, the forces of science prevailed and a view of the universe matured which, while excellent for accommodating measurable phenomena from solar eclipses to electromagnetic fields, was unable to find house room for magical powers or ghostly visitations. The Victorian scientists' cavalier dismissal of the supernatural element in man's affairs, which had held the stage for so long, may today seem to have been a trifle premature, but one has to admire their matchless optimism and total confidence in the triumph of the scientific method.

Curiously, it was at the high point of Victorian materialistic science that the first scholarly questionings of the physicalistic view were raised—not, however, using the old and largely discredited arguments of orthodox religion, but rather from the promising new field known as psychical research. There have been lots of attempts at pin-pointing the moment when this important movement got under way, and as with most events of historical significance there are numerous candidates for the office. My own favourite date is 13th November 1871, on which occasion two eminent Victorians, Henry Sidgwick and Frederick Myers, both formidable Cambridge scholars, took an after-dinner walk by starlight and found themselves discussing the nature of the universe and pondering its significance. It was cold and brilliantly clear, and both men were overwhelmed at the stupendous panoply of stars which swung across the sky. Myers, in an essay following Sidgwick's death in 1900, recalls that the unforgettable scene prompted him to turn to the senior man and ask him "almost with trembling" whether he thought that when all traditional, institutional, metaphysical and orthodox scientific methods had "failed to solve the riddle of the universe," as seemed to be the case at that moment, there might not be some alternative way which would help to resolve the problem? Could it really be that the universe was a huge machine, as uncaring of its components as a steam engine was of the individual molecules of metal which made up its pipes and cylinders? Was there not some sign, some fragment of evidence, which gave meaning and offered some significant role for man? In particular, Myers asked Sidgwick, was there not something enormously important in the phenomena of ghosts, spirits and other supernatural forces which had been reported since the beginning of history, and yet which were now rejected both by orthodox religion and by the materialistic dogma of science? Sidgwick pondered the question a while before speaking, and then revealed to Myers that he too had been thinking along these lines. "Steadily," Myers reports, "though in no sanguine fashion, he indicated some last grounds of hope." In these phenomena, he felt, there might indeed lie a key to the mystery of man and "from that night onwards I resolved to pursue this quest, if it might be, at his side."

And so it turned out to be. Myers and Sidgwick both devoted the remainder of their lives to a penetrating inspection of psychic phenomena, and by virtue of their impeccable academic reputation succeeded not only in drawing numerous other rebellious intellectuals into the quest, but also in converting the topic into a semi-respectable branch of science. A few years later they had founded the Society for Psychical Research in

London with the avowed aim of investigating supernatural phenomena. Its early membership consisted of an impressive roll of Fellows of the Royal Society, distinguished academics, and some of the most exciting intellectual figures of the day. The end product was a kind of scientific counter-attack against materialism, not, it should be pointed out, supporting the orthodox religious view, but rather advancing a radically different and in some ways more important role for man.

In surveying the broad and ephemeral field of the "supernatural," the Victorian psychical researchers found themselves with three main pathways down which they could travel. The first involved the study of peculiar talents of the human mind such as telepathy or thought reading, seeing into the future and so on. People had been claiming such talents for thousands of years, so perhaps the time had come to establish whether they really did exist and, if so, what their limitations were. The difficulty here was in finding suitable ways of testing people and, after testing them, in knowing what to make of any results that had been achieved. So little was known about the human mind that the discovery that it had the capacity for telepathic communication would not necessarily suggest that we lived in a non-materialistic universe. This avenue of exploration therefore tended to be ignored or played down by Myers and the other Victorian psychical researchers. In fact, the study of telepathy and other "extra-sensory" powers in a laboratory setting did not really get under way until the late 1920s or early '30s.

The second avenue, initially far more promising, involved the curious phenomena being widely reported from the seance room, which was leading to the emergence of a quasi-religious movement known as spiritualism or spiritism. Here there was not much doubt about the significance and likely interpretation of the phenomena, should they be verified. People calling themselves mediums were claiming to act as links between the world of the living and another world inhabited by the spirits of human beings who had previously died. Typically the spirits communicated with their living relatives, giving details, personal information and so on which could not have been known to the medium and which therefore established the genuineness of the link and the "reality" of the spirit personality. Even more striking were the phenomena allegedly involving the *physical appearance* in the seance room of materialized forms of the dead. Wives would be reunited briefly with dead husbands, parents would embrace the tiny form of their prematurely deceased child, and so on. That one could strike up a cheery conversation with someone who had died twenty years previously or walk around for a minute or so holding the hand of a materialized ghost, would to-day seem to be unlikely to the point of impossibility. In 1870, however, hot on the heels of the "starlight walk," it was another matter, and Myers, Sidgwick and others launched wholeheartedly into the investigation of mediumship.

Their third avenue of exploration was less sensational to begin with, but in an important way it was also inherently more plausible. It concerned itself with the vast amount of largely anecdotal, but still superficially convincing, evidence of what has since come to be known as spontaneous phenomena. This included the very widespread reportage of dreams in which the dreamer either (a) witnessed some event taking place in a distant part of the world, or (b) had a prevision of some event which would in due course turn out to take place. In both cases, assuming the anecdotes were true accounts, it looked as if under certain circumstances—notably in the sleep state—the barriers of space and time dissolved momentarily, often to advise or warn the dreamer of some momentous event.

Spontaneous psychic visions and dreams knocked spots off the spiritualist material in their plausibility. To begin with, they often occurred, quite without precedent, to people who had previously expressed absolutely no interest in psychic happenings, whereas the spiritist phenomena occurred under the most contrived conditions, and then only to people who were already convinced of their genuineness. Secondly, the dream experiences often had a chilling air of authenticity to them, being backed by much relevant circumstantial detail—dates and times of occurrences, etc—and often involved current or future disasters whose details could be documented. All this compared most favourably with the inherent silliness of much of the spiritualist material. Thirdly, for those, like Myers and company, who were simply looking for evidence that the universe had more layers to it than were built into the materialistic model, and yet who had no wish to revive the antiquated notions of traditional religions, spontaneous psychic experiences seemed to fit the bill admirably.

To gather data, Myers, assisted by another enthusiast, Trevor Gurney, placed an advertisement in the personal column of *The Times*, a newspaper they held to be taken by a reliable kind of reader, inviting anyone who had had a really remarkable experience involving an apparition or dream visitation to write in with full details. No doubt they expected a healthy response but their advertisement provoked an enormous flood of mail—literally thousands of letters, some written at great length. They were now left with the task of making some sense of it.

They applied ruthless filtering procedures, using a number of criteria to help them. Ideally they would have liked to eliminate all accounts of dreams, apparitions and other paranormal happenings which had not been fully written up within a few hours of the event occurring, thereby acknowledging the weakness of the human memory and its known tendency to play tricks on its owner. To their surprise and chagrin they observed that not one of the hundreds of accounts they received had been generated within a few hours of the reported occurrence, and the majority were only written down for the first time in response to the advertisement, which, in many cases, was years after the alleged event. In a similar survey carried out today, such a finding would have thrown the whole study under suspicion, for the fallibility of human memory is now even better recognized. But at the time Myers and Gurney merely found the non-contemporary nature of the reports disappointing, but nowhere near invalidating the host of otherwise suggestive material.

The second criterion which they held to be of the greatest importance was that the person telling the story should be a "reliable witness of integrity," and someone who could have no conceivable gain for fabricating a psychic personal experience. With this in mind, Myers and Gurney assiduously filtered out anecdotes from people who might be considered doubtful witnesses, or whose stories showed evidence of contradictory material. Thirdly, they decided to eliminate from their front-running cases any which were based purely on *one* person's single observation, unsupported by any independent evidence. And lastly they required that the anecdotes should have at least a modicum of verifiable circumstantial detail in them—facts other than those of the central theme, which could be checked later and thus provide a kind of back-up to the narrator's powers of observation and recall.

The original mass of responses was whittled down to a hundred or so enormously suggestive cases. There were stories of ghost figures seen by whole families, of apparitions which warned of coming death or serious accident, and numerous dreams which featured warnings of one kind or another. Myers and Gurney were in little doubt about the significance of what they had uncovered. Both in terms of the *number* of remarkable experiences they had received and the *quality* of the best of them, they felt that they had made the first solid scientific case for the existence of what might loosely be described as a paranormal world. During sleep, it seemed, and at other less predictable times, such as in moments of stress, the barriers of space and time could collapse and the rigid laws of the materialistic universe crumble. Slowly Myers and Gurney began to assemble the best of their cases for publication, and in 1884 the pick of them began to appear in the literary magazine *The Nineteenth Century*. Most of these were intriguing to say the least, but the ace of them all, *la crème de la crème*, and by general agreement at the time the most convincing "psychic anecdote" ever published, was the account of the apparition or dream figure that appeared to Sir Edmund Hornby. Sir Edmund was a former Chief Judge of the Supreme Consular Court of China and Japan at Shanghai. In this position he was one of the most senior and respected High Court Judges, and a man with a long and distinguished career. In 1884, after he had retired, he read the advertisement in *The Times* and put pen to paper with a brief account of an astonishing experience which he had had some years before. The account was initially so interesting that Myers and Gurney asked him to give a more complete and detailed story. Its substance was as follows:

On the evening of 19th January 1875, the Judge settled down after dinner to write a brief summary of the judgements he was proposing to deliver in court the next morning. This summary would then be made available, in strict confidence, to representatives of the press who would use it to prepare an account of the judgements for publication. This practice ensured that balanced and sensible accounts of the judgement appeared in the papers, and as in those days the lag between receiving news and the time it could actually appear in print was at least twenty-four hours, there was no danger of the judgements appearing before a Judge had actually delivered them. On completing his summary on this evening Sir Edmund sealed it up in an envelope, rang for the butler and told him to hand it over to the reporter who would in due course call for it. He then went off to bed before midnight. A verbatim account of the apparition or dream that he experienced as it was later told to Myers and Gurney follows, and deserves reading very carefully. I add my own comments on various stages of the narrative.

I had gone to sleep, when I was awakened by hearing a tap on the study door, but thinking it might be the butler—looking to see if the fires were safe and the gas turned off—I turned over. . .to sleep again. Before I did so, I heard a tap at my bedroom door. Still thinking it was the butler. . .I said, "Come in." The door opened, and, to my surprise, in walked Mr —. I sat up and said, "You have mistaken the door; but the butler has the judgement, so go and get it." Instead of leaving the room he came to the foot of the bed. I said, "Mr —, you forget yourself! Have the goodness to walk out directly. This is rather an abuse of my favour." He looked deadly pale, but was dressed as usual, and sober, and said, "I know I am guilty of an unwarrantable intrusion, but finding that you were not in your study, I have ventured to come here."

The fact that the Judge admits that he had actually been to sleep suggests that what he was experiencing was a dream visitation rather than an apparition. From an evidential point of view, of course, both are equally impressive. Note, however, the coherent, logical nature of the conversation between the two, and some important items of detail—for example the reporter is stated to be "deadly pale."

I was losing my temper, but something in the man's manner disinclined me to jump out of bed to eject him by force. So I said, simply, "This is too bad, really; pray leave the room at once." Instead of doing so he put his hand on the foot-rail and gently, and as if in pain, sat down on the foot of the bed. I glanced at the clock and saw that it was about twenty minutes past one. I said, "The butler has had the judgement since half-past eleven; go and get it!" He said, "Pray forgive me; if you knew all the circumstances you would. Time presses. Pray give me a précis of your judgement, and I will take a note in my book of it," drawing his reporter's book out of his breast pocket. I said, "I will do nothing of the kind. Go downstairs, find the butler, and don't disturb me—you will wake my wife; otherwise I shall have to put you out." He slightly moved his hand. I said, "Who let you in?" He answered, "No one." "Confound it," I said. "What the devil do you mean? Are you drunk?" He replied quickly, "No, and never shall be again; but I pray your lordship give me your decision, for my time is short." I said, "You don't seem to care about my time, and this is the last time I will ever allow a reporter in my house." He stopped me short, saying, "This is the last time I shall ever see you anywhere."

There are a number of features of great interest in this section of the narrative. These include the desperate persistence of the mystery figure in its attempt to get the details of the judgement, and the bizarre conversation which is pregnant with ominous phrases—for example, "Time presses" and the reference to the reporter never getting drunk again.

There is also an important mention of Lady Hornby, whom the Judge fears will be woken by the chatter which he notes from the clock was taking place at 1.20 in the morning.

> Well, fearful that this commotion might arouse and frighten my wife, I shortly gave him the gist of my judgement....He seemed to be taking it down in shorthand; it might have taken two or three minutes. When I finished, he rose, thanked me for excusing his intrusion and for the consideration I had always shown him and his colleagues, opened the door, and went away. I looked at the clock; it was on the stroke of half-past one.

(Lady Hornby awoke, thinking she had heard talking; and her husband told her what had happened and repeated the account when dressing the next morning.)

The Judge, in desperation, finally gives the judgement, and the figure thanks him portentously. Again the time is noted. Most important of all, Lady Hornby is finally awakened "thinking she had heard talking," and is treated to an account of the mysterious happening. This is further discussed by them both in the morning while dressing.

> I went to court a little before ten. The usher came into my room to robe me, when he said, "A sad thing happened last night, sir. Poor —was found dead in his room." I said, "Bless my soul! Dear me! What did he die of, and when?" "Well, sir, it appeared he went up to his room as usual at ten to work at his papers. His wife went up about twelve to ask him when he would be ready for bed. He said, 'I have only the Judge's judgement to get ready, and then I have finished.' As he did not come, she went up again, about a quarter to one, to his room and peeped in, and thought she saw him writing, but she did not disturb him. At half-past one she again went to him and spoke to him at the door. As he didn't answer she thought he had fallen asleep so she went up to rouse him. To her horror he was dead. On the floor was his notebook, which I have brought away. She sent for the doctor who arrived a little after two, and said he had been dead, he concluded, about an hour. I looked at the notebook. There was the usual heading: 'In the Supreme Court, before the Chief Judge: The Chief Judge gave judgement this morning in the case to the following effect'—and then followed a few lines of indecipherable shorthand."

A remarkable section of the narrative in which the central issue is raised: the Judge's visitor had died in the night at some time not earlier than midnight, but not later than 1.30 am, and, by inference, at about the time the Judge had his visitation. There is testimony from a doctor about the time of death, and a tantalizing entry in the reporter's notebook.

> I sent for the magistrate who would act as a coroner, and desired him to examine Mr —'s wife and servants as to whether Mr — had left his house or could possibly have left it without their knowledge, between eleven and one on the previous night. The result of the inquest showed he died of some form of heart disease, and had not and could not have left the house without the knowledge of at least his wife, if not of the servants. Not wishing to air my "spiritual experience" for the benefit of the press or the public, I kept the matter at the time to myself, only mentioning it to my Puisne Judge and to one or two friends; but when I got home to tiffin I asked my wife to tell me as nearly as she could remember what I had said to her during the night, and I made a brief note of her replies and of the facts.
>
> (Lady Hornby has kindly confirmed the above facts to us, as far as she was cognisant of them.)

Corroborative evidence of a very impressive kind is now being amassed. The Judge enlists the aid of a coroner because of the very peculiar circumstances of the case, and an inquest established that he could not have left his house at the critical time. The story is re-checked with Lady Hornby, who then adds her testimony in the form of a statement to Myers and Gurney. After the conclusion of the narrative proper, there follows a further statement from the Judge that his memory, normally excellent, is quite clear on all the details he has reported. He also says that he questioned the butler about whether he had bolted and chained the doors of his house at the usual time on the previous night and was assured by him that he had. It would have been impossible for anyone to have entered his house in the normal way.

And that is the substance of Sir Edmund Hornby's experience. To describe it as amazing is to risk being guilty of understatement. Indeed if one were to try to contrive a "perfect" anecdote of this kind, whether it be for the existence of ghosts, premonitory or psychic dreams or whatever, one could scarcely do better than this one. Compare its remarkable evidential features with those of most stories of this kind, with their almost total lack of self-consistency and corroborative evidence:

1 *The narrator was a "reliable witness of integrity":* A High Court Judge, whose years of experience at sorting out evidential wheat from chaff, and capacity for painstaking attention to the facts, would seem to make him supremely well qualified as a witness in this kind of happening.

2 *The lack of any motive for fabricating the story:* One can think of all kinds of reasons why people manufacture or distort stories—to extricate themselves from trouble, for financial gain or perhaps to achieve notoriety or fame. None of these motives would seem in any way credible in respect of Sir Edmund, who in fact was more likely to damage his reputation by coming out with a "vision" of this kind.

3 *The ring of authenticity about the tale:* This is slightly difficult to quantify, but there is no doubt that some tall stories have an inconsistent, phoney sound while others, of which this seems to be a perfect example, have a sustained, plausible ring to them. Possibly this is because of the wealth of fine circumstantial details that Sir Edmund supplied which imply that he was fully alert to what was happening and was not hastily recounting a vaguely perceived event.

4 *The corroboration of the tale by Lady Hornby:* This highly important feature lifts the story yet another rung up the ladder of acceptability. That the Judge's wife claimed to have woken by hearing voices and had then had a first-hand and immediate account from her husband of what had transpired seems to make the whole story quite unshakable.

5 *The highly significant temporal correspondences:* During his dream or vision the Judge "noticed the time" on at least two occasions. Later these times were established by independent testimony, both from the deceased's wife and the doctor, as almost certainly corresponding with the reporter's death. This chronological link is immeasurably important if it is argued that at the moment of death, accident or severe stress, "psychic" warning signals are transmitted to any suitable recipient, such as seems to be implied in this tale.

6 *The evidence of the reporter's notebook:* Although the details of the judgement were "indecipherable," the notebook contained a reference to a particular judgement which Sir Edmund was due to deliver the next morning. In a sense the whole story turns around this judgement, for it was presumably in order to complete his precipitously interrupted task that the spirit of the dead man attempted to contact the Judge.

7 *The independent testimony of the coroner and others:* A number of people provide secondary corroboration of the story—the coroner who "at the Judge's request" makes an inquiry and holds an inquest to ascertain the time, circumstances and cause of death; the reporter's wife who saw him apparently working "at around one o'clock" only to find him dead half an hour later, and various lesser figures, such as the butler who was quizzed by the Judge about the doors and had been given the envelope containing the judgement earlier.

8 *The evidence of the inquest itself:* No more satisfactory way could be found of checking the validity of many of the essentials of a story of this kind than to hold an inquest on the death of the principal party! The inquest would be expected to corroborate most of the key details, though presumably the Judge would not have reported his dreams as this could scarcely be relevant to the coroner's findings.

This formidable catalogue could hardly fail to impress anyone confronted with the story, and posed real problems for anyone wanting to provide a non-paranormal explanation—that is, one which could be cast within the framework of the mechanistic, materialistic model of the universe that prevailed at the time.

There were really only three ways of interpreting the data:

1 Sir Edmund Hornby was a thumping liar who was engaging in some kind of ludicrous hoax which had also involved a conspiracy between himself, his wife and, on a lesser scale, various other witnesses.

2 Sir Edmund was the victim of an appalling delusion and memory lapse, of a kind which it is hard to believe *any* human being would be guilty of, let alone a man whose powers of wisdom and observation had been tested over years of service in the judiciary.

3 A paranormal event of some kind did occur and at the time in question the Judge was either visited by the apparition of the dead or dying reporter, or had a dream in which he made telepathic or clairvoyant contact with him.

Anyone hearing the story would be obliged to make the choice between the three possibilities, and when the tale was first recounted in print there were few readers who did not plump, however reluctantly, for the third. To accuse the distinguished Judge of being an unprincipled liar, or a more-or-less total incompetent as far as his memory was concerned, would seem to be more unreasonable than to accept that the psychic event had actually occurred. It is little wonder, then, that all sage and balanced counsel declared that at long last an irrefutable psychic anecdote had been found.

But among the readership of the *Nineteenth Century* magazine was one Mr Henry Balfour, who, having read Sir Edmund's totally irrefutable, absolutely watertight anecdote, was unable to suppress a niggling doubt and so he decided to do a bit of detective work. He was quickly successful in tracing the reporter whose death had taken place under such dramatic circumstances. He was the Reverend Hugh Lang Nivens, who had been editor of the *Shanghai Courier*, the local English-language newspaper, and he had indeed died on 20th January 1875. So far so good, but then there emerged a completely unexpected finding: the Reverend Nivens had actually died at *nine o'clock in the morning* and not at around one a.m. as all the circumstantial details in the story were implying! In one fell swoop one of the major planks on which the anecdote rested was slashed away. But this was merely the beginning. Balfour quickly made three more startling discoveries: that *no inquest was ever held on the death of Reverend Nivens*; that Judge Hornby *did not in fact marry until some months after the incident*; and, finally, that there was no record of any such judgement being delivered the next day corresponding to the one that the Judge was supposed to have given to the reporter, rough details of which had been found "scribbled in his notebook." By now the whole story lay like a collapsed house of cards and what was lauded as an irrefutable account of psychic experience was shown to be totally valueless.

Actually, valueless is not the right word, for in many people's view the debacle was instructive in a most important way, and probably tells one more about the operation of the human mind than any laboratory psychological test. When asked to comment on Balfour's exposure the Judge, as might be expected, did the best he could to defend himself, and admitted that he must have had a dream which followed the event by some months and which his memory had subsequently misplaced in time. This admission is probably the correct interpretation, for the results of psychological research on human memory and testimony show it to be particularly prone to displacements of dates and times, and dreams which are reported as being precognitive have often been established as occurring some time after the critical event has taken place. Nor as a rule is this displacement deliberately made up by the dreamer. Most people sincerely believe in the story they are telling and are flabbergasted when confronted with the contrary facts. Judge Hornby's amazement apparently knew no bounds. As he remarked in a letter to the editor of the *Nineteenth Century*: "If I had not believed...that every word of the story was accurate, and that my memory was to be relied on, I should never have told it as a personal experience." Of course he wouldn't. The story, as Balfour found out, was simply too easily checkable for the Judge to have fabricated it hoping that no one would follow it up. It is only too evident that Judge Hornby, and no doubt his wife, sincerely believed that the events *had* actually occurred as he recounted them, and it was with supreme confidence in his memory and his reliability as a witness that he committed it to the public gaze.

And this surely is the moral of the tale. When human beings tell stories, no matter how superficially convincing, about ghosts, premonitory dreams, apparitions and the like, one should have little, if any, cause to believe them. The evidence of the paranormal, if it exists at all, must be drawn from some other source.

The ghastly exposure of the cream of Myers' and Gurney's case book did not, of course, deter them or other workers from continuing to amass data of a similar, if less exciting, kind, and in 1886 they published an enormous tome, *Phantoms of the Living*, which contains more than seven hundred accounts of peculiar happenings. None was a patch on Sir Edmund's story, and, like his, none has stood up under a really critical inspection. By the early twentieth century even psychical researchers were beginning to realize the terrible weaknesses of anecdotal evidence and the hopelessness of relying on human memory. Serious efforts were therefore made to establish research on a more scientific footing, if possible applying the tools and knowledge of the rudimentary science of experimental psychology. After numerous false starts this approach culminated in the founding of the justly famous Parapsychology Laboratory at Duke University, North Carolina, under the energetic directorship of Dr J.B. Rhine.

Chapter 7

PROBING THE PARANORMAL

THE STORY OF Rhine's gallant attempt to subject so-called paranormal phenomena to the rigours of laboratory testing is a fascinating one, which cannot be adequately told in this book on dreams. A very brief summary is essential, however, in order to appreciate the transition that occurred between the kind of investigation that Myers and company initiated, and the serious attempt made by a later generation of researchers to trap the psychic dream in a laboratory.

Rhine, a botanist by profession, was much influenced by the émigré British professor of psychology at Duke, William McDougall, and he saw that anecdotal evidence was not the pathway to establishing the reality of psychic phenomena. Experiences of this kind, while madly convincing to those who actually have them, carry little weight when offered up to dispassionate scientists. The only tactic likely to succeed was to treat the phenomena as though they were measurable psychological variables, and attempt to examine them in the laboratory in the way that memory, learning and normal sensory abilities are studied. In the early days of the establishment of his lab, this tactic seemed to be paying off handsomely. Rhine was able to announce that, using the technique of long runs of card-guessing (using the famous Zener cards, consisting of five symbols—star, circle, square, triangle and wavy lines) he was finding clear evidence of telepathic abilities in many of his experimental subjects. Unfortunately the early promise of the Duke studies was dashed when serious design flaws were found in the experimental procedures, and when psychologists of a sceptical turn of mind were unable to repeat Rhine's findings in their own laboratories. A huge controversy, not entirely resolved today, ensued throughout the 1940s, '50s and '60s, with the majority of the scientific world dismissive of the evidence for telepathy and other forms of ESP. A small but vocal minority, however, held that telepathy *had* been proved, and that the rest of the scientific world was conspiring to conceal or repress the facts because these were inimical to cherished materialistic models of the universe.

Even so, disappointing though the laboratory telepathy studies may have been, they did at least provide evidence which the scientific establishment was forced to consider, whereas the anecdotal material was no more convincing than the average ghost story told around the winter fireside. But was there any way in which the anecdotal material itself could be trapped in the laboratory? Obviously not, since almost by definition it occurred at unpredictable intervals and in any case never on command. The closest thing to controlling it was tied up with the spiritualistic experiments of the nineteenth century which, anyway, were easily shown to be due to fraudulent mediums rather than to any interaction between the worlds of the normal and the paranormal. The study of apparently psychic dreams, which are reported extremely widely and might be looked on as the most common type of allegedly paranormal phenomena, was just as inaccessible and intangible. How could one ever hope to study a dream while it was happening? Unless one could find either some way of telling on what night a person was going to get a telepathic dream or a way of knowing when the dream was actually taking place, there really were no means of quantifying the material and meeting the sceptics' objections. As a result the interest of psychical researchers shifted away from such phenomena altogether, and concentrated on the at least marginally promising card-guessing studies. And so things might have remained, with the study of psychic dreams never moving far beyond their status in the Judge Hornby era, had it not been for the work of Kleitman and his associates during the 1950s.

I have already briefly referred to Kleitman's lengthy researches in his "sleep laboratories" (Chapter 4), but have not mentioned the now well-known observation that during a particular phase of sleep, coupled with a characteristic pattern of brain waves, the eyes make a series of rapid movements (REMs) which persist for periods of thirty minutes or more. The discovery of REMs and their significance will be discussed later on, but I will briefly mention (in any case, it is now one of the best-known facts about sleep research) that if people are wakened when in these REM phases they will more often than not report a dream, while if they are awakened in non-REM phases the chances are that they will not. To this I will add the caveat that things turn out to be less simple when they are inspected in more detail, but for the moment we will let this simple observation stand! REMs seem to be a signal as to when the individual is dreaming.

When this discovery was made it was immediately obvious that a major breakthrough had taken place, and among the many scientists who found their curiosity awakened was one psychiatrist who swiftly saw the potential for psychical research. He was Dr Montague Ullman, a distinguished clinician and theoretician who was then director of the Sleep Research Unit at the huge Maimonides Hospital in Brooklyn. Ullman, though directly involved in scientific research into sleep, was also as a psychiatrist actively concerned with the treatment of patients both at the hospital and in his private practice. Not obsessively interested in paranormal phenomena, he had nevertheless come to the conclusion that telepathic powers really did exist. His conviction was based on observations made in the course of psychiatric consultation. Often—too often, he reckoned, for it to be due to chance—it seemed that patient and doctor would be aware of each other's thoughts. In conversation with his colleagues he discovered that he was not alone in making this observation, and that apparent telepathic rapport between doctor and patient was a fairly common occurrence in psychiatric sessions. Ullman also found that the patient's dreams, which play a very important role in much psychoanalytic therapy, would often correspond in strange ways to his own, as though the close bond which is naturally struck up between psychiatrist and patient forged an even closer link through their dreams.

It was the dreams that particularly intrigued Ullman, and while he was not the first psychiatrist to spot this slightly eerie mental rapport, he was certainly the first to see a way of investigating it more thoroughly and possibly turning it to some purpose. In essence, what he realized was that one should be able to make use of the REM phase of sleep to introduce an element of control into the dream process. His technique was ingenious, and was aimed at providing just the kind of breakthrough in paranormal dream research that the field had long been waiting for.

If one accepts the reasonable assumption that underpins most psychical theories of dreams, that during sleep the mind is more open to telepathic input, then one should be able to induce telepathic dreams by the following method: Wait until a person is in the REM state (and presumably dreaming) and then concentrate vigorously on something which one hopes to "transmit" into his mind. After a given period of time, wake the sleeper up and ask him or her to report his dreams. Then, inspect these accounts to see if they contain elements of the transmitted thoughts. In practice his design, which was based on the techniques of experimental psychology, was far more elaborate and carefully structured. The experimental subject was allowed to sleep on a comfortable bed in a quiet room which no one other than the experimenters could enter, and which could be monitored by closed circuit TV cameras. Before going to sleep the subject was kitted up with a pair of simple electrodes fitted close to the eyes which recorded the electrical signals given off by the eye muscles when eye movements were taking place. This device, known as the electrooculogram or EOG, is more or less essential for anyone wanting to do serious studies of REM sleep, and of course it allowed the experimenters, who had set up camp indifferent room, to monitor the sleeper's eye movement and immediately detect the onset of REMs and dream sleep. In a third room, again virtually isolated from both the experimenter and the subject, there sat the individual who was to act as telepathic transmitter for the evening. This individual was in possession of a set of sealed envelopes whose contents had been selected by yet another experimenter. They consisted of a set of pictures, photographs, reproductions of famous paintings, freehand sketches, cartoons or whatever, selected for this particular trial at random out of a total pool of about a thousand pictures. the experimenter on a given night did not know which of the cards had been selected for use as "target" for that occasion; nor, needless to say, did the subject.

As soon as the EOG of the sleeper showed the first signs of REMs, the experimenter would press a buzzer to tell the transmitter that the time had come for him to open his first envelope. This contained a single picture. Then, while the sleeping subject was presumably in the middle of a dream, the transmitter would concentrate on the target. This would continue for several minutes until the EOG signalled the end of the dream period. At this point the experimenter would go into the sleep room, wake the subject and immediately ask him to report any dreams. The subject's full report would be tape-recorded and only after he was satisfied that he had detailed the whole of his dreams, would he be allowed to go back to sleep. Later, when the EOG again indicated a dream period, the same procedure would be followed, the transmitter opening a second envelope and concentrating on another picture. The purpose of the various precautionary measures will by now be clear. The experimenter visiting the subject in order to extract a dream report would not know what picture had been selected and therefore would be unable to bias the subject intentionally or otherwise. The only person who knew which pictures had been chosen would of course not be allowed access to the subjects at any time—indeed would be unlikely ever to know who had been chosen as subjects for the evening's experiment.

The next day the assessment of the results of the experiment was carried out, also using a cunning double-blind technique to exclude fraud or carelessness on the part of the experimenter. Another individual, designated the judge, was given a set of six or eight pictures, one of which included the target in a particular experiment. The judge of course did not know which of the set had been chosen as the target. He was also given a complete, unedited transcript of the dream report, and was asked to say which of the eight pictures most closely matched the report. The selection of two pictures was not allowed, and no discussion was permitted with the experimenter until the selection had been made. Now, by chance, and assuming that no telepathy was operating, the judge would match the target picture against the dream report once in every eight occasions. If telepathy was operating, however, then one might expect the judge to do better than chance, for the dream report would contain at least elements of the target stimulus.

This, then, was the virtually foolproof design that Montague Ullman and his colleagues worked out, and which represented the first controlled assault on that most elusive phenomenon—the paranormal dream. To his great delight, and to the equal delight of the world of parapsychology, his first major series of tests carried out at Maimonides in the 1960s yielded results strongly suggestive of telepathic contact. The results, reported to major psychological journals, showed that the judges were choosing the correct picture not by any means on every occasion, but significantly more often than would be expected if chance were operating. Sometimes the correspondences between the pictures and the transcribed dream report were very striking indeed, but on other occasions just fragments of the pictures seemed to be embedded in them. Occasionally, and no less surprisingly, the judge would match up the dream report with a target that had *not* been chosen, and the correspondences here, when looked at afterwards, would also seem to be remarkable! Either the mind of the dreamer was somehow roaming around the total set of targets, not concentrating particularly on the one that the transmitter was looking at, or (and this is the hypothesis that the sceptics tended to prefer) when one reads more or less any narrative and compares it with more or less any picture, astonishing correspondences—caused by the mind of the viewer unconsciously interpreting the material to match his own ideas—will be found. But even if this were true (one does tend to read things into ambiguous material, as a glance through newspaper horoscopes will demonstrate) it still does not explain the correct matching of pictures and dream report in the main experiments.

It is not surprising that the world of parapsychology was agog. Progress in the field had been painfully slow since the '30s, when Rhine founded his lab and nothing much in the way of a repeatable experiment, the only type of experiment that would convince the world of science, had emerged. Perhaps here, at last, was what everyone had been waiting for, and Ullman's use of the REM phase of sleep was the key to the long-overdue trapping of psychic powers in the laboratory. But it was not only the rather small world of parapsychology that was interested. Other scientists, sceptical up to this period, began to prick their ears up, and when the Maimonides team put forward a proposal for funding to the National Institutes of Health, one of the major US organizations supporting research into medical and psychological phenomena, it was granted with few reservations. This in itself constituted another breakthrough, for it was the first time that any US government agency had specifically funded a research project involving telepathy or kindred topics. Bursting with confidence and enthusiasm, the Maimonides team began another programme of research, the first aim of which was to replicate the original dream studies, demonstrate that the phenomenon was repeatable, and afterwards find ways of applying it in the public good.

In a long and rigorous series of experiments, the Maimonides team repeated their studies only to find that the original successes did not reappear. Time and time again only chance correspondences between the judge's matches and the actual target stimuli appeared. Disillusioned and bitterly disappointed, the Maimonides group, now headed by Charles Honorton, a leading figure in parapsychology, changed to another line of attack—the study of possible telepathic ability under special conditions of sensory deprivation—and effectively closed the book on the dream studies. At the same time the NIH grant, itself a kind of breakthrough in parapsychology, ran out, and because of the failure of the dream repeats was not renewed. For a brief period a bright light had flickered and then failed. Tempting though it may be to do so, I do not propose to discuss the deeper significance of the failure of these studies, and will simply comment that this kind of event—the apparent discovery of some aspect of psychic phenomena that allows it to be demonstrated in the laboratory, followed by failure to demonstrate the phenomena reliably on subsequent occasions — typifies the tangled history of psychical research. Psychic powers, if they exist at all, will always, it seems, remain a haphazard component of our universe.

But even if we have to dodge the issue of the existence or otherwise of psychic powers, we can reasonably come to some conclusions on the matter of the telepathic or psychic dream. On the basis of a study of the anecdotal material, which is both the most voluminous and the most superficially impressive, there is little doubt that even the best of the evidence is extremely thin. This is because it rests totally on human memory and observational powers which, as the story of Judge Hornby emphatically reveals, are intractably prone to error. This, of course, does *not* mean that paranormal experiences of a genuine kind do not occur during dreams—no one knows enough about the large and complicated universe we live in to avow that they do not—but rather that if inarguable evidence for them is some day forthcoming, it will not be on the basis of personal human testimony. Equally, such experiments as have been conducted on telepathic dreams under laboratory conditions have, after a promising beginning, yielded little. Once again this does *not* imply that telepathy does not occur in dreams, but rather that there is at present no scientific evidence to suggest that it does.

Despite this formidable negative evidence, there is no doubt it is psychologically painful to have to reject such a fascinating facet of nature, and one's thoughts keep drifting back to personal experiences, or to the stories told by others (always more impressive than one's own). How many times have you heard about someone who has dreamed of a plane crash the day before he was due to go on a flight, has cancelled the trip and been suitably rewarded for his caution because the plane crashed? How many stories has one heard of people who dream vividly about someone "they hadn't thought of for years," only to open the paper next day to read about their death? The list is endless, and despite the mountain of scepticism which the Judge Hornby revelation creates, one still finds a voice niggling in one's mind: Aren't there just *too* many of these stories for them all to be fraudulent or, more simply, coincidence? As to the matter of fraudulence, this is very easy to rule out in many cases. Often (and there are a few well-documented examples) the person having the premonitory dream, say of an aeroplane crashing, will tell his family, his secretary, his boss of his dream and of his change of plans. Equally, the dream of the long-lost friend will often be told to a wife or husband. There is no need to give other examples, or labour this point any further. What one does need to do is to ask what is the frequency of *non-paranormal* dreams of this kind? By this I mean occasions where the person cancels his flight reservation and then feels a big chump when the plane steadfastly refuses to crash, or when one kills the fatted calf in expectation of one's long-lost friend turning up with the money he owes, only to find that he remains impenetrably hidden in the jungles of Borneo? It is hard to say since, naturally, no one is motivated to keep records of such dull non-incidents. But they are highly important in assessing whether apparently paranormal events really are paranormal or whether they are merely due to chance.

One way to tackle the problem might be for everyone to keep a detailed dream diary and make the records available to some central body for analysis. The first proposal for something as ambitious as this came from the mathematician J.W. Dunne, whose two books *An Experiment with Time* and *The Serial Universe* caused a flurry of popular interest in precognitive dreams in the 1930s. In his first, and most intriguing, book he detailed a number of dreams of his own and then hunted in newspaper cuttings for correspondences. He came up with some immediately striking hits, and pulled them all together in *An Experiment with Time*, urging his readers to document their own dreams carefully. If they did so on a regular basis, he promised, they would soon see evidence of precognitive material, often featuring events which were physically very remote and not involving the dreamer in any obvious way—an earthquake in Madagascar, for example. Numerous readers followed his example in a rush of enthusiasm, producing thousands of dreams, but none of this possessed any real significance. All that happened was that most participants soon realized that their dream lives were full of all kinds of incidents, sometimes mundane, occasionally dramatic, but which seemed to be more related to their personal lives, wishes, expectations, hopes and fears than to anything happening in the future. In fact, while Dunne's book is extremely impressive on the first reading, it is astonishing how poorly it stands up to a second, closer inspection. I first read it as a teenager in the late 1940s when the intellectual climate was much more favourably disposed to these things, and was immediately inspired to generate a dream diary which dredged up all kinds of inconsequential material but, as far as I could tell, nothing at all about the future. My memory of Dunne's book as containing a whole string of remarkable dream coincidences stayed with me, and it was only when I began to prepare the background material for this book that I read it through carefully again. To my great surprise, I found only one or two of his "precognitive" dreams to be even remotely interesting, and most of them to be thin to the point of insubstantiality. Any reader who was similarly impressed by Dunne's book on a first reading is invited to try the experiment of re-reading it and to be prepared for a great disappointment.

More recently, a systematic attempt at gathering precognitive dreams on a large scale came from something which started off as the "*Evening*

Standard Premonitions Bureau." This was founded after the appalling disaster in Aberfan, Wales, in the mid-'60s, when a coal tip collapsed and buried the village school together with many of the local school children. After this ghastly event numerous people wrote in claiming to have had precognitive warning dreams of one kind or another. Realizing that, true or false, a precognitive dream which is only announced *after* the event has happened is but tenuous evidence, the science editor of the London newspaper the *Evening Standard*, Peter Fairley, launched a serious campaign inviting people to send in any spectacular dreams they had *as soon as they had them*, and allow them to be matched up against any events that occurred later. Significantly, after fifteen years or so of operation, the Bureau had gathered together many thousands of letters of one kind or another, but nothing that could be offered as scientific evidence for the existence of precognitive dreams. A few unusual dreams did, of course, occur, but against the huge background of non-events they amounted to no more than one might expect by chance.

But what do we mean by chance? How could it be established how many dreams of an apparently paranormal kind would occur "by chance" against how many apparently non-paranormal ones? Ideally one would need to know the total number of dreams about a particular subject occurring in the whole population, and of these the total number that appeared to relate to some future event which subsequently came true. Needless to say, such a monumental task is beyond the scope of even the most dedicated researchers, to determine how often an apparently precognitive dream will occur "by chance," but a serious attempt has been made at answering it, with interesting results. In 1965 an American psychologist had a vivid dream about a friend whom he claims he had not thought of for some time. He was awakened from his sleep by the phone ringing, only to find that it was indeed his friend who was calling him, for no particular reason, from Hawaii. The correspondence between the dream and the phone call was so amazing that for a while the psychologist was convinced that he had had a psychic experience. The odds against the coincidence were simply so astronomical that it was absurd to attribute them to chance. Had he not been trained as a scientist with a grounding in statistical methods he might have let things end there and become a convert to what one might describe as the psychic cause. But instead he sat down and did a bit of thinking. What actually *were* the odds against such an event happening? Clearly it depended on a number of factors of which the principal ones were the number of dreams he had, the number of friends he had, the number of telephone calls he normally received, and so on. But he also had to take into account the number of *other* people who were dreaming, the number of friends *they* had, etc., in order to establish what the likelihood of an event like that occurring by chance might be. When he did all the calculations—the exact figures have been published in the famous journal *Science* and have never been disputed on mathematical grounds—he found that while it was very unlikely indeed that the experience would happen to him or to any other individual, over the whole of the continental USA, *several thousand people* would be having just such an experience on any given night or morning. It is rather like the odds against winning the football pools: they are literally millions to one against in the case of any individual, but because such a vast number of individuals are taking part, the cumulative odds mean that one or two are successful every week. Of course the individual to whom the pools win actually happens — like the individual who is struck by lightning — considers it remarkable that it should have happened to *him*, and might even think that he was especially favoured by fortune. But the hand of fortune is in fact nothing more than the remorseless, inflexible and, to most people, mysterious law of chance in operation.

In the last three chapters we have been looking at the second great cluster of theories which attempt to say something about the nature of dreams, and, by implication, of sleep. It has been necessary to spend some time in this territory because widespread popular belief holds that there may be a strong element of the psychic and paranormal in many sleep experiences. Furthermore, scientific interest in this area has not been negligible. This interest has tended to concentrate on two areas—the anecdotal reports of precognitive or telepathic dreams, and, more recently, on gallant attempts to trap the telepathic dream in the research laboratory. Both strategies are entirely legitimate areas of study, but they are also areas which have failed to yield anything in the way of reliable, useful information. This does not mean, as I have said earlier, that there is no such thing as precognitive or telepathic dreams. Some day hard evidence for them may be forthcoming, though I personally doubt it. But whatever the final outcome, we should not at present feel obliged to take this particular view into account in seeking a new understanding of the mysteries of sleep and dreams. That said, we can move on to consider the third and final theoretical approach—the psychological.

Chapter 8

THE PSYCHOLOGICAL VIEW: ENTER
SIGMUND FREUD

WE HAVE NOW looked at two of the three principal theoretical approaches to the enigma of sleep and dreams and examined their inadequacies. The first, the *physical*, actually says very little about dreams, and tends to concern itself with the functions of the body and with describable anatomical and physiological states. The *psychical* approach, on the other hand, is more tied up with the theories of nature and the universe and requires little in the way of physiological back-up. In the present chapter we shall look at theories which could be described as being primarily *psychological*, and to do this we will of necessity be concentrating on the ideas of the best-known psychologist of all, Sigmund Freud.

The story of Freud's lifelong investigations into the nature of the human mind, of the extraordinary resistance he encountered in the course of his studies, and of the very real insights which he achieved en route is a riveting and revealing one, and has been told in a number of biographies. Here I shall look only at those aspects of Freud's life and career which are closely relevant to an understanding of dreams.

The first and most important concerns the frequency, range and nature of the sexual experiences reported by so many of Freud's patients. Vigorous sexual feelings were in his time supposed to be the prerogative of men, and even then of men who had no proper control over themselves. Women were supposed to be largely unsullied by such matters, unless they were in some way depraved. The finding that tangled but powerful sexual emotions were clearly revealed by his respectable, middle-class women patients undoubtedly jolted Freud at first; though he could see the dangers of pushing deeper into this territory, he was too courageous to back off as so many others must have done in the past. Freud's second major observation surprised him even more. A large number of the memories recalled by his patients during free association sessions dated back to childhood and often involved a sexual advance or even assault by the young girl's father. Facing up to these astonishing findings, Freud made the only reasonable deduction: hysterical and neurotic behaviour was due to a trauma which was implanted by the shock of sexual parental assault. Where a childhood trauma was not revealed, a sexual conflict, frustration or aggression could be traced to some event later in the patient's life. Having uncovered these findings and come to these conclusions, he began to give lectures and publish papers on his thesis, that most, probably *all*, hysterical and neurotic behaviour originated in some sexual trauma or conflict. It is not hard to envisage the consternation and horror that greeted these inimical pronouncements. Freud was cold-shouldered by his university colleagues, spurned by fellow physicians and rejected by an increasing number of patients. This hostility had the predictable effect of strengthening his resolve and luring him deeper into the treacherous waters of the unconscious mind.

The heroic nature of the task he had undertaken—we shall be casting a very critical eye over his findings and his conclusions later—cannot be overestimated. Quite apart from challenging the establishment view of a particular branch of science—a risky business at the best of times —Freud was also putting forward ideas which would ultimately rock the foundations of nineteenth-century society. In the first place he was questioning the sexual role of women in a society which wished, for one reason or another, to deny that role altogether. In the second place, by suggesting that the traumas of childhood could affect people in their adult life, he was stating, by implication, that children were capable of sexual experience, if only of a rudimentary kind. From this was to emerge the theory of infantile sexuality, now widely accepted on the basis of physiologicial and anatomical facts, but in the late nineteenth century rejected as a degradation of the purity of infancy. Thirdly, he was obviously implying that sexual drives, emotions and needs played a vital role in a "normal" human life—an assertion that was diametrically opposed to the moral and religious precepts of the time. Finally, he was coming to recognize the significance of unconscious mental processes in determining human behaviour. Once again this was a notion which went against the ethos of the time, not just of the closed, complacent Viennese circles in which Freud moved, but virtually the whole of the western world. It is at this point that we come to the crux of the Freudian position, and in particular those aspects of his theory which throw light on the mystery of dreams. But to understand this properly we need to penetrate a little more deeply into the body of the theory.

Freud's uncompromising stand on the aetiology of the neuroses, to the effect that they were *all* caused by sexual frustration or conflict, was in large part based on his clinical observations. Patient after patient, in the course of the technique which began to be known as psychoanalysis, ultimately revealed some sexual trauma lodged in their past history, and more often than not in some childhood incident. The evidence was too compelling and too clear-cut for it to be ignored. But not only was it too compelling, it was also, he began to perceive, too frequent. The stories of infantile seduction, rape and perversion allegedly committed by fathers on their infant daughters piled up endlessly until they assumed a frequency which was altogether improbable. Another suspicious observation was that tales of such sexual traumas were rarely, if ever, found in the delirious ramblings of psychotics. This would imply that they were significant only to the aetiology of relatively mild disorders, a suggestion which Freud found hard to accept. Finally, to reinforce the pattern of doubt, there was the fact that a high percentage of his analytical treatments were failing to reach a satisfactory conclusion, despite the fact that the key traumatic episodes whose identification should discharge the neurosis were apparently being uncovered. The only conclusion which would fit with the framework of his ideas was that either the childhood traumas were *not* the key episodes—in which case something even more horrid and startling was remaining hidden—or that the traumas were not at all what they seemed. Gradually Freud came to the unpalatable conclusion that despite the vividness of detail and the relish with which they were often related, the "memories" of sexual assault which his women patients were dredging up were not real memories at all. They must be fantasies which had, in some totally puzzling way, assumed the garb of reality in the patient's mind.

As Freud himself later acknowledged, his reaction to this discovery was "helpless bewilderment." His first temptation was to give up in despair and go back to his former dull but unthreatening career of a general practitioner. Fortunately his underlying convictions overruled this. If the simplistic version of the theory no longer matched up to the facts, then what was required was a modification to make sure that it *did* match. And there was little doubt as to what form this modification would take:

"If hysterics trace back their symptoms to fictitious traumas," he wrote, "this new fact signifies that they create such scenes of fantasy, and *psychical reality requires to be taken into account alongside actual reality.*"

The italics in his final phrase are mine, and serve to emphasize the historic importance of this remark. The idea, of course, is that there are at least two levels of reality. The first is that of the external world which is perceived by all men and is normally referred to as objective reality. The second is internal, psychological or, as Freud puts it, psychical reality, which is that perceived only by the individual and never directly by anyone else, and which is normally referred to as subjective reality. The distinction between the objective and the subjective is one that was made in the very early days of philosophy, but the bold inference that Freud was making was that there were aspects of the mind, the personality, that perceived both objective and subjective matters but which were incapable of discriminating between the two. Both, to put it plainly, were equally *real*. Once he had ventured down this path he was drawn towards another conclusion: the conscious mind being primarily concerned with objective reality, as it was this that it had most contact with in day-to-day life, would only act on the basis of experiences coming to it from the objective world. But any part of the mind which was incapable of distinguishing between subjective and objective reality would, of course, act sometimes on the basis of one and sometimes on the basis of the other. And just as both were, in its terms, equally real, so its actions and decisions would have the force of reality and would affect the individual accordingly.

This concept, once formulated, was earth-shaking. For thousands of years, indeed since the birth of organized religion, human beings were taught to believe that they were essentially two entities, a physical and mortal body, and a non-physical and indestructible soul or spirit. The purpose of life was to test the fortitude of the soul in the face of the temptations of the physical world. In principle, there was no reason why any human being should not be capable of overcoming all these physical trials. It was a matter of a kind of spiritual potency which within the Victorian ethic was better described as will-power. No human being, in other words, could really be excused for yielding to temptation—at least not for very long. A wicked man was wicked because he *chose* to be, a spiritual man was weak because he lacked the moral courage to do what he knew was right. And even the most wayward could, with the right kind of spiritual incentive, regain control of his own affairs. The essence of life, therefore, was personal responsibility summed up in the saying: "I am the captain of my fate and master of my soul."

What totally horrified any contemporaries who read Freud's writings on the subject was that he appeared to be propounding a view which denied this notion. What he was saying was that there was some aspect of man's mind or personality which was not a complete slave to the mind or will and that had wishes and needs of its own which it would strive to fulfil. Worse yet, these hidden or unconscious forces were often unrecognized by and unknown to the conscious mind, which would be taken aback when the body, over which it fondly believed it had absolute control, proceeded on an apparently independent, even irrational, path of action. Excellent examples of this were the behaviour pattern manifested in phobias and compulsions which are characteristically quite outside the subjugative power of the conscious mind. As if to compound the tangle, the motivating forces which drove the unconscious mind into these actions operated on a plane to which the conscious mind appeared to have no access. In this way the behaviour was not only uncontrollable but also incomprehensible.

Once he came to these dramatic conclusions, Freud was in a position to understand his patients' most irrational and bizarre behaviour. The tortured beings who came to his consulting room for help were suffering not from disorders of their spirit which could be checked by willpower, nor from neurological or pathological disorders of the brain, but from conflicts between their conscious day-to-day selves and powerful, irrational forces which lay in the unconscious portions of the mind. There now remained only one path open to Freud: he must find some way of penetrating the crust that separated the conscious and the unconscious, in order to communicate with the hidden forces that lay beneath. Hardly had he come to these conclusions when the solution, or rather *a* solution, was revealed to him.

In the course of free association the subject matter of patients' ruminations would often turn out to be the memory of a recent dream. The frequency with which dreams turned up, either directly reported or after subsequent questioning, intrigued Freud who became even more interested when he began to look at the raw material or narrative of the dream. Sometimes no obvious pattern emerged, and the narrative or plot followed a familiar haphazard plan, a finding which accorded with the contemporary "scientific" view of dreams as the ramblings of the partially conscious mind. On the other hand, there were occasions when they contained a simple, inarguable message. The first example he reported on was based on the dream of a medical student who for some time had been extremely reluctant to go to the hospital in the morning. Once, when woken by his landlady, he went back to sleep and dreamt that he had got up, dressed and made his way to the hospital. This kind of dream is one that most readers will be familiar with: its most common form is encountered when the need to urinate becomes urgent in the middle of the night, when the forces of sleep and the comforts of a warm bed are still overpowering. The resulting dream can take two forms—either one has got up and is urinating, or one is getting up and looking all over the place for suitable places to urinate. The latter dream, perhaps fortunately, is the more common version. It did not take Freud long to distil the essence of the dream: it served to gratify or fulfil a wish, the wish to go off to the hospital without actually having to take the trouble to get out of a warm bed to do so, and without the inconvenience of waking the sleeper. Having discovered one inarguable principle lying behind dreams, the next step was to see whether the principle would hold for other dreams as well. Unfortunately (or perhaps in the long run fortunately) other dreams were far less forthcoming in the way they announced their purpose. Most were far from obviously concerned with wish fulfilment and in some cases seemed to be running on almost the opposite lines. This was irritating because it implied that there might be several, perhaps a great many, principles operating to determine the nature of dreams.

His next tactic was to look more deeply at the structure of the dream, trying to peer beyond the narrative and the "obvious" factual building blocks to see if a wish striving for fulfilment might somewhere be revealed. In doing this he was accepting the fact that in between their occurrence and the time of their recall, the details of the dream would inevitably have been corrupted through the weaknesses inherent in the memory process. A period of thorough analysis of both his own and his patients' dreams followed through the closing months of 1894 and right into the summer of 1895. And then, on the night of Tuesday 23rd July in that year, he had a dream which was so fascinating and bewildering that he made it the subject of an intensive analysis on the following day. Since immortalized as "The Dream of Irma's Injection," the full text can be read in Freud's own classic *The Interpretation of Dreams*. But it and the case history which was a part of it can be summarized without losing its flavour or its importance.

In the weeks before the dream Freud had been treating an attractive young woman who was also a family friend. Some headway had been made and her anxiety attacks had lessened, but it was by no means certain that the case was wrapped up. Before closing up his practice for the summer vacation, however, he told her where he felt the roots of the trouble lay and, even though she did not seem terribly convinced, treatment came to a temporary halt. While they were on vacation, a doctor friend named Otto who had recently been staying with Irma and her family came to see Freud. When the latter asked how Irma was he replied, in what seemed to be a slight tone of reproof or disapproval, "She's better but not quite well." Later that evening, slightly irked at Otto's manner, he wrote out Irma's case history in detail, intending to send it to another medical friend, a Dr M., with the vague aim of justifying his own treatment. That same night he had the celebrated dream.

He was in a large hall where numerous people were mingling, among them Irma, whom he immediately took aside and said, "If you've still got pains, it's really only your fault." To this she replied, "If you only knew what pains I've got now in my throat and stomach." Noticing how ill she looked, he "took her to the window and looked down her throat." On the right side of her mouth he saw a big white patch, and some "extensive whitish grey scabs upon some remarkably curly structures which were evidently modelled on the turbinal bones of the nose." Fearing that he had missed some serious organic trouble in his original treatment, he called over Dr M. who in the dream looked very different from his normal self, being pale, clean-shaven and walking with a limp. The other doctor Otto was also present and he began tapping her chest saying, "She has a dull area low down on the left," and pointed out that there were signs of a disease on the skin of her left shoulder. Dr M. now said, "There's no doubt it's an infection, but no matter, dysentery will supervene and the toxins will be eliminated." Earlier (in the dream) Otto had given her "an injection of a preparation of propionic acid...trimethylamin," and in the dream the formula for this appeared before him printed in heavy type. The dream closed with Freud thinking to himself that "injections of that sort ought not to be made so thoughtlessly, and it was also probable that the syringe had not been clean."

The dream is a hotchpotch typical of the kind we have all, at one time or another, experienced. The principal characters may be well known to us, though they may be bizarrely changed in certain respects, and the setting may be a vaguely identifiable one. The *dramatis personae* sometimes perform sensibly, while at other times they act in ways which are foreign to their nature. The whole thing is carried along with a definite but peculiar grammar of its own. Small wonder that the naive view has always been that these are little more than the ramblings of a partially conscious mind. But to Freud's quizzical inspection a definite and discoverable logic was beginning to emerge. In the first place he noted that the identifiable characters in the dream had figured in his life on the previous day, if only because they had been the subject of thoughts or conversations, but mainly because they had actually formed the subject of actual experiences. Irma, for example, had obviously been at the forefront of his mind as the subject of an important and worrying conversation with the young doctor known as Otto. Dr M. too, while not physically presenting himself to Freud, was to be the recipient of the case history of Irma specially written out for him. So far so good, but what of the other features of the dream? What was the nature of the odd conversation between the dream Freud and the dream Irma? What were the peculiar marks and growths in her throat? Why was Dr M. so peculiarly metamorphosed, and what was the point of Dr Otto's percussions? Even more peculiar, what was the significance of the remark about dysentery, the injection of propionic acid with its formula? And why the remark about the dirty syringes?

In considering all this, Freud was faced with a crucial choice: he could take the easy way out and say that while some dreams represented wish-fulfilment, others were just jumbles of odd events that had occurred the previous day. Or he could stick to his original hunch that *all* dreams represented wish-fulfilment, but that the nature of the wish was not always as explicit as one would like. The second alternative was by far the more challenging and the more difficult to demonstrate, and Freud, of course, opted for it. The result was that after a very devious analysis he managed to produce an interpretation of the key events in the dream which did indeed fit in with the theory of wish-fulfilment. From that moment on the psychoanalytic approach to dream interpretation—and, one might as well add, just about every modern approach to the subject—was launched into being. The following is a rough précis of his interpretation with the numerous, but closely linked, wish-fulfilments revealed.

The presence of Irma needed no explanation, nor the conversation with her. Freud is reproaching her because she had brought her troubles on herself (his wish, of course, is that this would be proven to be so). She makes references to pains in the stomach, very much the hysterical symptoms she had complained of (and Freud was "wishing" that she would recognize what they were). His examination of her and discovery of definite physical signs represented his "wish" that she did indeed have some organic illness which would absolve him from responsibility for her cure. The scabs in the turbinal bones might be interpreted in the same light, but why the turbinal bones (these are the tiny structures which hold up the bridge of the nose)? By an interesting twist of interpretation Freud sees these as referring to his own predilection for co-caine, which he was using at the time in an attempt to relieve some swelling in *his own nose*. The strange appearance of Dr M., clean-shaven and limping, seemed peculiarly puzzling, but on reflection he realized that this was a kind of dream amalgam, a fused image of the real Dr M. and of Freud's brother who was indeed clean-shaven and walked with a limp. The reason the two men were blended in the dream was simple: he had been annoyed with both of them recently about a rather similar matter. The appearance of Otto similarly needs little interpretation. True to Freud's hidden wish, Otto's presence and general activities are confirming that there is something physically the matter with Irma, who indeed showed some organic condition on her shoulder. This logic is pursued with Dr M.'s remark "It's an infection," and Freud later recalled that he had found a mild infective condition present in her at the time of first examination. The medically nonsensical remark about dysentery eliminating the toxin was more obscure. Ultimately Freud tracked it down to a patient whom he had been treating earlier for a severe gastric symptom which he was confident was hysterical. The patient had gone off on a trip to Egypt from where he had written despairingly saying that he was crippled with dysentery. Again Freud suspected hysteria, but the fear that he had made a wrong diagnosis was playing on his mind and found itself flowering in the dream.

We now come to the injection sequence. This is obviously built up of a number of layers, all of which are linked to his friend Otto. In the analysis Freud remembered that during his stay with Irma's family he had been called to the neighbouring hotel to give an injection to someone who was unwell. The substance of the injection, however, had not been trimethylamin, whose formula had appeared so vividly in the dream. After sifting through various possibilities Freud gradually began to put together an exotic interpretation. The only context in which this chemical rang bells in his memory was a long discussion he had once with his friend Wilhelm Fliess, an ear, nose and throat specialist, who had told him that one of the products of the sexual metabolism was trimethylamin. Fliess, incidentally, was a brilliant crank who had influenced Freud greatly and who, amongst other things, was propounding a bizarre hypothesis that there was a link between disorders of the nasal and the genital organs. Hence the strong role played in the dream by the mysterious structures "like the turbinal bones of the nose" in Irma's mouth. At the time too, Freud was himself devoting a lot of psychic energy to advancing his own controversial ideas about the sexual basis of neuroses, which he assumed must underlie Irma's troubles. There now remained to explain only the reference to the "thoughtless" giving of injections, another implied criticism of Otto, and the "unclean syringes." In the latter case Freud tracked down the image to an injection which he had given a day or so earlier to an old lady suffering from phlebitis. At the time Freud had thought to himself that the phlebitis was caused by a dirty syringe, and rather smugly congratulated himself that, in the whole of his medical practice, he had never caused an infection through unclean equipment. Once again the episode served as a back-up testimony to his medical powers and correctness.

As soon as he achieved this analysis Freud was struck with the certainty that he had discovered the true nature and meaning of dreams. There are numerous references in his own writings and correspondence that testify to this. After revisiting the hotel where he had the dream he wrote to Fliess:

> Do you suppose that some day a marble tablet will be placed on the house, inscribed with these words: "In This House, On July 24, 1895, the Secret of Dreams was Revealed to Dr Sigmund Freud"?

Many years later Freud was to sit on the terrace of the hotel with his biographer, Ernest Jones, at the very table where the self-analysis had taken place and jokingly remark that the tablet had not yet been erected. Nor was it ever. No matter, for Freud erected for himself monuments far more durable than any block of marble and one of them is almost certainly his classic book, in which dozens of other dreams, some more remarkable but none so historic as "Irma's injection," are painstakingly analysed. All follow the line that the dream, in part and in whole, acts to fulfil a wish of some kind, in the Irma case the over-all "wish" being that Freud's own professional judgement would be vindicated. The wish in this case, incidentally, is clearly an amoral one, typical, as Freud was to find out, of the unconscious which has few ethical scruples or any sense of compassion for others. Woven into the tapestry were numerous other sub-thematic wishes which there is no space to explore here. But all in all, in Freud's own words, the interpretation showed "that dreams really have a meaning and are far from being the expression of a fragmentary activity of the brain. *When the work on interpretation has been completed, we perceive that the dream is the fulfilment of a wish.*"

This simplistic yet elegant view remained the main prop of Freud's theoretical approach for the rest of his life, and it became incorporated into the dogma of the Freudian school of psychology where it has remained, relatively unchanged, to this date. This is despite the fact that it has certain grave limitations which we shall be looking at more closely very shortly. Its staying power is due to one central fact: it was the first coherent, workable theory offering an explanation of both the nature and the function of dreams. All previous efforts were at best partial explanations, and at worst cavalier guesses which were untestable, unusable and often self-contradictory. The Freudian argument had a logical power which could not be denied and offered genuine explanations of otherwise totally mysterious events.

Like many revolutionary ideas it fell on deaf or, to be more exact, selectively hostile ears. Freud was ignored by his colleagues, even snubbed, and his practice, patchy enough anyway, began to dwindle to vanishing point. Scandalous rumours were spread not only about his motive for writing the book—such as it being a sensationalistic way to make money—but also about his involvement with the sex lives of his patients. This frigid boycott of his work and ideas was deeply distressing to him, though he was perspicacious enough to understand many of the reasons for the hostility he was facing. He cannot, therefore, have been too surprised at the size of the audience when he gave his first formal lecture on dreams on 14th May 1900. Today, of course, a lecture by Freud on just about anything would fill Wembley Stadium or the Houston Astrodome, but his audience on that historic occasion was so small that we can actually name it. Present were a Mr Hans Konigstein, a Miss Dora Teleky, and a Dr Marcuse. Sitting self-consciously in the first row of the dreary lecture theatre, these three were present when psychology turned a corner and a seminal philosophical movement was born. And what about all the others who should have been there, those bearded and self-opinionated colleagues who had more important things to do that May evening? Too bad for them. They missed it.

Before moving from what may seem to be a rather laudatory view of Freudian thinking, and launching into a critical evaluation of this theory of dream interpretation, I want to recap on Freud's contribution to psychology as a whole. Over the course of his life Freud evolved a comprehensive theory of mental life in which not only the conscious workings of the mind but also its unconscious and sleeping operations were described and analysed. He saw the mind as a multi-layered structure, each layer having distinctive mechanics, principles of operation and a degree of autonomy. Nevertheless, the independence of one layer from another could be considerable, particularly in the case of the distinction between the unconscious and the conscious. Freud is often credited with the "discovery" of the unconscious mind, but the concept was actually floating around in nineteenth-century literature decades before he began to work with it. The poet Wordsworth seems to have been the first to use the word in the English language around 1800, and the German equivalent, meaning roughly "unconsciousness," was commonly used in philosophy and in the early psychological literature. The scholar F.W.H. Myers, whom we met in Chapter 6 because of his pioneering work on psychical dreams, played around with the term quite extensively and introduced the idea of a "subliminal self," which he believed was responsible for such phenomena as dreams, hallucinations, psychoses, hypnotic behaviour, automatic writing and even poltergeist activity. As for dreams themselves, Ralph Waldo Emerson in 1883 remarked, "A skilful man reads his dreams for his self-knowledge. However monstrous and grotesque their apparitions, they have a substantial truth," and odd remarks of a similar kind pop up from time to time in the Victorian literature. Freud's real contribution was in exploring the idea of the autonomous unconscious with real thoroughness and then incorporating it into a wider theory. In the course of doing so he became the first to realize the huge power of the unconscious, and it is for this that he will always be remembered.

Over the course of time Freud's multi-layered model began to acquire detail. He saw most psychological behaviour as representing a struggle between two partly autonomous facets of the mind, the Ego and the Id. The latter is the more primitive and the more fundamental, representing virtually the whole of the mind at birth. Being an amalgam of all inherited instinctive needs and behaviour patterns, the Id is preoccupied with self-gratification —the primary instincts necessary to assure its survival—and remains so throughout life. Its actions are blind, yet purposive, unconcerned with, perhaps even unaware of, the needs of others, and amoral in the strictest interpretation of the word. As the individual moves out of infancy into childhood, however, the phenomenon of unconsciousness begins to emerge, together with ways of behaving, thoughts, wishes and so on which are not purely instinctive. With their emergence the Ego—in adults the component of the personality that is self-aware, the part that thinks of itself as "me"—begins to develop and in due course becomes the greater part of the conscious mind. The Ego has little access to, even little awareness of, the unconscious, but is unable to avoid interacting with it whenever its wishes conflict with those of the largely unconscious Id. One might instance the very common situation where physical hunger triggers off Id drives to eat, and yet the Ego wishes to continue on some conscious activity until an appropriate "eating time" appears. Here the clash of wills is not likely to be serious, and the Ego resolves the problem to the discomfiture of the Id, by "repressing" the Id's "Eat now!" demands, shoving them temporarily out of consciousness.

By this model the whole of life can be looked on as a tussle between Ego and Id, often on trivial, easily resolved matters, but sometimes on more serious grounds. In the case of food, for example, no real conflict is likely to ensue because the gratification of the Id will never be too long delayed—at least in affluent societies. But anyone who has had a weight problem and has been condemned to dieting for weeks or months will know how powerful, how overwhelming on occasions, Id forces can be. An even more potent example is drug addiction, where the Id requires gratification so badly that it will overwhelm Ego resistance, making the sole goal of life the quest for the drugs it desires. Somewhere in between lies the example of sexual deprivation, less critical than food deprivation because it does not lead to death. After a period in which the Id's sexual needs are not satisfied the Ego resorts to its tactics of repression—refusing to allow them to drift up from the unconscious into the conscious. But this tactic will only work for a limited period, and in due course tension builds up in and around the Id which bursts forth in some other mode, in particular, according to Freud, in the form of hysterical or neurotic symptoms. Identifying the precise nature of Ego/Id conflicts through psychoanalysis should allow the problem to be resolved.

Later on in the evolution of his psychodynamic theory, Freud introduced a third major "mental activity"—the Superego. This is only fleetingly involved in dreams, but I will explain it briefly because it can be looked at afresh in the light of the computer-based theory I shall be expounding later. The Superego, which is represented more or less equally in the conscious and unconscious segments of the mind, consists of the demands that the outside world makes on both the Ego and the Id—the pressures to conform to the wishes and needs of others and of society in particular. The larger part of the Superego is made up of parental injunctions and prohibitions which begin to impinge on the personality at an early age, and it is almost always diametrically opposed to Id needs and often those of the Ego. In the march through life therefore the other forces blend, squabble and interplay continuously. The "sane," "happy" persona, broadly speaking, is one who manages to balance the three out with the minimum of disruptive conflict, while the disturbed, "unhappy" individual is one who cannot achieve this balance and who resorts to denying or repressing any conflicts that do occur rather than attempting to resolve them openly.

These are the main mechanisms of the Freudian theory of mental dynamics. Simplifying them still further they go as follows: Man is a creature of instincts, but he lives in a world where selfish, blindly instinctive behaviour conflicts with the needs and requirements of the society of which he is a part. Conflicts ensue, many of which are shelved by suppressing them into the unconscious. From here they continue to exert their power, with varying strength, and also reveal themselves in dreams which arise when the conscious mind is off guard. In that way dreams reflect the working, and in many cases the conflicts, of the mind as a whole, and act, in Freud's imperishable words, as the "Royal Road to the Unconscious." The theory is immensely attractive because it does seem to allow one to unravel the bizarre world of the dream. Wishes, needs and desires that are incompatible with the realities of personal or social life are pushed down out of consciousness where they no longer bother the Ego. In sleep the wishes achieve vicarious discharge through the dream, which not only reduces internal pressure but also saves the Ego from having to continue to exert pressure during the day keeping the repressed desires bottled up. The need for a regular nightly session of dreaming to cope with the unfulfilled wishes of the day is understandable, and accounts for Freud's finding that the raw material of the dream is invariably composed of elements of the previous day's experiences. The narrative structure of the dream is determined by that portion of the unconscious that devotes itself to these things which Freud called the "dream work."

On the basis of everything we have been saying, dreams should be relatively simple to interpret and should all feature obvious (and not so obvious) expressions of an unfulfilled wish. Perhaps for reasons of internal economy the wishes might all be dealt with in one grand scenario, no doubt producing the kind of Alice-in-Wonderland narrative that runs through most complex dreams. But once one has peered through this barrier, the message of the dreams should be extremely direct. That this is clearly not the case is evident to anyone who has spent any time at all examining their own dream life. Dreams, even making allowances for their peculiar logic, do not always signal their message with clarity; in fact clear messages are the exception rather than the rule. Freud himself soon came to accept this, arguing that the message often required interpretation, the Irma dream being an excellent example. But why should the message be blurred to the point that it required interpretation? Having been pushed down into the unconscious, why should it not emerge as a more or less direct replica of its original form, allowing for minor distortions due to memory failings and so on? Clearly this is a puzzle which must be solved if the wish-fulfilment theory is to stand, and Freud faced up to it immediately.

The importance of the dream, he said, was *to preserve the state of sleep*. The bottled-up wishes stewing away below the surface would need to be discharged gently if the conscious mind, and in particular the Ego which had spent all day keeping the lid on them, were not to be alerted to what was happening. In many cases the discharge could be effected easily if the wishes, and hence the content of the dream, were not particularly threatening. But in some cases—perhaps the majority—the nature of the original wishes was such that their discharges would be so alarming as to cause the sleeper to awake. To meet this problem Freud proposed that in the course of the dream, the most threatening and anxiety-provoking wishes would be disguised or transmuted into a form which would be acceptable and unlikely to arouse the sleeping person. With this fertile notion, Freud immediately dealt with all those dreams or portions of dreams which did not instantly reveal their wish-fulfilment message. Any enigmatic dreams represented wishes whose true nature would be so shocking if dreamed in their raw state that the sleeper would wake and the whole purpose of the exercise would be ruined.

This solution was ingenious, to say the least, and did indeed allow the theory to stand in its original form. But it also brought problems in its wake, as we shall see in the next chapter.

Chapter 9

CRACKS IN THE FREUDIAN EDIFICE

COMPELLINGLY ELEGANT THOUGH it was, Freud's theory was not beyond criticisms, the most powerful being tied up with the problem of determining the rules for penetrating the dream's disguise. If the technique of dream analysis was to be a fruitful one, allowing the analyst to identify the anxieties which the Ego had shoved into the unconscious, one obviously had to discover the transformation rules by which the disguise mechanisms operated. Because of their frequency of occurrence, some of these were, in Freud's view, easy to identify and categorize, and they have since become the famous, or infamous, symbols which feature in just about every book on dream interpretation. They are so well-known as to be almost wearisome to repeat: the snake, staff, or any elongated object to represent the phallus; the shoe, cave, door the vagina; the empty house the body, and so on. Their very familiarity is a born testimony to the extent to which Freudian ideas have penetrated our present culture, and something of a hurdle in the way of an objective appreciation of their validity. Is the tremendous plausibility of this kind of symbolism simply because one has been exposed to the idea for so long and because they have featured in numerous novels, articles, films, and paintings? Or is it because we *do* have some intuitive understanding, however fleeting, of our own internal mental processes which signals the validity of the symbolism? My personal hunch is the latter, but leaving this aside for the moment one now begins to perceive a grave difficulty for the Freudian approach. If one accepts the notion of disguise and deliberate distortion of the dream forms so that the horror of their true nature is never revealed to the dreamer, one then has to ask how the intepretative dictionary is compiled by the analyst in the first place. Who is to declare that the serpent is a disguised representation of the penis, or a dark room the womb to which we are all supposed to crave to return? Is this catalogue of symbols the fruit of a fertile imagination on the part of its compiler?

Followers of Freud reply that the symbols are verified by objective observation. Once the dreamer appreciates them for what they are then the message of the dream becomes obvious and the root of the conflict is removed. But pressing the point reveals that things are not as simple as all that. Who decides, for example, whether the message *has* been correctly interpreted? The simplest response would be that if as a result of the interpretation the patient was able to eliminate the conflict and make a complete recovery, then the interpretation must have been correct. But things rarely work themselves out in that clear-cut way. The occasions when the interpretation of a dream leads directly to a dramatic cessation of hysterical symptoms are few and far between. Such sensational catharses may have taken place in the very early investigations, and no doubt Freud once hoped that things would always work out that way, but they are not, alas, a feature of modern psychoanalytic therapy. An alternative answer, albeit one fraught with terrible pitfalls, is that a dream interpretation is considered to be successful either when it is declared to be such by the dreamer or by the analyst; in other words, when either or both feel that the interpretation makes sense within the Freudian scheme. The dangers of this strategy are that the whole exercise becomes self-fulfilling, and that one interprets a mystery dream in more or less whatever way one wants—a tendency which has become one of the most unfortunate features of psychoanalysis and which has laid the method and theory open to ridicule. Anyone doubting this should riffle through the pages of psychoanalytic texts from Freud up to the present day when it will be obvious that in the quest for the latent wish-fulfilment elements in a dream the most far-fetched interpretations are resorted to. Some dreams, such as the Irma one, do indeed lend themselves to a ready interpretation, but others can only be revealed as "significant" with the wildest and most freewheeling interpretations —interpretations which are greeted with ribald amusement by most people uncommitted to the Freudian point of view (though not necessarily antagonistic towards it). Just how easy it is to produce interpretations to fit one's own theoretical framework can be seen by anyone who wants to try out the exercise on the Irma dream. It will swiftly be seen that Freud's interpretation was a purely personal one and by no means the only possible view. The famous injection sequence, for example, which Freud argues is related to Dr Otto's injection of someone who fell ill while he was staying with Irma's family, could be interpreted differently, although entirely in keeping with the Freudian ethos. Would it not be just as easy to see the hypodermic syringe as a phallic symbol, implying either that Freud was anxious to impregnate his attractive young patient, or perhaps that he suspected Dr Otto of wishing to do so? The comment about the syringe being "dirty" could then be looked upon as indicating Freud's disgust at his own base and unethical desires, while the remark about "injections of this kind ought not to be made so thoughtlessly" becomes self-explanatory.

The arbitrary interpretation hypothesis is clearly only too easy. Furthermore, the logic of the Freudian view — that the theory of wish-fulfilment provides a comprehensive theory of dreams and that all dreams can be expressed on this basis — means that the analyst is more or less obliged to provide an interpretation of *every* dream. Where the dream is "obvious," then all is well and good. Where it is obscure, the principle of disguise must be operating and the hidden meaning must be unravelled. Where the dream is downright peculiar or apparently trivial, then the disguise principle is clearly at work even more cunningly and the latent content may be of even greater significance. There are some exotic examples of the determined interpreter's craft, where the most incomprehensible and irrelevant details in a dream are transformed into points of fundamental significance while the most simple and straightforward features find themselves metamorphosed into tangled obscurities. One of many that could be chosen comes from Freud's own *magnum opus, The Interpretation of Dreams,* in which an intelligent and cultivated woman is reported as describing the following dream to him:

> She dreamt she was going to market with her cook, who was carrying the basket. After she had asked for something, the butcher said to her: "That's not obtainable any longer," and offered her something else, adding "this is good too." She rejected it and went on to a woman who sells vegetables. She tried to sell her a peculiar vegetable that was tied up in bundles but was of a black colour. She said, "I don't recognize that — I won't take it."

If one simply took the line that dreams reflect memories of events which had occurred the previous day then one might expect to find that the woman had been shopping the previous day and had been unable to get what she wanted. Such a finding would fit quite nicely with the basic Freudian idea—frustrated over her failure at the market, she was pursuing the topic in her dreams. In fact, on questioning her, Freud did find that she had gone to the market but had found it closed. The weakness here would be that this would only explain the main theme of the dream and not its rather bizarre component details. Because of this he was forced to persist with a more involved and convoluted approach. In the first place, he asked, what is the over-all message of the dream? Well, it could be summed up in the phrase "The meat shop is closed." Actually, one can think of several other ways of distilling the message, from the most obvious "The market is closed" to "I have been unable to buy any food for my family." But for the purposes of the argument let us accept Freud's view that "The meat shop is closed." Now, if one takes the *opposite* of that (the freedom to move to opposites if the main sense is not what one is seeking is but one of the devices by which psychoanalytic dream interpretation proceeds), then what one finds is "The meat shop is *open*." This, Freud says, reminds one of the vulgar Viennese, "*Du hast deine Fleischbank offen,*" which means "Your flies are undone." The butcher's remark "That's not obtainable any longer" is something Freud said to the patient in a previous session when he told her that childhood memories were "not obtainable any longer as such." The phrase "I didn't recognize that" was a remark which she happened to have made on the previous day to the cook to which she had added, though it did not appear in the dream, "Behave yourself properly." It is this phrase, even though it did not figure in the dream, that Freud seizes on, commenting that it is just the kind of remark she would have made if someone had appeared before her with his flies open! As for the peculiar vegetable "tied up in bundles and black in colour," this "could only be a dream combination of asparagus and black radishes." "No knowledgeable person of either sex," Freud declares portentously, "will ask for an interpretation of asparagus." One assumes that he is implying the asparagus is a phallic symbol—which might be more plausible if that were the only vegetable figuring in the dream. And the radishes? Here things get really interesting. The German for black radish is "*schwarzer Rettich.*" This could alternatively be seen as an exclamation, says Freud, such as "*Schwarzer rett dich,*" which freely translated is "Blacky be off!" This, he believes, is another reference to the butcher's open flies and in particular the horrified housewife's response. "We need not now enquire," Freud confidently concludes, "into the full meaning of the dream...the meaning was far from innocent."

Viewed now with the perspectives of the late twentieth century, this tortuous interpretation, squeezing the dream into a sexual mould which is only one of a number of rival possibilities, is partly laughable, partly pitiable, but it is only too clear that Freud and his followers took it with enormous seriousness, as many still do today. With the hindsight of almost a century it is easy to pick holes in the psychoanalytic thesis, and I can only hope I have stressed that there is much in it that is constructive and enduring. But Freud was in many ways an autocratic individual, passionately convinced that he had uncovered a number of basic "truths" which should not be modified or watered down. This was especially true in the case of his fundamental thesis that the origins of *all* neuroses lay in some sexual conflict. But once again it was all a matter of interpretation. Indisputably, many of the cases Freud dealt with involved sexual conflicts, which must have been extremely common among the repressed Jewish middle class who formed the bulk of his clients. On the other hand, as other workers soon began to realize, some cases simply did not have such unequivocally psychosexual roots. To this Freud would reply that the roots were there if only one dug deeply enough. Even a conflict over money or a disastrously unhappy work life would ultimately be found to have been precipitated by some sexual frustration, and where no discernible cause of *any* kind was discovered, this must be because the roots were desperately deep. Many of his colleagues were perfectly prepared to go along with this tortuous thesis, but it was in the nature of the psychoanalytic movement, because of its invigorating assault on establishment ideas, that it attracted imaginative and unconventional brains to its ranks. Many of these people found it hard to toe any kind of party line, and if pressed too far showed the capability of splitting away and forming psychoanalytic movements of their own.

The first to break with Freud was Alfred Adler, an otherwise minor figure who nevertheless made a big splash at the time by publicly denying the sexual aetiology of neurosis, substituting as the main dynamic spring of human behaviour the quest for "power." After he had emigrated to the USA he had the temerity to write to Freud, begging him to reconsider his position and adding that by downgrading the sexual component he had made psychoanalysis far more acceptable amongst professional physicians and psychiatrists in America. To this Freud sardonically replied that if the goal of the exercise was to be "acceptable," then the whole psychoanalytic movement had better pull down the shutters and go home. Adler is best remembered because he introduced the concept of the "Inferiority Complex," but he had little to say about dreams except, of course, that they reflected the struggles of the self in its quest for power and achievement. Far more important, and far more interesting because of the new twist it gave to dream interpretation, was the defection of Jung.

Of the talented band that spontaneously gathered themselves around Freud in his most innovative period, by far the most remarkable was Carl Gustav Jung. The son of a crushingly orthodox clergyman, he graduated to medicine through science and before long found himself specializing in the relatively young field of psychiatry. In 1900 he had read *The Interpretation of Dreams* without making too much of it, but on picking it up again in 1903 he was much more intrigued. Jung was nowhere near convinced about Freud's assertion that the origin of all neuroses was some sexual trauma, but at the time was unable to offer anything more convincing as an alternative and hitched his wagon to the older man's with a tempered enthusiasm. Before long his sparkling intellect had endeared him to Freud who, for a period at any rate, looked upon him as his "successor" as leader of the psychoanalytic movement. Unfortunately for this plan Jung was too wilful and independent to fulfil the role of intellectual yes-man—which is what dynastic successors are often groomed to be—and the two men fell out on a number of different occasions. Once in 1910, not long before their final break, Jung had been bickering with Freud over some matter and the latter, suddenly becoming very animated, said to him: "My dear Jung, promise me never to abandon the sexual theory. That is the most essential thing of all. You see, we must make a dogma of it, an unshakable bulwark." Jung, who did not like the idea of dogma at the best of times and particularly not within the context of psychoanalysis, asked what it was supposed to be a bulwark against. To this Freud replied in a shaking voice: "Against the black tide of mud—of occultism!"

It was an unfortunate remark to make to Jung who was extremely interested in the occult, using the word in its literal sense of "hidden," implying those aspects of the universe not readily understood through traditional science. For most of his life he had felt a deep awareness that the world as we perceived it was but a minute fragment of some total reality, and even as a child had been prone to visions, hallucinations and apocalyptic dreams of one kind or another. All this had led to an outspoken interest in paranormal phenomena which Freud had accepted in an avuncular manner, hoping no doubt that his clever young colleague would in due course grow out of it. But it was not to be. Jung could no more give up his interest in the supernatural than he could suppress his growing feeling that there was something crankily dogmatic about Freud's insistence on the sexual aetiology of *all* neuroses. On the matter of the supernatural the two men maintained a kind of friendly antagonism, but the real falling out between them came about, perhaps fittingly, as the result of a dream. Jung categorized it as one of the most important of his life: He was in an unknown house of two storeys which he knew belonged to him. The upper floor was furnished in rococo style with fine oil paintings, and on the ground floor everything was "much older," dark and with medieval overtones. Exploring the rest of the house he found a "heavy door" behind which a stone stairway led down to a cellar. Here was a beautifully vaulted room which seemed incredibly ancient, dating perhaps from Roman times. Set in the floor of the cellar Jung now saw a ringed stone slab which, on being lifted, revealed yet another flight of stairs. Descending still further he came upon a low cave cut into the rock. "Thick dust lay on the floor, and in the dust were scattered bones and broken pottery, like remains of a primitive culture." Here were two human skulls, very old and half disintegrated. At this dramatic point he awoke.

Anyone at all familiar with Jung's work will recognize this as an absolutely classical Jungian dream, just the kind of dream that patients in Jungian analysis regularly report. (Needless to say, patients in Freudian analysis regularly report "Freudian" dreams.) When told about it, Freud immediately seized on the two skulls, repeatedly asking Jung whether he could uncover any "wish" connected with them. Realizing that he was fishing around in the hope of discovering a secret death wish and not wishing to disappoint him, Jung finally lied and said they reminded him of his wife and his sister-in-law. Newly married at the time, Jung honestly believed that he harboured no kind of death wish against his wife, but Freud "seemed greatly relieved" at the reply. In other words he was pleased to find an explanation which fitted his theories. At this point it seems that Jung effected the real psychic break with the founder of psychoanalysis. The ease with which Freud had accepted this glib interpretation seemed to him to be an example of how to miss an important point by several miles. To him the dream was the symbolic statement of something totally different, and when he had worked out exactly what this was he was ready to move off and found a psychoanalytic movement of his own.

To Jung the house represented an image of the psyche, the top floor with its "inhabited" feeling referring to consciousness, while the ground floor stood for the "first level of the unconscious." The deeper he went the more alien and dark the scene became, with the cave representing the very lowest level of the unconscious. Here the skulls and the other remains of a primitive culture symbolized the world of primitive man which still existed in the deepest layers of the mind. The most important features of the dream were the successive levels of the house and the increasing antiquity that each level revealed, which Jung saw as a kind of history of the evolution of the conscious and unconscious mind.

The top level was the consciousness of this lifetime, the other floors reflecting aspects of consciousness which had been laid down at earlier phases of the history of mankind. In other words he was beginning to play with the twin, but not totally separable, concepts of archetypal images and the collective unconscious.

Many of the central ideas of psychoanalysis have passed into the public vocabulary where their meaning has become distorted or lost. Good examples include the words "subconscious," "repression" and "overcompensation." But none can match the way the concept of the collective unconscious has got lost in the mists of imprecision. Most psychologists regard Jung as being a mystic beyond the pale of rational thought. One of the main reasons is because of his views on the collective unconscious, which most people assume is some kind of lagoon in psychic space whose contents can be tapped by the unconscious mind and whose images make themselves felt through dreams, fantasies or, if one is unlucky, through psychotic hallucinations. All humans, therefore, are linked in psychic brotherhood through the collective unconscious, and the common images they experience are known as archetypal images. From this huge pool are drawn not only the delusions of madness but also the creative visions of artists, poets and mystics. This interpretation of Jung's great central idea is erroneous and misleading, for although much disposed to the notion of telepathy and even weirder concepts outside the scope of this book, he had a much harder view of the nature of the collective unconscious. He argued that one had to look upon the psyche as a real thing in much the same way as one looked on the body as real. The psyche might only be a manifestation of that magnificently complex organ, the brain, and might be impossible to weigh, measure or photograph, but it was nevertheless an entity whose presence had to be taken into account in human psychology. And just as the human body had evolved over time, changing in response to the subtle pressures of evolution, so had the psyche followed a process of evolution. Furthermore, just as there were traces of our evolutionary past to be found in the anatomy of present-day man, so there were vestiges of primitive psychic structures to be found within the psyche, and these would from time to time manifest themselves in dreams and the like. Anyone taking more than a dilettante interest in the dream-life of himself or others would be bound, sooner or later, to come up against these vestigial forces. Indeed, Freud himself had spotted them, recognized them more or less for what they were (he used the phrase "archaic vestiges" to describe them), but had dismissed them as being irrelevant, or of only trifling interest. Jung, on the other hand, spurred on by the power of his dream of the skulls and numerous others of an equally weighty nature, says that what he was looking at were the archaeological sub-structures of the mind. Treated with imagination and insight, they must throw as much light on the evolution of the contemporary psyche as do the archaeological remains of buildings and the works of art of the past on the evolution of our present culture.

Jung undoubtedly found the widespread misunderstanding of the collective unconscious very irritating, particularly when this misinterpretation was used by others to beat him for his "mystical ideas." He had no objection at all to being termed a mystic, where and when the term was applicable, but in the case of the collective unconscious he felt that he was dealing with a scientific concept in a typically scientific way. Starting with the strikingly common observation that humans shared certain common images and symbols which were to be seen not only in their dreams but also in the creative and artistic output, he simply set out to provide a sensible explanation for their existence. Each human mind shared psychic structures with all other human minds, and it was the morphological correspondence of these structures that caused the common images to appear in the conscious and unconscious. Looked at in these terms the idea is not merely a valid speculation, but an insight which ranks with Freud's equally intuitive hunch about the huge reservoir of power lying within the unconscious. The trouble was, and still is, that it is not easy to see what neurological or anatomical form these inherited psychic structures might take, or—a very important consideration—what was their purpose within the mechanistic operation of the mind. Jung did in fact have a few ideas about this, but they tended to drift into the genuinely mystical. The structures might act as sources of inspiration, links between the physical world and some other less substantial reality. Carrying the whole thing a step further into the occult, they might be seen as the bridges by which God communicated with his creatures. This partly explained why dreams of this kind, with their momentous images, often appeared prior to some great disaster affecting either the individual or his society. Jung, for example, had a number of dreams in which he saw the entire lowland of Europe covered in a great sea of blood, these occurring portentously in the years just before the start of the First World War. Most open-minded people taking the trouble to read Jung's original work could go along with the notion of the collective unconscious but in the absence of some model which could incorporate it into the structure of modern psychology and physiology, this powerful idea has had to wait in the wings without being able to play the role it deserves. In Chapter 18 we will try to see how it might be incorporated into our knowledge of brain function, but to close this chapter we will briefly summarize the psychoanalytic view of dreams to see what can be retained as "useful" and enduring from the original ideas.

The Freudian view has the incomparable advantage of removing dreams from the realms of random, meaningless happenings, more or less equivalent to "noise" in the central nervous system, and out of the spuriously tempting world of the supernatural. In place of these we are given a rational view of dreams as intelligible reflections of internal mental processes, which for a number of reasons choose to reveal themselves when consciousness is lost in sleep. In Freudian terms the mind is seen as an uneasy amalgam of three quasi-autonomous entities, Ego, Id and Superego. The Ego is largely concerned with conscious waking behaviour and is only marginally aware of the Id and the huge territory it dominates, the unconscious. Powerful instinctive drives, mainly governed by the Id, which are to do with survival in a presocial, primitive world being incompatible with present-day experience, have their strength deflected or suppressed mainly by the Ego forcing them into the unconscious. Bottled up inside they try to push to the surface when consciousness is absent and they are experienced in the dreams their activity creates. Applying certain principles, their latent content can often be determined and their "meaning" understood. In the case of Freudian theorizing, the meaning of the dream will be found to be a frustrated wish, more often than not of a sexual nature. In Jungian psychology, dreams, while perceived to be messages from the unconscious and often of conflicts lying therein, may also reflect important features of the psyche as a whole, normal and abnormal, and may reveal the structure of the psyche of ancestral man.

Viewed as objectively as is possible with such an emotive subject, it is obvious to anyone who has inspected the marvellous landscapes of their own dream life that this view has a great deal in its favour. But it is also terribly easy to pinpoint its prime weakness which, by a quirk of fate, is also somehow its strength. All psychoanalytic theories lean heavily on the fact that most, probably *all*, dreams are of fundamental significance to the dreamer—otherwise the conflicts that underlie them would never have been pushed into the unconscious in the first place. Unfortunately it is only too obvious that many dreams are not only trivial in their content but also seem to be simply a kind of muddled re-run of the day's events. Freud himself recognized this, and to explain their innocuous nature claimed that this was merely a facade behind which lay a heavily disguised version of reality. This was an unshakable defence—the more trivial or bizarre the dream, the more devious its nature — but also a hopeless weakness because it made the theory untestable and incapable of providing firm predictions. Tests and predictions that were actually made and which subsequently failed could be rationalized as being due to mistaken interpretations in the first place. In the same way a course of psychoanalysis which failed to come to a successful conclusion could be rationalized on the grounds that what had *seemed* like correct interpretations of dreams had been erroneous ones. Where treatment was a success, of couse, the correctness of the interpretation was self-demonstrable. These very arguments, it should be added, are still applied today, when the questionable status of psychoanalysis as a therapy is being debated more hotly than ever. Where Freud had claimed that dreams gave a truer picture of the individual personality than his normal day-to-day utterances and general behaviour, Jung suggested that the human race shared a significant number of rudimentary dream patterns, in the same way as they shared more overt psychological behaviour patterns such as breathing and eating.

Thus, psychoanalysis did us all the favour of showing that dreams were relevant, structured and could reveal some messages from the unconscious. With those broad premises few will now disagree, and the thesis of this book is strongly in accord with them. But in an effort to provide a single, economic and all-embracing explanation of dreams, psychoanalysts got trapped into attempting to interpret all dreams by a single yardstick—that of wish-fulfilment—a yardstick which is at best only applicable to some of them.

PART TWO

A Change of Direction

Chapter 10

OF MICE AND MEN AND OTHER SLEEPERS

SO FAR THIS book has been largely given over to what might seem to be an iconoclastic assault on the various established approaches to the problem of sleep and dreams. Of the three main systems considered, the physical or physiological concentrated on the phenomenon of sleep and had virtually nothing to say about the dream. The psychical, on the other hand, was strong on dreams but had little to say about sleep. The third approach, the psychoanalytic, considered sleep to be a phenomenon with its own discrete function, during which time certain important psychological processes took place which, when they emerged into consciousness, were known as dreams. This psychoanalytic view, particularly the Freudian, tends to assume that dreams reflect disturbances of the internal mechanisms of the psyche, and should therefore not occur at all if the warring triumvirate of Id, Ego and Superego could settle their differences.

All these approaches, then, tend to treat the dream state as in some way abnormal. The sole possible exception to this is the Jungian, but even in this case too much of the material dredged up from the multi-layered unconscious is touched with madness and the mental detritus of generations long dead, and best left undisturbed. This tendency to see dreams as mistakes, malfunctions, disturbances or oddities which would not be present in a perfect world is understandable, and is partly due to the peculiar nature of most dream material which hints at chaos rather than cohesion. It is also due to the fact that all the approaches we have been considering have been built on, at the very best, the most limited physiological and psychological data. Most of the central questions which need to be dealt with before anyone could hope to get a convincing theory together have been simply unanswerable with the limited exploratory tools available. To give some examples: Does every human dream? How long do dreams last? At what period in the sleep state do dreams take place? Is there any correlation between the amount of dreaming and age, intelligence, sex, or other similar variables? Do animals dream, and if so do all species dream or just some? What happens if you prevent people from dreaming? All these questions are clearly germane to any discussion of the function of dreams and yet hardly any of them was in the past amenable to inspection. Central to the problem, of course, was the fact that dreams are essentially phenomena associated with sleep and with the lack of consciousness, and thus cannot easily be studied without disturbing the state and, by definition, destroying the subject matter of the experiment.

Only two avenues of exploration, both of them narrow and limited, lay open. The first, widely used by Freud and colleagues, relied on a *post hoc* analysis of the contents of dreams. The main weaknesses of this approach were that one had to (a) rely on those dreams that were remembered in the morning and which presumably were only a smallish selection of the night's total; (b) beware of and make allowances for distortions of memory occurring between the dream proper and the time of its reportage; and (c) take account of the fact that there would inevitably be selective reporting of dreams by the subject, who would choose very carefully which dreams he chose to relate and which fragments or portions he decided to present to the analyst. Freud, as we saw earlier, was well aware of these pitfalls and did all he could to avoid them, but with only partial success.

The second avenue of approach involved direct monitoring of the brain's activity during sleep through the technique of electroencephalography, which we described in Chapter 3. The main problem here is that even though the technique was successful in detecting the presence of non-random electrical signals from the cortex, there was practically no way of linking the different types of signals to specific cerebral processes. The sole exception, perhaps, was the alpha rhythm, which was obviously related in some way to the mechanism of attention. Similarly, even though an expert interpreter of the EEG could reliably tell, by looking at the EEG print-out alone, when the individual had passed from the waking state into one of sleep, and even (roughly) what stage of sleep he was in, that was about all. To say that he was in level three rather than in level two did not add much to one's knowledge of the sleeping brain, and told one absolutely nothing about such crucial matters as whether he was dreaming or not. How often did the electroencephalographers peer wistfully at the frenzied scribblings traced out by the pens of their elaborate devices wondering which, if any, of the multitude of rhythmic patterns indicated the presence of a dream? The discovery of such a pattern would be the key to the Aladdin's cave.

★

But before getting to such subtleties as dreams one really ought to look more closely at what is known about sleep to see if that provides any useful clues. So let us digress for a moment and look sideways, or rather downwards, from man to other sleepers.

We have already remarked that sleep is a near-universal phenomenon of the animal kingdom, if not of all life. It is sometimes said that plants sleep, in that they enter a period of what might be described as quiescence and insensitivity with the decline of the sun—curling petals and leaves as they do so—but it is carrying things a bit far to call this period "sleep." For example, unlike sleep in animals, one cannot "arouse" the plant by prodding it or stimulating it in any way other than by some photoluminescent source. Furthermore, plants go into their quiescent state whenever light is reduced below a certain level and, conversely, will stay in full bloom as long as light is present. Animals, on the other hand, will sleep after a given period of wakefulness whatever the conditions of luminance and show grievous withdrawal symptoms, which we shall discuss in a moment, whenever they are prevented from doing so. Furthermore, while most animals elect to take up their sleep quota during the hours of low illumination, there are a number of animals who come awake at night when they prey on any other creatures foolish enough to be out of their nests at that time. Perhaps the most striking dissimilarity between the two states is that whereas in the case of plants it is a kind of convenience (being a period where heat and water loss are reduced and the chances of accidental damage minimized by petal withdrawal at a time when the processes of photosynthesis cannot take place), in the case of animals sleep seems to be a profound necessity. Since the word "animal" covers an immense spectrum of life on this earth, one needs some qualification and explanation here.

The animal kingdom consists of a huge number of species, themselves further placed into larger groups known as phyla, ranged on a scale of complexity from the simplest one-celled creatures like amoebae to creatures such as man. Even this complex scale is a bit ephemeral, but roughly speaking it relates firstly to the number of individual cells in an organism and, as a parameter, to the number of different types of specialized cells which make up the whole. These specialized cells include blood cells, muscle cells, bone cells and, most important of all, nerve cells or neurones. If one wanted to, and it is likely that some physiologist or zoologist has already attempted it, one might devise some kind of formula for complexity, expressed in the ratio of the total number of cells in the creature's body to the number of different types of cell occurring. By this scale a creature such as the jellyfish, which has quite a big total cell population but relatively few different *types* of cell, would come low down on the complexity scale, whereas creatures like man would come high up on it. Zoologists and those interested in classifying animals by their special characteristics have already got a crude system, of a much more *ad hoc* nature, which they term the phylogenetic scale, and along which all creatures are ranked according to their evolutionary heritage. Broadly speaking, those species which retain a great number of primitive structures (that is, those which were present in the creature's primitive ancestors) and which do not have a highly evolved central nervous system—the two features tend to go hand in hand—are ranked on the low end of the phylogenetic scale, while those in which primitive features have largely been eliminated and where a complex central nervous system is present are ranked high.

It is a characteristic of sleep that it appears to be most urgently required in animals at the top end of the phylogenetic scale, and to occur with decreasing frequency as one moves down the scale towards the simpler or primitive species. As a rough rule of thumb, the primates seem to require the most sleep, while of the rest of the mammals the carnivores need the next most, followed by the herbivores. Amongst other phyla, birds need a fair amount of sleep, and so do reptiles. Fish too require periods of sleep. Even the most primitive of fish, the shark, which records its evolutionary age by the fact that it has no skeletal structure and only a gristly tube for its backbone, is now known to snatch periods of sleep when it finds itself in a secure and quiet spot. But when one gets even lower down the scale to molluscs, insects and so on the evidence for the existence of sleep becomes much thinner. Some simple creatures like sea snails seem to have a period of relative quiescence from time to time, but this appears to be related very directly to environmental conditions—still water, low levels of luminescence, particular water temperatures—and might have more in common with the quiescent phase in plant life than the very strange phenomenon we call sleep in higher animals.

It should by now be apparent that there is enormous difficulty in (a) defining exactly what one means by sleep and then (b) deciding whether it is present in an animal or not. In the case of humans it might seem to be simply a matter of asking them, but even that, as we shall later find out, is an unreliable guide. With a dog or cat one assumes that if one can arouse it from its dormant state by kicking it, then that dormant state probably was sleep. One might try the same technique on alligators and sharks, and the underwater explorer Jacques Cousteau, a brave man, applied just this technique to sluggish sharks that he found tucked away in marine grottos. One might even try it on the bigger molluscs such as octopuses and, indeed, some workers claim to have observed sleep-like behaviour in these interesting animals, but the problem grows when one sets out to test sleep/wakefulness cycles in such creatures as the oyster, the limpet, the spider or the earwig. Most insects appear to exhibit nothing that looks like sleep, tending to be relatively active or relatively inactive at all times, the phases of activity being determined more by the presence of food, appropriate external temperatures and so on.

Of course, as we have learned, there are less crude ways of assessing sleep than by prodding or kicking the dormant animal to see if it wakes or not. By far the most promising is to take recordings of the electrical activity of the brain and note whether the appropriate changes in the nature of its activity are occurring. This tends to be quite easy with humans, who will generally submit to sleep researchers' funny requests and more or less uncomplainingly spend several nights in a laboratory with wires attached to their scalps. Animals will not toe the line so willingly, and the electrodes have to be implanted into the cranium so that they cannot be scratched or rubbed off. Once one attempts to extend one's study downwards to the smaller, simpler creatures, the problems of electrical recording compound rapidly. Imagine trying to detect the electrical impulses in an earwig's minuscule brain without damaging the creature in some way. In fact, experiments have been carried out using microelectrodes and extremely fine wires inserted in the "brains" of insects, but they reveal none of the characteristic signals which are common in the higher species. In sum, sleep appears to be a characteristic of the phylogenetically higher animals only and a behavioural feature which is linked to the presence of a brain or bundle of integrated neural tissue in the central nervous system. We must now consider how important sleep is to those creatures which do indulge in it, and in particular what happens to animals when they are deprived of it.

Chapter 11

SLEEP DEPRIVATION

IN PHYSIOLOGY OR anatomy, if one wants to discover the function of some particular organ one can employ the drastic technique of removing that organ and then seeing what function is lost in the deprived animal. The technique does not always work, or at least not in the most informative way—extricating the heart, for example, will cause the loss of many kinds of functions, while removing a great chunk of the brain will sometimes produce no behavioural effects at all—but as a technique it is better than nothing. By the same argument, one might hope to get some clue as to the function of sleep by preventing a human or animal from achieving its regular quota. The first concerted experiments in this direction were performed in the latter half of the nineteenth century by the physiologist Marie de Manaceine. She kept puppies awake for periods from four to six days and found to her surprise that this killed them. The physiological cause of their death was hard to establish, but their red blood cell count had dropped markedly and there were capillary haemorrhages in their brains. They also suffered from hypothermia (lowering of body temperature). A few years later the Italian scientist Tarozzi, thinking that Manaceine's fatal results might have been due to the young age of the dogs, kept three adult dogs awake. The first died after nine, the second after thirteen, and the third after seventeen days. Curiously he found no cortical haemorrhages on post mortem. Nathaniel Kleitman, the Chicago sleep researcher, repeated the Manaceine experiment in the 1920s using twelve puppies from six weeks to three months in age, keeping a careful daily record of their body weight, blood sugar, alkaline reserve and so on in case these were found to have any bearing on the matter. At the end of seven days, with all the puppies still alive, he terminated the experiment, killed half of them to look at their brains, and let the others go to sleep. Of these, two of the little creatures died without awakening and Kleitman found no obvious pathological changes in the brain. Similar experiments performed using rabbits, rats and other unfortunates showed roughly comparable findings: most of the animals died in due course, though the death was often due to some subsidiary cause. Rats, for example, get so irritable when sleep-deprived that they fight each other, often to the death.

What does the cause of sleep research have to show for these grisly experiments? The first and most important finding is, of course, that death seems to be the drastic penalty for prolonged sleeplessness; en route to death there are behavioural disturbances—restlessness, irritability, photophobia, peculiar attitudes to food (either under or over-eating)—and bizarre reactions including fearfulness, strange posturing and so on. The second finding, admittedly of lesser import, was that depriving an animal of sleep is not an easy task. Manaceine and Tarozzi kept prodding and walking their animals, but even then they would often doze off for brief periods if left unguarded. Later experimenters used more ingenious systems: Bunch's rats had to swim endlessly in water mazes while Webb's rats trotted unceasingly in a rotating wheel. These ruthless techniques led some to the view that it was physical trauma to the body or nervous system that led to death rather than the effect of sleep deprivation *per se*, but in most cases pathological changes in brain or nervous system were negligible, if present at all. Thirdly, one other finding emerged quite strongly: the younger the animal, the more resistant it was to sleep-death. Older animals succumbed much earlier than their younger counterparts.

The next question, and one which is in principle far less easy to establish, is what are the effects of prolonged sleep deprivation on *humans*? Obviously, the rather brutal tactics which can be performed on animals (I make no comment on the ethics of this) cannot be employed on humans, though there is anecdotal evidence that one of the favourite tortures of the ancient Chinese was to deprive their victims of sleep until the wretches became first mad, and then died. The technique was also known to the experts of the Spanish Inquisition who used the *Tortura insomnia*, as it was called, allegedly to the death. Even if one accepts the anecdotes at face value, one still has the problem of deciding how much of the death can be blamed on sleep deprivation *per se*, and how much on the ruthless physical indignities that are required to keep a person fully conscious for one or two weeks. Making a person balance on a plank to avoid falling into a pit of alligators may well keep him awake without too much trouble, but one can easily imagine how the side effects could hasten death. There is no way, then, of repeating the animal experiments and seeing if depriving humans of sleep—however that were done—would result in death. On the other hand, it is a characteristic of human beings that they are prepared to take chances with their health and well-being in the pursuit of scientific knowledge, of novelty or of publicity, and with these triple goals in mind, many people have been motivated or induced to undergo prolonged periods of sleeplessness for experimental purposes.

The first true scientific experiment on human tolerance to sleep deprivation was performed by G.T.W. Patrick and J.A. Gilbert in 1896, and their finds were published in the journal *Psychological Review* that year. They kept three young men awake for a total of ninety hours (just about four nights without any sleep), watching closely to make sure that none of them nodded off and performing a variety of psychological and physiological tests on them—sensory acuity, reaction time, learning ability and so on. They found a slight decrease in efficiency in all the psychological factors, though nothing to get too excited about, and an over-all reduction in body temperature. One of the subjects did, however, report very striking and peculiar visual hallucinations, seeing animals that were not there and claiming that one of the experimenters was making faces at him. At the end of the ninety hours all three were allowed to sleep, did so for a straight twelve hours and then woke up refreshed and apparently unmoved by the experience. The experimenters concluded that the slight decrement on tasks involving mental concentration was the least that could be expected, and the only mildly unexpected finding was the hallucinatory experience of one of the subjects.

Nothing much else happened in this field for about a quarter of a century, when E.S. Robinson and S.O. Herrmann reported in the *Journal of Experimental Psychology* that people could be kept awake for as long as sixty-five hours (missing three nights' sleep) without any important changes in performance on tasks similar to those Patrick and Gilbert had tested. About the same time the diligent Kleitman, then just beginning his distinguished career in sleep research, tried something more ambitious. Over the course of some months he studied no fewer than thirty-five subjects, mainly students, all of whom stayed awake for sixty-five hours. Just to show that what was sauce for the goose was also sauce for the gander, Kleitman himself joined in, staying awake for over a hundred hours. Except for the fact that it was found to be exceedingly difficult to keep subjects from taking cat-naps when they got half a chance, little new material emerged. The tendency to hallucinate or "dream while awake" was, however, widely reported. A particularly common observation was that the experimenter would notice the subject making inapposite remarks and when questioned he would report that he had believed he was having a conversation with the experimenter to which the remarks would have been pertinent. On pondering the matter, however, he would then often remark that he must in fact have been dreaming. As we shall see when we come to a discussion of the nature of dreams, this was really a very revealing finding, but in the 1920s it passed the researchers by without much comment. In all cases, a good night's sleep following the deprivation seemed to restore good health and normal mental states.

A much more spectacular experiment, if one can call it that, and the first of the "marathon" sleep deprivation studies was carried out in 1935 by the psychologists S.E. Katz and C. Landis. They had been contacted by a 24-year-old man who claimed that he could stay awake indefinitely. Sleep, he believed, was merely "a bad habit" and like all bad habits could be broken if one simply had enough will power. Katz and Landis thought him a bit odd when they first met him, but decided that the opportunity was too good to miss and agreed to co-operate. Curiously, they elected not to use a laboratory as their experimental site—possibly the subject objected for reasons of his own—and no really satisfactory procedures were adopted for ensuring that he remained awake at all times. Instead he was allowed to remain at home and was given a time clock to punch every ten minutes. This would certainly make sure that he did not have any prolonged stretch of sleep, but of course it had no deterrent effect on cat-naps and those brief snatches of unconsciousness lasting as little as ten or fifteen seconds which are now known as "microsleep." Armed with his punch clock the young man kept going for a total of 231 hours with, at the very least, greatly reduced sleep which was at the time by far the longest period of deprivation recorded. Periodic monitoring of weight, pulse, blood pressure and all the other obvious physical signs showed no big deflections from the normal. By the fourth "sleepless" day, however, he was hallucinating fairly vigorously and on the fifth and sixth days he began to develop delusions, the most common and persistent of which was that the psychologists were deliberately trying to ruin the experiment and prevent him from proving his point. Eventually his behaviour became so bizarre, not to say dangerous, that Katz and Landis declared the marathon over and persuaded their subject to go off to sleep. For various reasons follow-up studies were not possible so it is not known how long it took for the hallucinations and delusions to subside, but the experiment did at least show that people may go for something like ten days with, at the most, small intervals of sleep and suffer no physical collapse. On the other hand it was fairly clear that psychological disturbances are a striking feature of that kind of deprivation.

Hallucinations and what is sometimes known as pre-psychotic behaviour are unquestionably common, if not absolutely universal, manifestations of any period of sleeplessness lasting more than about four days in total, and there seems to be evidence that where the individual is predisposed to psychological disturbances, the hallucinations may be more intense and frequent. Schizophrenic patients, for example, who "volunteered" to take part in sleep deprivation experiments showed a marked exacerbation of their symptoms, and epileptics (though this may be a totally different matter) tended to have more epileptic episodes. One might argue that none of these findings is particularly surprising: they are merely indicative of the fact that if one abuses the brain it will malfunction. But why should there be hardly any loss of efficiency in performing the kinds of activities one would intuitively expect to suffer in an "overtaxed brain" such as learning lists of verbs or counting the number of blips that appear on a radar screen? And why should such dramatic symptoms as hallucinations and paranoid delusions come into play?

Because of the unpleasant side effects, studies of more than four or five days without sleep have rarely been undertaken by responsible scientists, and then only with medical supervision of the participants. On the other hand there is no law to stop people trying to stay awake for six weeks, six months or six years if they want to, and such is the nature of mankind that there are always plenty of people willing to have a try. The first of the truly public ventures of this kind is attributed to Mr Peter Tripp.

Behind the stunt was a plan to raise cash for the US National Foundation for Polio Research in 1959. Tripp, a well-known disc jockey on a New York radio station, elected to stay awake for two hundred hours —then undeniably a record—in return for public pledges of financial support. The enterprise involved people ringing up the station beforehand and announcing that they would give ten cents, a dollar or whatever for every hour that Tripp stayed awake beyond a certain point. Pledges could be accepted at any time during the "wakeathon" and to keep public interest on the boil Tripp planned to continue with his daily shows which would be broadcast live as usual, but with the intriguing variation that they would go out from the window of the Army Recruiting Office in Times Square. This allowed a high degree of audience participation in the spectacle, which attracted large crowds morning, noon and night. Enough being known about the peculiar effects of much shorter-term deprivation, it was decided that a public experiment of this kind could only go ahead with adequate medical supervision. So a team of psychologists and psychiatrists from the Walter Reed Army Hospital in Washington DC, where a good deal of sleep research had previously been carried out, set up camp in the Hotel Astor across the Square. They made all the usual measurements before, during and after the event, including heart, blood pressure, blood and urine analysis and electroencephalographic recordings, and also kept a close eye on Tripp to see he remained awake. Once in a while he would leave the booth and pop into the Astor for a wash and a change of clothes, during which time he was also watched to prevent cat-naps. Needless to say, the crowd outside the window was equally watchful and entertained Tripp constantly by rapping on the glass, making unusual faces and so on.

For the first few days the pattern was much as expected: Tripp gradually became more and more sluggish, fluffing his normally fluid DJ patter, and by the end of the fifth day had to be given Benzedrine to keep going. Minor hallucinations—for which he had been prepared—had begun on the third sleepless day. He saw cobwebs on his shoes and these were later felt brushing across his face. A rabbit sat with him for a short period in the window. Small insects marched across his studio console. These failed to bother him because he was at that time able to identify them for what they were. He *saw* the cobwebs, the rabbit and the bugs, and told listeners about them, but at the same time he accepted them as being objectively unreal, simply the creations of his sleep-deprived brain. With the passage of the hundredth hour of wakefulness, however, a subtle change took place. The hallucinations, when they occurred, were no longer treated with such cheery abandon. When one of the Walter Reed experts came in on a routine visit, Tripp shrank back in horror and disgust because it appeared that the doctor was wearing a suit made of crawling worms. On another occasion a nurse who was taking his blood pressure seemed to be drooling saliva all over the place. Insects were no longer seen as Disneyesque jokes, but as dangerous, threatening creatures. When opening a cupboard in the hotel to get a change of clothes he discovered that its interior was a mass of flames and for a moment inspired a panic that the hotel was on fire.

His mood now changed sharply, and his normally benign personality exhibited signs of paranoia. The blaze in the cupboard was no longer accepted as being hallucinatory, but was a real fire started by one of the doctors to test him. When medical staff visited him he backed up against the wall in suspicion and terror. The clock in the booth began to keep Alice-in-Wonderland time and its face took on the appearance of Dracula. Tripp now announced that people in general, including the crowd making faces on the pavement, were out to prevent him from achieving his goal, though, curiously, when the time came for him to perform his broadcast he refrained from uttering his suspicions on the air. His hostility to all those engaged in the experiment grew markedly, so much so that a conference was called to decide whether his paranoia was bordering on the psychotic, in which case the experiment should indeed be terminated. The majority feeling—based mainly on his more or less normal vital signs (heart, blood pressure etc.)—was that he could take a bit more, and in due course he passed the two hundred-hour goal. Shortly after this Tripp suffered a real psychotic episode. When an anxious doctor came in to examine him, bearing for some peculiar reason an umbrella, Tripp took him for an undertaker and ran out into the street screaming for help. At this point everyone decided that enough was enough, and the DJ was escorted to a comfortable bed at the Astor, where, after a bit of grumbling he slipped off into a thirteen-hour sleep. On awakening all hallucinations and delusions had gone, though he declared himself to be "a bit depressed." This feeling of mild depression lasted for about three months, during which time it gave doctors some anxiety in case he had suffered irreparable psychological damage. Fortunately he had not.

Not surprisingly, in view of all the publicity, one wakeathon swiftly led to another. Within a year Rick Michaels of another radio station in Michigan was staying awake on behalf of the Muscular Dystrophy Fund, again aided by scientific and medical advisers. He reached 230 hours, suffering much the same kinds of hallucinations as Tripp including bursts of flame spurting out from the walls and furniture of his room. There were also a number of unsuccessful attempts in which the experiment was either stopped by worried doctors or, more often, by the subject succumbing to the overpowering demands of sleep. In at least one case the subject—another disc jockey—had to be hospitalized for a few months because of some kind of depressive hangover. After this the craze died away for a few years until it was revived by a seventeen-year-old student named Randy Gardner, who undertook his world record attempt as part of a high school science project. This time there was no public display of symptoms, the whole thing being conducted at home with only doctors and family in subdued attendance. No stimulants were used and stress was deliberately kept to a minimum. Even so Randy gradually developed all the familiar symptoms and on the ninth day became convinced that he was a giant negro football player—a most inflammatory delusion in those times. Nevertheless he saw it through to 268 hours—a record which was to stand for many years—and did not suffer much in the way of post-experimental symptoms.

Publicity and charitable aspects aside, all these adventures added up to very little, serving only to confirm two important things: prolonged sleeplessness is an unpleasant and, in the end, intolerable experience; and the subsidiary fact that it is invariably accompanied by psychological disturbances. On the other hand, they did make it clear that sleep is not just a "bad habit" that can be broken by deliberate exercise of will. Since the Randy Gardner episode, possibly because his 268 hour record looked so hard to crack, interest in wakeathons has declined. Subsequently a South African housewife managed to push the total up to 280 hours but medical supervision was only partial and the record is mildly suspect. The current edition of *The Guinness Book of Records* lists Mrs West of Peterborough, England, as being the current holder with a remarkable figure of over four hundred hours. Unfortunately there was no medical or scientific supervision of her sleeplessness record bid so it is impossible to be sure that she did not take regular cat-naps which it is known can occur while the eyes are open, while the individual is engaged in some rhythmic and undemanding task (such as rocking) and, most important of all, without them realizing they are occurring. Nevertheless, she saw the usual zoological parade, including pink elephants and green cats, but despite all this managed, after thirteen days, to sally out for a Chinese meal before settling down to sleep at home.

But the undoubted world record for sleeplessness—an unenviable record as it turns out—is held by a young Frenchman who was admitted to hospital in 1973 suffering from a very rare illness known as fibrillary chorea, of which one of the symptoms was a virtual inability to sleep. In the hospital he was watched closely night after night and continuous EEG recordings were taken without revealing any evidence of sleep as we normally understand it. Sleeping pills, even of a fairly potent kind, failed to knock him out. During the day he felt moderately well, but at night he would drift into regular hallucinatory episodes, some of which lasted as long as an hour. He also had to endure a series of brief hallucinations, numbering as many as fifty in a night and lasting a minute or so each. Some of the longer hallucinations featured recurring dreams, one of which involved a trip to the moon. The hallucinations were extremely unpleasant, partly because he felt himself to be fully awake and yet could do nothing to prevent them from running their course. After about six months in hospital, during which he got very little sleep, he died of a not very clearly defined disease of the brain.

Chapter 12

THE NATURE OF HALLUCINATIONS

THE ONE FEATURE common to all the experiences we have just been describing is, of course, the hallucinations. Psychologists distinguish, on the whole successfully, between illusions and hallucinations. The former are misperceptions of a generally predictable kind, as when the vertical line bisecting a horizontal line of equal length is invariably judged as being longer, or as when the larger of two boxes of identical weight is invariably judged as being the *lighter*. The essence of an illusion is that the brain, either because of its nature or its past experience, makes an automatic misjudgement, and on the whole illusions tend to be universally perceived by humans, and to about the same extent. A hallucination is something quite different, and consists of a perceptual experience which appears to be internally generated and not precipitated by some feature of the environment likely to mislead the brain. A hallucination (like an illusion) can engage any of the senses singly or in combination, and psychologists normally class something as a "genuine" hallucination only if the person experiencing it is convinced at the time that it is "real" and does not recognize it as hallucinatory. When Peter Tripp was watching beetles marching across his table, joking about them and at the same time not really believing in them, they were not true hallucinations. When his wardrobe "caught on fire," however, and he rushed out in alarm to warn everyone, his hallucinatory experience was genuine. To make any sense of these weird psychological states one has to find some kind of reason for their occurrence. The first step one might take is to see where and in what other circumstances hallucinations tend to occur reliably. There are a number that can be identified.

The first is, of course, the one that has been hinted at several times in the previous chapter—the hallucinations which are a common feature of psychoses and the more serious mental disorders. The major psychoses, of which schizophrenia is the paramount example, are surprisingly common forms of illness, and in most cases they require a period in hospital for specialized treatment. They are characterized by delusional states including bizarre beliefs of the "I am Napoleon" variety, and paranoid conditions where the individual believes the world or some segment of it is out to inconvenience or destroy him. Sometimes hallucinations interpreted as mystical or inspirational experiences have been used by poets, artists and writers as platforms on which to build magnificent aesthetic superstructures. William Blake, for example, a man often treated to glimpses of different worlds, became adept at tapping them for his own ends: when an old man repeatedly appeared at the top of his stairway, he ended up giving us his fabulous drawing of Job and the Creation; a treeful of angels seen when a child equally inspired some marvellous graphic art. There is little doubt that Blake believed in the objectivity of his visions—they were true hallucinations—nor is there much doubt that we are all the richer for his deflected schizophrenia. Nothing of comparable merit has emerged from the hallucinations of sleep-deprived humans (perhaps something might turn up if an artist substituted for a disc jockey) but the parallel between the two sets of experiences, one experimentally induced, the other involuntary and mainly unwanted, is obvious.

A second major catalyst for hallucinations is to be found in drug-induced states, and here again the types of visual, auditory and tactile experiences closely parallel those of sleep deprivation and, indeed, various forms of madness. Hallucinogens have been used by man in one form or another for thousands of years, and their mood-altering properties and, more important, their capacity to induce visions and unearthly experiences, have had religious significance in many societies. Of these drugs the most common are mescaline and its near neighbours derived from the peyote cactus, and the altogether milder marijuana which tends to produce dreamy reveries rather than vivid hallucinations. Both were used extensively in the religious ceremonies of early American societies, and the visions achieved were almost always assumed to involve messages from gods or spirits. The compelling reality of peyote-induced visions was first commented on formally by Aldous Huxley in his influential book *Doors of Perception*, which popularized the notion that the hallucinations might provide a genuine widening of psychological horizons and even have therapeutic value in certain mental illnesses. The visual, auditory and other sensory hallucinations experienced with LSD have often been described. They have been compared to those accompanying the psychoses, and indeed LSD is sometimes classed as a psychotomimetic drug—one that induces a psychotic state. Their greatest significance from the point of view of this book lies in the fact that they are hallucinations which can be achieved at will, and thus allow their investigation on a scientific basis. Large numbers of accounts of LSD-based hallucinations now exist, many of them provided by psychologists and physicians, and they conform very closely to those experienced during sleep-deprivation and, of course, in psychotic states. Sometimes the hallucination, particularly if it is visual, seems to be a kind of "overlay" on the normal backdrop of experience, believable at one level and yet unbelievable at another because of its bizarre quality. Typical, for example, is the observation by one girl that her "toes were dripping blood." The drops of blood, sometimes gushes, could clearly be seen and were aesthetically disturbing to her. Nevertheless, on one plane she was able to attribute the phenomenon to the fact that she had vividly painted toenails and that the hallucination was amplifying this in some way.

The third area of psychological experience in which hallucinations are likely to occur also involves drugs, but in this case features their absence rather than their presence. In particular I am talking about the spectacular hallucinations which often accompany the withdrawal of the chronic alcoholic from alcohol, and which are commonly known as delirium tremens. Similar hallucinations may be suffered during withdrawal from any central nervous system depressant, including barbiturates, but the alcoholic symptoms are the best known. These may be accompanied by paranoid delusions, but their most striking feature is their overwhelming believability to the person experiencing them.

The fourth area where experiences of this kind are common is a particularly unusual one and merits a slightly more detailed discussion. It concerns the effects of what is known as "sensory deprivation" and it was the subject of a certain amount of controversy in academic psychology in the 1950s. The issue first came to a head shortly after the Second World War when the American Air Force introduced a new range of extremely high-flying jet bombers whose operation threw novel loads and stresses on their crews, a few of whom began to report peculiar symptoms. Mostly these involved airmen who were isolated in such places as the observation globe at the front of the aircraft, and most commonly of all where the pilot was the only occupant of the plane. Jets in flight are dramatically less noisy than propeller craft, and there is also a marked absence of vibration. At forty or fifty thousand feet there is also an almost total absence of the kind of buffeting that is a characteristic of flight through clouds. In these conditions, where the visual environment is also featureless, airmen frequently reported bizarre and unsettling hallucinations, sometimes visual, sometimes auditory and very often tactile. For example, one pilot, sitting in his translucent dome at forty thousand feet, his headphones silent, poised apparently in motionless space, began to feel that his body and the aircraft were "blending into one," and his limbs were extending out to stupendous size. In other cases "phantom" radio signals were heard, and in more disturbing instances flight instrumentation was seen to give false readings, or the pilot's spatial perception outside the aircraft was distorted. Air Force medical staff became accustomed to these odd reports which were sometimes of a one-off nature, but it later became evident that there was a certain type of pilot particularly prone to the experiences. These unfortunates found themselves permanently grounded as a result. Uncommon though they were within the millions of flying hours accumulated by the personnel of the USAF, they were nevertheless studied with great interest by scientists who were already thinking a bit further out than forty thousand feet—those involved in the USA's embryonic space effort of the 1950s.

The common feature precipitating the hallucinations seemed to be either a great reduction in input to the pilot's senses or, alternatively, the lack of any change in the individual's sensory environment. If this sensory isolationism could come into play in high-flying aircraft, might it not be even more violently effective in the remoteness of outer space? If there was anything about the conditions of space flight that was likely to precipitate uncontrolled hallucinations in astronauts, now was the time to find out about it before a billion dollars' worth of equipment was put at risk, to say nothing of the lives of the astronauts themselves. Accordingly, military authorities—then the prime movers in the US space effort before the Russian triumphs forced the creation of NASA—began to instigate and sponsor programmes of research into the effects of isolating human beings from their normal ration of sensory input. These experiments, the famous "sensory deprivation" studies, were conducted at a number of military establishments in top secret, and in a more open but no less determined way at some major universities. The results were surprising, even sensational. Subjects—in the most extreme cases they were garbed in astronauts' suits and suspended in a bath of water at body temperature in a room from which sound and light were totally excluded—began to have vivid and unsettling hallucinations of all kinds. In many cases these grew so disturbing that they would press the emergency button to tell the experimenters to release them. Even highly-motivated, well-trained airmen succumbed in dishearteningly short periods of time. In one study where university students were employed, large sums of money, increasing steadily with the passage of time, could not persuade anyone to stay in "the black room," as it came to be called, for more than twenty-four hours. As one academic drily remarked, "One would have thought that my students would have been delighted to be paid huge sums of money to do nothing, particularly as the more nothing they did, the more they would be paid!" But the hallucinations and delusions—bugs and beetles, multi-coloured animals, weird faces, eldritch sounds, meaningless images and so on—were too much for even the most impoverished and the most indolent. The theoretical explanation advanced for this quite unexpected manifestation of hallucinations was ingenious: the brain, it was argued, was a device which literally fed on stimulation through its senses, and from birth to death it was accustomed to an unlimited diet. Deprive it of its sustenance, however, and it would be seriously disorientated, so much so that before long it would "create" stimuli in order to satisfy its need. Hence the hallucinations which represented the brain's strivings to instil some action into the scene. As far as I know no one made the connection, but it might equally have been argued that dreams were just the same kind of phenomena, induced by the brain during the hours of reduced sensory input known as sleep. In fact the theory, while ingenious, proved to be little more than that.

The fifth context in which hallucinations may occur is in states which for the want of a better word one might describe as mystical or trance-like. Some may prefer the more fashionable phrase "altered states of consciousness" which is used these days to describe a whole ragbag of phenomena from hypnosis to mantraic meditation. One must be careful not to sound dismissive, for although much, perhaps the vast majority, of what is said, written and done in the name of mysticism is no more than hot air, there is a kernel of significant material that at least merits inspection. There is the undoubted control of autonomic functions such as pulse, respiration and blood pressure which can be achieved by trained yogis, and it is also clear that when appropriate meditational or introspective steps are followed (there are a variety of rivals claiming the true path), decidedly unusual states of mind may be achieved. Often these feature convincing visual and auditory experiences which in other conditions would be termed hallucinations. The yogic argument is that these are objective experiences which represent a glimpse of another world or plane of existence into which initiates may delve and which merely highlight the multi-layered nature of the universe. Without taking sides on this question, which seems to be largely a matter of personal belief and has little to do with scientific knowledge, it is enough to recognize the technique as being yet another way of invoking, this time under partial control, hallucinatory experience.

One final area remains to be discussed: the hallucinatory experiences that occur in the transitional zones between sleep and wakefulness. These need to be distinguished from the kind of reveries that most people have while dropping off to sleep, those with all the autonomous and sometimes illogical qualities of a true dream but which are somehow perceived to be "unreal" and from which it is always possible to rouse oneself. Not everyone, perhaps fortunately, experiences this kind of hallucination. I have myself had only one or two in my lifetime, one visual and one auditory, but they are inarguable and memorable when they occur. Children are particularly prone to have them, and as the young child has a poorly developed ability to discriminate between "external" and "internal" reality they may be especially terrifying. The worst examples are known as night terrors. Typically, these hallucinations—they are known as hypnagogic when they occur prior to sleep and hypnopompic when they occur in the morning on the threshold of wakefulness—intervene when the individual feels that he or she is not asleep. Many of the normal features of wakefulness may be present. For example, the person may move the head or the limbs, even sit up in bed, and yet the image persists. Their content is often bizarre, sometimes horrific. On the other hand, like most hallucinations they may sometimes have a kind of pertinence. A scientist who had been wrestling with a major theoretical problem for some months and making agonizingly slow progress, told me that he had been greatly cheered one morning to be favoured by a most convincing hypnopompic hallucination in which a parade of the great scientists of the past—including Newton, Galileo and Darwin—marched past his bed telling him not to despair and that all would come out in the end. He was realistic enough to accept the images for what they were, internal fantasies externalized in some especially vivid way, but was also human enough to take comfort from the apparitions' encouragement. He did resolve the problem in the end, by the way.

This concludes the catalogue of circumstances in which hallucinations of one kind or another may occur. Occasionally the experiences we have talked about straddle the boundary between hallucination and fantasy, particularly where, as is the case with hypnagogic imagery, the person experiencing them is partially conscious of their subjective nature. Nevertheless the types of phenomena reported in all cases have great similarity, so much so that one is led to suspect they are served by some common mechanism or function. We will explore that possibility in the chapters ahead. Before doing so it is important to refer to one other kind of psychological state where internal events featuring striking, often bizarre, imagery occur, and where the mind is in a more or less permanent state of acceptance of their reality. Although they fit the general description of hallucinations very well, we have never traditionally treated them as such. I am referring, of course, to dreams.

Chapter 13

THE TRAPPING OF THE DREAM

THE STORY OF how the elusive, ephemeral dream was first and finally trapped in the laboratory is one of the great anecdotes in the history of psychology, perhaps even in the history of science. It has been told before, in detail and in generalized outline, and there will be many readers who are thoroughly familiar with it. No book on dreams, however, would be complete without it, and I offer it up once again with no apologies.

In the early 1950s a young student, Eugene Aserinsky, working on his doctoral thesis in the laboratory of the great sleep researcher Nathaniel Kleitman, was making some casual observations of the sleeping postures of young babies. What he was actually looking for was some evidence of cyclic body movements which might tie in with the different levels of sleep as spelled out by the electroencephalograph. Instead, what almost immediately caught his attention was that one of the babies was making strange movements of the eyes while still apparently fast asleep. The movements were clearly visible because the corneal bulge, the "window" on the front of the eyeball, raised the skin of the tiny closed lids as the eyes moved from side to side. Movements of this jerky, spasmodic kind are sometimes seen as a precursor of an epileptic seizure of the *grand mal* variety, but there was nothing about the baby's relaxed posture to suggest that anything of the kind was occurring. After a period the eye-movements died away and the baby continued an apparently undisturbed sleep. On a hunch Aserinsky now decided to look at the other babies —there were plenty of them around in the hospital—and before long he had spotted eye-movements in some of them too. Later in all the infants. The next step was to inform his boss, Kleitman, who showed due scepticism at first but later conceded the validity of Aserinsky's discovery. Then began a more systematic study from which it was deduced that the eye-movements occurred in bursts of roughly thirty minutes at regular intervals throughout any sleep period, and made up in all well over a quarter of the infants' total sleeping time. They were universally present with roughly the same frequency of occurrence in all babies.

Looking at scientific discoveries in retrospect, and with all the hindsight of the raconteur, it is amusing to think that Aserinsky, Kleitman and company at first assumed that the phenomenon was a characteristic of babies' sleep only. Why should they think otherwise? It is not clear who made the crucial suggestion that someone should take a look to see if they occurred in adults as well; but someone did and, lo and behold there were the bursts of rapid eye-movement (it was some time before they were immortalised with the acronym REMs) occurring in all adults, of all ages, at frequent intervals throughout the night. And from here on the project snowballed. Some time was now spent in speculating on the nature of the phenomenon, not the least important question being just why no one had ever noticed it before. Subsequently it was realized that these eye-movements had in fact been noticed and reported on a number of occasions as far back as the nineteenth century, but no one had spotted that they were universal in sleeping subjects and their potential significance had been missed. The team was now joined by a physician named William Dement, and it was he who performed the first experiments involving waking people while in REM sleep and in non-REM sleep as a control, and establishing what differences, if any, showed up in their introspections. And there was a difference. In the non-REM state subjects showed just the usual muddled irritability of anyone woken from a comfortable snooze, while those in REM sleep reported, almost invariably, that they had been having a dream.

It might have been assumed that during REM sleep the person was actually on the threshold of wakefulness (which might account for the frenzied movements of the eyes) and was experiencing the kind of part-sleep, part-wake fantasies or reveries which occur on the boundaries of sleep but if so the rhythmic nature of the REM cycle and the even (roughly thirty-minute) duration of each bout of REMs made little sense, for the REMs would surely appear at the beginning and end of the sleep period rather than at rhythmic intervals within it. And when REM records were coupled with standard EEG data it was found, as we anticipated briefly in Chapter 3, that they occurred next to the periods of deepest sleep and that while they were in progress muscles were exceptionally relaxed. Only the brain, with its high-voltage, ultra-fast rhythms, suggested a vast amount of internal activity. The only plausible conclusion was that Aserinsky, Kleitman and Dement had between them found a way of telling when someone was dreaming without having to disturb him to find out!

The discovery was not only interesting in itself, but allowed a whole string of questions to be posed and answered: Does everyone dream? How often does one dream? How long do dreams last? Does one dream more at a particular time of night? The Chicago team swiftly produced some answers. All humans, even those who believed that they never dreamed, *did* dream and did so every night for a substantial part of the night. Even the most recalcitrant non-dreamer could be converted to this new point of view, for all one had to do was to persuade him to spend a night in the laboratory, wait for the first burst of REMs and wake him up. The team also found that dreams—as measured by REM periods—were more common in babies and young people than in adults, with very old people perhaps dreaming a little bit less. Questions about the content and duration of dreams were not susceptible to such snap answers, but were taken up with enthusiasm at other universities in various parts of the world as soon as news of the basic findings had spread. A whole range of imaginative experiments could now be performed. For hundreds of years people had wondered whether external factors occurring while a dream was taking place could influence the content of the dream. There appeared to be anecdotal evidence that they did; many people have observed that the alarm clock which wakes them in the morning sometimes features in an appropriate way in a dream—an ambulance bell ringing or something of that kind. What researchers now did was to wait until their sleeping subjects were showing REMs, and then introduce some fairly positive outside stimulus—calling their name softly, or that of a close friend, sprinkling them with water or wafting an unpleasant smell into their nostrils. They then woke them up and asked what they had been dreaming. Not all the stimuli found their way into the dreams, but some undoubtedly did. Water dreams were often associated with swimming or rainstorms, and in one or two cases the speaking of a familiar name led to that person featuring briefly in the interrupted dream.

All this was very interesting, but in itself it added little to an over-all understanding of the mechanism of dreams, let alone sleep. The most important, and possibly revealing, single finding was the very high proportion of the night that was actually spent in REM sleep. This turned out to be something between a fifth and a quarter of the total-sleep-time, depending upon age and one or two other factors. This was a far, far higher component than anyone had even contemplated before, and hinted very strongly at the idea that the dream itself might be performing some vital function. Biological systems are notably economical in the way they apportion their structure and function, and nothing occurs on a regular basis in a normally operating system which does not have a very good reason for doing so. Before long Dement had devised an experiment to investigate this. It was an experiment that was to throw up an amazing result and which brought the topic out of the relatively small world of science and into public prominence. Curiously, its results, while superficially compelling, turned out in the long run to be misleading, but as is so often the case with basic scientific research, misleading in an ultimately helpful way.

Dement's experiments proceeded as follows. Two groups of subjects were invited to sleep in the laboratory, the only restraint on them being that they had to wear small electrodes against their eye sockets. These detected electrical signals given off by the eye muscles when they were in action, and thus, with the help of an electro-oculogram, gave a clear record of when REMs were taking place. The first group were woken up immediately they showed any sign of slipping into REM sleep. After being thoroughly wakened, they were allowed to return to sleep but only until the REMs reappeared, when they were woken up again, and so on in this disagreeable way throughout the night. The other group, the control, were awakened an equivalent number of times and at an equivalent duration of time, but during non-REM periods. The question was, would there be any measurable difference in the behaviour or the psychological capabilities of the two groups? The answer was apparently yes. The group who had been refused the opportunity to dream, so to speak, began to show signs of fairly severe psychological stress, while those who had been deprived of non-REM sleep were no more irritable than you would expect after several nights' constantly interrupted sleep. The worst effects took at least a week to show themselves, and there was a certain amount of argument among the experimenters as to what they should classify as stress or "troubled" symptoms. But the picture seemed clear enough for them to publish their findings in a reputable psychological journal, together with Dement's remarkable but reasonable inference that the dream served some critical function which related in some undefined way to the mental well-being of the sleeper. So after thousands of years the secret was out. Dreams, it seemed, were not aimless patchworks of fantasy caused by a disrupted sleep, but served some function vital to our mental life. Man *needed* to dream.

Follow-up experiments appeared to clinch the matter. When subjects deprived of REMs for several nights were finally allowed to sleep undisturbed, it was noted that the amount of time they spent in the REM phase of sleep was significantly increased, this increase being particularly marked on the first "recovery" night. If anyone had any doubt that

REMs, and presumably dreams, were vital, these doubts should have thereby been dispelled. These findings touched off a wave of speculation about their interpretation. So man needed to dream—but what purpose did the need serve? Numerous suggestions were offered, varying from the possibility that during REM sleep the brain was recharging itself with the proteins that underlie the memory process, to the suggestion that REM sleep was an "alerting" exercise designed to prevent the sleeping brain from drifting into an ever-deeper coma. None of these suggestions, intriguing and plausible though they were, lent itself to easy testing. One question which might help to eliminate some hypotheses and promote others was whether animals also had dreams, or whether they were exclusively human. Speculations about animal dreaming had always previously been just that—speculations—and had been largely based on the charming observation that dogs twitch their paws when sleeping by the fireside. Unlike humans, animals cannot be woken up and asked whether they were dreaming or not, but it *is* possible to watch them to see if they go through the same eye-movement rigmarole, and to everyone's delight the animals obliged by exhibiting obvious REMs when this little test was made. By animals we are referring to dogs, cats and other domestic creatures, and in later experiments monkeys and other members of the primate family. With the herbivores—sheep, horses, cows and so on—REMs were also present but less easy to detect and on the whole less common. Nevertheless, they were present, which made it clear that whatever function the dream-period served for man served for many of the higher animals too.

The next step was to try out the dream deprivation experiments on animals but here the experimenters, who by now were in action in laboratories all over the world, came up against a few problems. Although it was fairly easy for the most part to gauge whether an animal was in REM sleep or not, in order to do this one had to watch the creature closely and stand by it all the time—a tedious requirement which made experiments with large numbers of animals impossible. The electro-oculogram method did not have the accuracy that it had with humans, and furthermore few animals take kindly to having electrodes pasted to the side of their eyes. The only reasonable alternative was to attempt direct electrical reading from the brain itself. This is science in its least attractive garb, for by far the most satisfactory method of monitoring the brain's complex electrical output is to insert electrodes directly through the skull and into the cerebral cortex, or even deeper structures. The electrodes tend to be encased in plaster of Paris, and after a while most animals get used to the indignity. There is no suggestion that they feel any pain for the brain itself is free of pain receptors. The experimental method is certainly not pleasant, but it is, nevertheless, just about the only way to gather such elusive data.

In the early days of the EEG studies it was noted that during sleep the brain seemed to move through a series of phases or "levels," each marked by a characteristic pattern of energical activity. Typically, the deepest sleep would be associated with slow, rhythmic waves of fairly high amplitude, but occasionally these would give way to periods of more dynamic activity in which the waves were faster, smaller in amplitude and more erratic in rhythm. During these periods the body musculature would become extremely relaxed, almost flaccid, despite the evidence that the brain itself was apparently engaged in the most vigorous activity. Because of the jagged, arhythmic quality of the records, this phase became known as "desynchronized" sleep by some workers. Others, puzzled by the apparent contradiction between the active brain and the totally inactive musculature, termed it "paradoxical sleep." More recently there has been an international agreement to use the terms "active sleep" (AS) and "quiet sleep" (QS) to describe the two states. Active sleep, by the way, tends to correspond, in those animals which exhibit it, with REM sleep, so it serves as an excellent, and in some ways more satisfactory, indicant of "dreaming sleep" than the eye-movements themselves.

Most experiments on the dream state in animals, therefore, were conducted by the method of direct sampling from the cortex, and in this way a huge variety of animal species could be studied. By these means it was established that all mammals experience active or dream sleep —AS—this being somewhat more prevalent in the primates and the carnivores than in the herbivores. Birds also dream by these criteria, though to a lesser extent, and so do many types of fish, reptiles and the odd amphibian. In reptiles—the "lowest" types of animals in which AS has been found—eye-movements are seldom present and the only evidence one has of their capacity to dream is from direct electrical recording. In some animals, like the frog and the owl, which simply do not have the oculomotor mechanism promoting eye-movements, one obviously cannot expect to find REMs. Both show AS, however. Lower down the phylogenetic scale—the molluscs are more or less the next step down in the ladder—sleep is sometimes present but AS has not yet been discovered. Caution is required in interpreting this evidence as the difficulties of recording directly from the rather small brain of an octopus, let alone an oyster, should be fairly obvious and one could not be entirely sure that small periods of AS were not occurring which one's recording techniques were too coarse to detect. Below the molluscs (one has to be very careful about where one places animals on the phylogenetic tree, and talk of "higher" and "lower" animals is apt to be risky) one finds insects, worms and so on where there is little evidence even of sleep, and absolutely none of dreaming.

The over-all interpretation of this work, which took up some years of highly concentrated research during the 1950s and '60s, could be summarized thus. Sleep is divided into two main types, synchronized or quiet (QS) and desynchronized or active (AS) and this dichotomy is present in all animals from the primates down to reptiles and some amphibia. In animals other than reptiles the AS is accompanied by bursts of REMs, and in mammals AS may occupy as much as one quarter of the total sleeping period. Below the reptilia, sleep may be present but there is as yet no evidence that any component of it falls into the category of AS. Both sleep and AS are features which occur in animals with well-developed nervous systems. The high percentage of the sleep state which is given over to AS suggests inevitably that it serves some vital function to do with the operation of the nervous system. But what function?

The best approach to this problem might be selectively to deprive the animals of AS, in roughly the way that humans were so deprived by Dement in his pioneering studies. The expectation would be that the same kind of psychological disorders would appear as appeared in humans, taking due account of the difficulty of deciding what constitutes psychological distress in animals. A concerted research programme was instigated to do just this. The results were frustratingly inconclusive. Some animals when AS-deprived, behaved in extremely bizarre ways, becoming comatose or hyperactive, refusing food or eating ravenously with no consistent pattern other than that the behaviour was abnormal. Other animals of the same species seemed relatively unmoved and stoically endured literally weeks of "dreamless" sleep without ill effects. Only two phenomena appeared as consistent features of these states. The first we have already referred to as the rebound phenomenon. Without exception, animals deprived of AS devoted a significantly greater proportion of their recovery sleep in the AS or dream state, this being particularly marked on the first few recovery nights. Clearly the creatures' violated nervous systems were catching up on something they had missed. But what? The second consistent factor, far less easy to speculate about, concerned the behaviour of curious electrical patterns known as PGO spikes. This term refers to very characteristic and easily identifiable bursts of sharp activity which are found in various parts of the brain, particularly those known as the pons, the lateral geniculate body and the occipital cortex (where the processing of visual information takes place), and which frequently occur just prior to the onset of dreams or AS, and continue intermittently throughout the AS period. These PGO spikes were particularly frequent during the increased AS or the rebound period. More significantly, perhaps, they began to appear uncharacteristically during QS or *non-dreaming* sleep with increasing urgency in animals which had been lengthily deprived of AS. They were even seen to appear in AS-deprived animals during wakefulness. In other words, some component of REM sleep was evidently not being totally eliminated from the animals' electrocortical repertoire even during the most arduous deprivation experiments. This in turn suggests that the apparent lack of major catastrophic effects may be due to the fact that such deprivation is not really total.

This possibility might go some way to explaining the curious results which greeted attempts at replicating Dement's original work on humans. One of the first to provide contrary findings came from Anthony Kales and his colleagues on the West Coast of America. They took a number of subjects, deprived them of REM sleep to the best of their ability for several days, taking care to keep them in a subdued and quiet atmosphere the whole time. Under these circumstances they found little evidence of any peculiar behaviour or psychological disturbances, and the AS-deprived group seemed to be more or less the same as those who had lost an equivalent amount of QS, or non-dreaming sleep. Kales' findings were confirmed—more or less—by other workers, and even Dement himself, in later replications of his own work, had to admit that his earlier assumption of a simple relationship between dream deprivation and psychological disorder, not to say psychotic behaviour, had been a hasty one.

The mood of naive optimism which had pervaded sleep research was now dampened. The most promising theoretical approach to understanding the nature of sleep and dreams that had ever been formulated—that the brain had an overpowering need to dream which, if frustrated, would lead to mental malfunction, madness and in due course death—seemed to be dashed into dust. This glum mood was short-lived, however, as a further reappraisal of the position confirmed the importance of the original study. On consideration it was concluded that all that had been destroyed was the initial hunch that Dement and his colleagues had made, which was that a precise equation could be made between the REM state and dreams, and furthermore, that it was the REM state, or active sleep, that was the most important single component of the sleep process. Research has continued, but today, about a quarter of a century after the fledgling Dr Aserinsky first noted babies' eyes moving under their lids, we are not all that much wiser about sleep, dreams and their function. In the chapters that follow, I shall propose a theoretical approach which I believe takes account of all the central findings of sleep research, up to and including the various dream deprivation experiments. Before moving on to this, though, it is worth summarizing exactly what the central findings are so that we know where we stand when we come to appraise them. There are twelve of them in all.

First: Sleep is a phenomenon which involves a period of relative quiescence on an animal's part, and in particular a loss of consciousness and responsiveness to stimuli which puts it, in principle and often in practice, at considerable risk of its life.

Second: Despite the risky nature of the exercise, sleep is an exceedingly widespread phenomenon in the animal kingdom, being present in all mammals, birds, reptiles, fish and in some amphibia. There is no evidence of its occurrence to any significant extent in molluscs, insects and the numerous phyla equipped with primitive nervous systems. It does not appear to be present in plants.

Third: There seems to be a rough equation between the amount of sleep taken and the complexity of the species' central nervous system. Those species such as the mammals which have highly evolved brains and are capable of elaborate sensory discriminations and psycho-motor responses, spend large parts of their lives asleep. Birds need less sleep, but still indulge in it. Reptiles and fish need even less. Among the mammals the carnivores on the whole need more than the herbivores.

Fourth: Sleep is not a period when the central nervous system lapses into inactivity. The relative immobility of the body during sleep is misleading, for the brain is highly active for much of the sleep period.

Fifth: Sleep does not appear to be one continuous process, but is made up of a number of different types of activity whose individual characteristics are not properly understood. In purely descriptive terms most of the sleep period is dominated by rhythmic, rather slow electrical patterns. Between a fifth and a quarter of the total time, however, features vigorous, rapid and irregular patterns when muscle activity is absent, with the curious exception of the eye muscles which give rise to the burst of rapid eye-movements.

Sixth: This differentiation into what is sometimes known as REM and non-REM sleep, sometimes as desynchronized and synchronized sleep, and more recently as active sleep (AS) and quiet sleep (QS), occurs only in those animals with highly evolved nervous systems, notably mammals and birds. It is only controversially present in reptiles and fish.

Seventh: Animals deprived of sleep for any substantial time exhibit symptoms of behavioural disorder, and in the case of humans hallucinations occur, plus delusions and bizarre trains of thought. If animals are deprived of sleep for long periods they tend to die, and death occurs sooner than death from food deprivation. There is anecdotal evidence that man too dies from prolonged sleep deprivation.

Eighth: The effects of sleep deprivation appear to be more marked with older than with younger animals, though the *very* young are particularly seriously affected. Young human adults have gone for as long as 250 hours without sleep and suffered no detectable long-term effects, but hallucinations etc. make the process an unpleasant one.

Ninth: The sleep requirement falls off steadily with age. Babies and very young animals need the most sleep, and the elderly (when healthy) need the least.

Tenth: REM periods or active sleep are almost always associated with the mental process known as "dreaming" in humans. It is not, of course, possible to make the same assumption about animals.

Eleventh: Animals and humans may be deprived of REM periods for days and even weeks with no conclusive evidence of dramatic long-term psychological or behavioural disturbances. On the other hand, when animals and humans are allowed to sleep normally following lengthy REM-deprivation they spend a significantly greater proportion of the recovery sleep in the REM phase. Other electrical activity such as the PGO spikes, normally associated with AS, also appears in greater frequency and may "burst through" into QS during deprivation and even appear in the waking state.

Twelfth, and finally: There are very striking similarities between the hallucinatory and ideational disturbances that occur in sleep deprivation and those seen in certain drug-induced states, in the peculiar transitional zones between sleep and waking, in mystical experiences and, of course, in many mental disorders and psychoses.

These twelve features do not represent an absolutely exhaustive list, and there are a number of other, lesser facts which have been gradually accumulated by sleep researchers from Freud onwards. But they *are* the prime factors and serve as building blocks upon which any really effective theory of sleep and dreams must be constructed. They serve also as challenges, for no effective theory can fail to take any of them into account, and if it does so it is really evading fundamental issues. As can be seen by surveying the various approaches covered in the first part of this book, no existing theory builds fully on these factors or helps to explain them. We now move on to consider one that, in the view of the author, accepts them all gratefully as building blocks, and at the same time accepts the challenge that they pose. If it is not an absolutely watertight theory, then it must be said that any theory which appears watertight on the basis of the incomplete evidence we have at present is automatically suspect. The theoretical approach—perhaps that is a fairer description than theory *per se*—is one that takes over where all its predecessors leave off, and at the same time promises to extend its powers beyond the study of sleep and dreams and into the whole of mental life.

PART THREE

The Computer Theory

Chapter 14

EVOLUTION OF AN IDEA

NEWS ABOUT THE Dement-Aserinsky-Kleitman discoveries filtered through to me rather slowly. In 1960, the work had infiltrated the professional literature but had not yet reached the text-books I was then studying and only a stray reference to the work in a lecture alerted me to its intriguing possibilities. Initially I was sceptical. In retrospect I suppose this is because at the time psychology was on a particularly featureless plateau, with very little of interest being discovered, so that one viewed with great suspicion anything that seemed to constitute any kind of a breakthrough. This mood of indifference changed suddenly with a very odd experience that I had in the early summer of 1960, a few weeks before I was actually to sit the critical final exams. By that time I had abandoned lectures altogether, and immersed myself in text-books for about fourteen hours a day. On the day in question I was reading on the flat roof of the house I was sharing with some other students when I noticed that a human hand, followed by an arm, had appeared through the small door in the skylight. The hand groped around and picked up my wristwatch which was lying amid the scattered oddments around me. Then a face, that of an eleven or twelve-year-old boy, peered round the sill, gazed at me for a moment and withdrew hurriedly, taking the watch with it. The apparition was so unsuspected that it was several seconds before I could give chase, and by that time it was, of course, too late.

Reporting the theft to the police on such flimsy evidence seemed a pointless formality, but the watch had a personal sentimental value and on the vague off-chance that it would turn up somewhere I went along to the police station and said my piece. It was while I was in the middle of it that I discovered to my amazement and fury that I did not know the make of the watch, despite the fact that I had gazed at its face, and presumably its name, on what must have been thousands of occasions. The chances of getting the watch back, slender enough at the outset, were reduced to absolute zero, and I went back home in a state of great disappointment. But there was also a thread of considerable curiosity, spurred by my training in psychology and by my interest in the mechanisms of human and animal memory which I considered to be one of my strong areas. In particular I wondered if the affair threw any light on the venerable problem of how much of the information we receive in our lifetime is actually permanently stored, and how much rejected as being irrelevant. My incapacity to remember the oft-viewed name of the watch suggested that this kind of information, although it must have been received by the brain on passage up from the retina, was *not* stored, presumably because some sorting mechanism treated it as irrelevant and unnecessary clutter. But on what basis was the sorting and rejection mechanism conducted? This was—and still clearly is— one of the central problems in understanding human memory.

That night I woke suddenly in the midst of a vivid dream. It seemed that I had been looking at the face of my watch, in a kind of expanded close-up. The hands, numbers and other features, even the metallic sheen of the casing were brilliantly visible. So too was its name, clearly spelt out in capital letters in the centre of the face—BIFORA. This was indeed the make of the watch, and I now remembered having seen it clearly laid out on countless occasions. The next morning I trotted eagerly to the police station with my news and was quite offended to note the relative unwillingness of the constable on duty to get out the report book and make the necessary amendment. The news that I had received the information in a dream was treated with even less enthusiasm.

It struck me that there were a couple of rival interpretations of the event. The first and most easily dismissed was the notion that the dream represented some kind of "psychic" experience and that the watch was "signalling to me" clairvoyantly not only its name, but perhaps also its location. I mention this unlikely interpretation only because I have found that it is one which quite a large number of people seem to find quite reasonable, and it is, of course, a possible view of the circumstances, but not one I give any house room to. The alternative explanation is that the name of the watch was located in my memory somewhere and, while for some reason not accessible to my conscious mind, could be dredged up in a dream. Experiences of this kind are not at all uncommon. Almost anyone who has written about dreams has quoted a fair number of such cases. Havelock Ellis, in his now rather rare book *The World of Dreams*, has a nice example from his own dream life: In his dream he was in Spain, attempting to book a train to a town called Zaraus. On waking he remembered the dream vividly but could not place Zaraus as being anywhere he knew in Spain or elsewhere. Maps did not help him to locate the town, but his natural interest in dreams made him decide to push on further. He ploughed through various Spanish guidebooks and railway timetables, and at last to his delight and amazement, he saw that there was indeed a tiny station name Zaraus lying between San Sebastian and Bilbao. Although he still had no conscious memory of the place he realized that he would have passed through it on a train journey to Bilbao about nine months previously. There are endless examples of this kind, but my own and the Zaraus story suggest most strongly that during sleep, and in particular during dreams, the brain's memory or data banks are opened up or scanned in some way, and that even trivial information, apparently long forgotten or which may not even have emerged into consciousness at all, is stored.

The BIFORA incident provoked other questions: *how*, for example, had the watch name been arrived at? Clearly the loss of the watch was preoccupying me greatly and my irritation at being unable to remember its name produced added motivation for whatever forces were at work in the part of my brain which had the power to scan through its memory banks. And evidently the motivation was sufficient. But why should it only be possible to reach such data during sleep? And what was the brain doing poking about in its own memory system at night, when one might have expected it to be inactive? These questions arose naturally out of a consideration of the experience, and they had the effect of putting me on a particular line of thought which subsequently led to the development of the computer-based theory I will be discussing in the next chapter. The thought was this: perhaps during sleep, the brain, for reasons of its own, spent a good proportion of time looking through its filing system. Indeed perhaps the dream was in some way a reflection of this nightly browsing.

This was, of course, not a particularly original thought. Freud, among various other theorists, recognized that much of the raw material of a dream consisted of references to the previous day's events—an observation that is easily confirmed by inspection of one's own dream life—which implies that the data banks are being sampled in at least a moderately formal way by the dream mechanism. But suppose one accepted the idea that some kind of memory scanning was taking place during sleep, how would this tie in, if at all, with the Dement findings which showed that the dream, with its frequency and pattern of occurrence, was playing some highly significant role in the brain's functioning—a role which was disrupted in sleep deprivation with apparent catastrophic results? But what role was it serving that might have something to do with memory? There are other relevant facts about sleep and dreams which might tie in with this. The first is the fact, experimentally verified, that material learned just prior to going to sleep is better remembered than equivalent material learned during the day. In other words, the sleep period seems to have the effect of facilitating or consolidating the memories. There are, of course, a number of possible explanations for this, but it does suggest some direct involvement with memory traces during sleep. Secondly, there is the curious finding that some memories, particularly of dreams themselves, seem to slip away out of consciousness on waking, no matter how hard one tries to preserve them. Freud used this phenomenon as the basis for his important idea of repressive amnesia: unwanted or threatening thoughts as would normally be found in dreams are pushed down into the unconscious as soon as possible where they could no longer threaten the Ego. The third fact concerned the apparent evidence that humans — and animals — were equipped with two distinct memory systems, a short-term and a long-term.

I began with the central assumption of Dement's work, that during the REM period some operation or operations were being performed which had some important psychological constituent. I then moved to the "dual memory" hypothesis and made the following proposal: suppose that the short-term system could hold information circulating, so to speak, in an immediate-access store, but that the system was unable to keep this information indefinitely "on hold." At night, with sensory input reduced, some part of the brain would now get to work on the data pool, sorting out the material into "wanted" and "unwanted," filing the data according to whether it would be needed for immediate-access or long-term store. The REM periods with their accompanying phases of hyperactivity might represent the sorting and transferring process.

The theory (if one can grace it with the name) did have some attractive features: first it suggested a plausible function for the dream process, provided that one was able to accept the notion of a two-stage memory system in humans and animals. The sorting out and transferring from immediate-access to long-term store would have to be carried out at some time and there would be certain advantages, not overwhelming but nevertheless advantages, in carrying this out at a period when sensory input was reduced to a minimum and the contents of the short-term store could be inspected uninterruptedly. In the second place, the theory also gave a plausible explanation of the peculiar effects of prolonged sleep deprivation, and in particular the hallucinations which so rapidly accompany it. According to my view these were due to the fact that the brain was overloaded with new information and the hallucinations were either some kind of spilling-over effect or, more likely, a desperate attempt on the part of the sorting mechanism to do its job while the individual was awake. A third intriguing feature is that it offers—I still believe for the first time—a clear statement about what a dream exactly is: a momentary interception by the conscious mind of material being sorted, scanned, sifted or whatever.

This last point is very significant, for it led me to a realization of the important distinction between the process actually occurring in the brain during REM sleep, which is the dream *proper*, and the relatively small segment of that process which gets sampled by the conscious mind when the first process is intercepted, and which is merely a glimpse of the dream. The distinction would not be so important to make were it not for one remarkable fact. All human thinking about dreams, from the earliest philosophers through Freud and beyond, has concerned itself largely with, and been based on, the second aspect of dreams, the intercepted part, and furthermore has considered that aspect to be the root and heart of what dreams are about. This is neither surprising nor reprehensible. After all it is, or has been, the only aspect of dreams that has made itself available for study, and it is only with the Dement/Kleitman work that we have realized that this aspect is but the tip of the iceberg.

It is clear, therefore, that we have to realize that it is no longer sensible to refer to dreams as one process, but two. The first, let us call it Dream Type A, is the vast bulk of the phenomenon, and consists of whatever function is taking place during REM sleep (and possibly at other times) and thus is totally untouched by consciousness and therefore never experienced in the common understanding of the word. The second, Dream Type B, is nothing more than a subsection of Type A, modified to some degree by the interposition of consciousness and the vagaries of memory, and is the thing we talk of over coffee and toast in the morning and on which all theories have erroneously and misleadingly been based. The distinction is a most important one and should be kept in mind during the chapters that follow.

Chapter 15

THE BRAIN AS A COMPUTER

I SAW MY first computer when I joined the National Physical Laboratory in 1963. The venerable electronic computer ACE (an acronym for Automatic Calculating Engine) was still working away at full steam, though it was getting a bit long in the tooth and was subject to disconcerting lapses of memory. It had been designed by a gifted team of NPL scientists and engineers in the late '40s and early '50s, and it was at one time the fastest and most powerful computer in the world. The mighty system (I suppose you could fit its microprocessor equivalent into your pocket without too much difficulty today) was housed in a huge room, originally part of a wind-tunnel, and it was a magnificent sight indeed—the last of the Hollywood computers as someone put it. In the centre of the glass-bricked room was the console, shaped rather like a cinema organ, while ranging halfway round the room, twelve feet high and in a glorious sweeping curve, were its memory banks consisting of tens of thousands of electronic valves or tubes. Banks of lights flashed here and there and spools of tape turned from time to time. These were the system's main memory, the electronic valves—though apparently arrayed in vast numbers—being only sufficient for the system to hold a bit of information prior to, or just after, a calculation. By far the greater part of ACE's memory was stored in the form of magnetic signals on tape and the information on these could be transferred in relatively small chunks, to the electronic valve memory for calculation purposes. Equally, when the information stored in the valves was dealt with it could then be transferred on to one of the tapes for what was known as archival storage. The reason that the swopping had to take place in computers was that the valve store was too small to handle all the information that the computer needed to store. The slow, magnetic tapes were merely a rather inefficient backup device only in existence because the fast, electronic store was limited by the large size of the storage units themselves. The parallels with my extremely rudimentary theory of dreams and dreaming described in the last chapter are inescapable, but the important question is, do such storage problems exist in the brain?

*

We tend to assume that not all information fed into the brain is perpetually stored, and this is based on two observations. The first is that so much of what has been experienced does not seem to come to mind by the normal processes of memory. This applies even to quite recent experiences, for example, the telephone number which is "remembered" for long enough to be able to dial it, but which an hour later appears to be totally lost. The second is the vague feeling we all have that the quality and accuracy of the memory fades as a function of time, the long-winded process known as forgetting. Memory for past events is said to be "dim" or softened by the passage of time. There are some anecdotal experiences which seem to contradict this, notably the way in which old people often report that they have been dredging up thoughts which haven't entered their memories for decades and which they honestly believed they had forgotten. Such anecdotes, like all others, need to be taken with a pinch of salt, but the implicit suggestion that the material has not been lost but has merely been inaccessible in some way, was supported strongly by some extraordinary work carried out at McGill University in Montreal two or three decades ago.

The studies were conducted by the great neurosurgeon Wilder Penfield and they involved the direct stimulation of the brain of conscious human beings. This is not as unlikely as it seems: in many cases where surgery has to be performed on the brain—say for the removal of a cerebral tumour — there are various medical reasons why general anaesthesia should be avoided if possible, and since the brain itself is insensitive to pain the surgery is often performed under local anaesthetic and the patient is fully conscious throughout. This provides a unique opportunity to examine the properties of exposed parts of the cortex, mainly by inserting minute electrodes into specific parts, delivering tiny electrical shocks to them and noting the patient's responses. In many cases the findings of these stimulation experiments were in accord with expectations. When tiny areas within the motor cortex were stimulated, the patient would exhibit a motor response—twitching a muscle on the face, perhaps, or making a small involuntary movement of a limb. In other areas the patient would report hearing sounds, experiencing smells or tastes, and these experiences would tie in with what was previously known about the areas of the cortex handling these senses. When, however, the temporal cortex (roughly speaking on the side of the brain over the ears) was stimulated, it was memories that were evoked rather than specific sensory experiences. More interestingly, the memories that were evoked were often described by the patient as being of events which he or she had believed had been totally lost. One woman heard her mother calling to her in the kitchen when she was a little girl, a man saw the features of a friend whom he had not seen since boyhood and who, because of the small part he had played in his life even then, he believed had been dismissed totally from memory. Apart from this, there was other incidental information of considerable interest: for example, Penfield and his co-workers found that even if they stimulated precisely the same spot in the cortex a second and third time, they rarely (if ever) evoked the same memory again, which suggested very strongly that a particular event was not permanently located in a particular segment of the brain.

The inference that one can make from the Penfield work is that memories which appear to have been forgotten do seem to lie latent in the brain and are accessible to consciousness only under unusual circumstances, and that the brain has a near-infinite storage capacity. Regrettably, no one—psychologist, anatomist, or physiologist—has the faintest idea as to how the brain stores the information it receives through the senses. The principles of sensory operation—how the eye captures information and passes it on to the brain, or how the ear does the same with auditory information—are moderately well understood. There is also some less clear-cut knowledge as to roughly which parts of the brain are responsible for the receipt of this information. Even less clear-cut, almost to the point of being vague, is our knowledge of where the information is actually stored. Weakest of all is our understanding of the form in which the storage takes place. For over a century it has been known that the basic unit of operation in the brain and central nervous system is the nerve cell or neurone, a long thin strand of tissue which has the capability of transmitting electrical signals from one end of its length to another. The brain, particularly the cerebral cortex, is a huge tangle of neurones—at a conservative estimate a billion of them—all twisted together like a huge pot of serpents, their ends touching up against each other at curious junction points known as synapses. On the face of it, a thousand million cells is an awful lot of individual units, and it is not surprising that early theories assumed that some great proportion of them would be given over to information storage. A number of hypotheses were advanced as to how this storage might be achieved, most of which leaned on the enormous complexity of the total neural system and the colossal number of pathways which the multiple interconnections of each neurone provided. One billion is a very large number, but assuming that one "fact," whatever that might be, was stored in each neurone—in the way that one bit of information is stored in each binary switch of a computer—this would scarcely be enough to store the stupendous mass of material which human brains need to go about their business through several decades of existence. A fair amount of binary storage is needed to handle just one word, let alone a complex language, and it is doubtful if a billion binary switches would be enough to handle every aspect of a single spoken language, let alone all the other information that a brain requires just to tick over. Theorists, therefore, were forced to argue that the memory system, whatever it was, was somehow able to avail itself of the colossal number of discrete pathways that the interconnecting neurones made available. As each neurone interacted with at least a dozen others, the number of separate pathways down which information could flow rises into astronomical figures. There are in fact more individual pathways available than there are atoms in the whole of the universe, which means that if one could think of a way of utilizing these pathways as individual storage units, the brain could cope with everything that was put into it and still have room for a billion times as much again.

As a psychologist and a computer scientist, thus having my feet in both camps as it were, I was particularly eager to pursue any parallels I could find between brains and computers. Of course I was not the first person to attempt this synthesis, not by a very long chalk. Charles Babbage, whom many people hold was the inventor of the general-purpose computer, and who was busy constructing one out of brass cogs and wheels as far back as 1820, made several references to the functional, if not the structural, similarities of his machine and the brain. During the war, one of the most creative intellects of the century, the mathematician Alan Turing who worked on Colossus and later on ACE, devoted a lot of thought to brain/computer parallels, as did Norbert Wiener (sometimes known as the father of cybernetics) and the outstanding mathematician John von Neumann. In fact at one time the subject became so fashionable amongst the élite of the computer intelligentsia, that the phrase "electronic brain" slipped into the English language as a synonym for a computer, and has only recently slipped out of vogue. Most computer scientists tended to be irritated by the phrase, as it happens, for it seemed to suggest that all they were doing was attempting to construct synthetic miniatures of biological brains, whereas they were actually designing totally novel systems from the ground up. Those few psychologists who were interested in the topic at all tended to be equally irritated, feeling that the computer engineers could have little understanding of the vast complexity of the living brain, and the sheer hopelessness of attempting to make a copy of it out of valves or relays. Partly as a result of these negative feelings, and also partly because of the palpable weakness of early brain/computer models, parallels of this kind have dropped out of fashion. Nevertheless there are fascinating points of contact between computers and animal and human brains.

To begin with, both brains and computers are information-handling devices, although that on its own doesn't actually say too much. The main problem here is that one must first define information, which is by no means a simple task. To most people it probably means "facts," the kind of assembled material that one gets in a newspaper or a television news or documentary programme. This actually refers only to a special type of information, but if one pursues this line a little further one can begin to get some clues as to its wider meaning. The first point to grasp is that newspapers as such, or television transmissions, do not themselves contain any "facts" at all—all they are are bits of paper with marks on them or waves in the air. So, how does one proceed from there? Since we know that newspapers can actually convey facts, then it is obvious that the marks printed on them are not random but have been structured or "ordered" in a particular way according to the rules known to the person who wrote and/or printed the paper. This structuring or ordering is such that if the writer picks up the paper some time after it was written, he can immediately understand the purpose behind the structuring or ordering when he first put it there. Furthermore, the rules of this structuring being known to other people who speak his language, his purpose—or "message" if you like—can be understood by anyone else picking up that paper who has learnt the rules. We might say, therefore, that the reader of the paper has, by the act of picking it up and interpreting its structure (reading it), received some information which was originally in the mind of the sender and which he was anxious to convey to any readers of the paper. The accuracy with which the information is passed from the sender (the writer's brain) to the receiver (the reader's brain) is a function of a number of things: the clarity of the communication channel, in this case the newspaper; the efficiency of the coding and decoding mechanisms, say his typewriter or printing set; and at the other end, factors such as the reader's intelligence, the amount of light on the page when he is reading, the efficiency of his eyes and so on have an effect.

This may seem rather a long-winded way of going about describing the purpose of a newspaper, but it serves to illustrate two purposes. The first of these is to highlight how complex is the act of communicating between one human being and another. We do it so automatically that we take its multiple levels of operation for granted. Secondly, it serves to indicate that a "fact" or information is not a thing which exists in itself, but merely something which comes into being when certain processes have taken place according to certain rules. These rules, to recap, are: (1) A sender must generate a signal of some kind, (2) code this in a manner suitable for transmission across the physical universe we live in, (3) this signal (suitably coded) must now be observed by a sensing system, (4) decoded according to rules known to the receiver, and (5) finally arrive in the receiver's brain.

Up to this point we have been talking about rather grandiose manipulations of information, but it is important to realize that information can pass from non-living things to each other, from living things to non-living things, and from non-living things to living things. When two computers communicate by passing details of bank balances from one bank to another, they are following all the rules of information transmission and reception (the fact that humans are behind it all is not actually relevant if you think about it). When a man types a sequence of instructions (a program) into a computer and the computer responds, information exchange is equally taking place. It is also true to say that when the sun sends out its rays at dawn to a plant, causing it to open its petals, it too is generating information and this information is being acknowledged and received. Information is obviously a feature of the interaction—not necessarily sentient—between complex systems in our universe, and it is not a feature unique to brains. Brains, however—and computers—are magnificently well equipped to handle information. Indeed it is their primary task in life. One can go further: not only are brain and computers information-handling devices, but there are also close parallels in the *process* by which both kinds of brain perform their tasks.

However powerful or ingenious or "intelligent" a computer might be, everything it "knows" and everything it can do depends on a program (the collective name is software), which is a set of instructions to specify a course of action at any given time. Modern computers are equipped with thousands—even tens of thousands—of programs, many of them stored within their own memory system. As the computers become more complicated and powerful, the programs that control them need to get correspondingly more elaborate and intricate; and they need constant revising and updating as the job the computer has to do changes slightly from day to day.

When I joined the National Physical Laboratory I began to look systematically at parallels between the operations of computers and those of the living brain. My most productive contacts were with the computer expert, Ted Newman, one of the pioneers of computer development in this country, who it turned out had the same kind of consuming interest in drawing analogies between electronic and biological data as I had. Rather casually over lunch in the summer of 1964, we wondered if there were any processes in these great analytic machines that paralleled sleep. Offhand, the answer seemed to be "no." They do frequently have to be switched off for servicing and replacement of dud components, but this is not quite the same. There is one set of operations, however, which has to be performed fairly regularly with the biggest computers which did suggest an exciting concept. These are the operations concerned with program clearance and classification.

Computers, as I have said, are controlled by vast sets of programs which are effectively instructions on how the computer should use its brain. Now if it is a fairly stolid device, dedicated to one or a few particular tasks, then these programs remain static and unchanged—as long as the task is unchanged. Early computers tended to be used in this kind of way, but as technology has advanced their inherent flexibility has been progressively better exploited, and modern systems tend to be employed on a really enormous number of different tasks, all controlled by distinct and separate programs. After a while the software bank for any individual computers builds up to very considerable proportions, and the machine becomes a tremendously powerful device, capable of tackling a remarkably divergent range of tasks.

So far so good: but now a complication arises. The world changes steadily from day to day, and at the same time the tasks which the computer is called upon to do also change—necessitating, of course, constant minor or major modifications in the program. With small computers supported by limited software these modifications tend to be infrequent and unlikely to affect the course of the computer's work, but with very large systems the amount of rewriting, updating and testing of new programs becomes considerable. There is an interesting further complication.

For various reasons it is advantageous, and in some cases absolutely necessary, for this process of updating, rewriting and testing of programs to be done when the system is, to use a technical expression, "off-line." This is a piece of computerese which means not that the system is switched off, but rather, uncoupled from the environment. Data from the outside world is not fed into it, and, even more important, *it cannot itself operate on the outside world.* This is a very important concept to grasp, for it represents something rather special in machine terms. The system can be working away like mad and yet not interacting with the environment in any way.

Now, in this off-line mode, programs can be rewritten and tested without the consequences of this testing etc. being dramatized in the ouside world. Take computers that control wage and salary systems for a large firm. As wages increase, taxes change and the number of employees varies, the computer's programs must be constantly altered. So the computer operator takes the computer off-line (uncouples it from the task it is controlling), then runs the programs through and makes modifications where necessary. It is imperative that the computer be off-line, otherwise the experimental or modified programs will do the job they were intended to do *as they are being run through.* If the computer were not taken off-line we would get sets of peculiar pay packets issued at the wrong time of the month. Worse, if the computer were controlling a chemical factory, the running of test programs when the system was on-line might lead to some peculiar chemical compounds being mixed and, sooner or later, no doubt, some pretty spectacular explosions would occur. There are all kinds of other examples that one might think of.

Up to now I've been talking about what happens in computers. Let's now switch to brains, which are after all biological computers with a fabulous bank of software—painfully acquired since birth—and a spectacular degree of flexibility. The principles of operation of brains may be very different in kind from those that apply in the case of computers, but nevertheless they must still be controlled by programs of some kind. Furthermore, these programs—because of the brain's role in a rapidly changing world—must be constantly and regularly revised and updated.

Sleep is the period when the brain comes off-line, cutting itself off from the sensory input, and restricting psychomotor input. In this off-line period, the great software files of the brain become open and available for revision in the light of changes that have taken place as the result of the horde of new experiences which occur every day. Thinking about this led Ted Newman and me to the conclusion that in sleep, man with his own tremendously advanced computer—his brain—might be performing an operation similar to and as vital as the modern computer program clearance. On that afternoon in 1964, our joint paper "Dreaming: An Analogy from Computers" began to take shape.

Chapter 16

PROGRAMS OF THE MIND

NOW IS THERE any evidence to suggest that the brain resembles a computer in having a stock of programs? If so, what are they? Why do we need them?

Two recent lines of research suggest part of the answer. The first came from the laboratory in Lyon of the French neurophysiologist Michel Jouvet who has managed to glean some fascinating insights into the nature and purpose of dreaming in cats. Normally the sleeping cat—like us—is physically relaxed and inert. But by careful surgical methods Jouvet has been able to modify the brains of experimental animals (a procedure totally unthinkable of course with human subjects) so that their muscles continue during sleep to respond to neural instructions to move. Then Jouvet wired electrodes to the animals' heads so that he could record REM patterns. He then waited for his cats to fall asleep. During REM periods—those mentally highly active phases in which dreams are known to occur—the cats would suddenly jerk into life and, still sleeping, perform a number of highly distinctive movements. They would tense themselves. They would stalk, crouch and then spring at imaginary mice. They would behave, in other words, as predators in their dreams. And that is not all. Even cats reared in cossetted surroundings with good, regular food supplied to them and who had never had to hunt in order to eat would—during REM sleep—also show this preoccupation with predatory exercises. Is this, wonders Jouvet, the cat running and re-running, checking and re-checking one of its most basic programs for survival—that concerned with maintaining a food supply—in the event that it may need it in the future? Does the cat have a "predation strategy" program built in that it strives to keep in good working order in case it is suddenly called for?

Humans, of course, do not need food-catching programs. But, according to another psychologist, Nicholas Humphrey of Cambridge University, what we do need are many strategies for social survival. Dreams are, he speculates, like dress rehearsals for events we can expect, hope for or fear in everyday life. Situations present themselves in which the dreamer is an actor, playing a part, coping with the often strange twists of the plot, keeping abreast of the unfolding drama. Could these regular bouts of nocturnal histrionics be, like the cat's predatory behaviour, the running through of basic human programs? We are, after all, social creatures, whose lives are highly-coloured if not ruled by personal relationships and situations. If, indeed, we are to stay mentally and emotionally well-adjusted we have to accommodate others, fit into our multiple roles, both major (lover, employee, parent) and bit parts (optimist, cynic, nuisance), and be prepared to do so quickly and effortlessly. Do we then need, among others, special "social facility" programs in the way a cat needs its food-catching instructions? Here of course we are undeniably in the realm of speculation. Indeed such colourful theorizing is unavoidable, given the nature of our subject. Nevertheless, these are not speculations without substance and support, some of which begins to build up into a cogent argument for a computer-brain theory of dreams.

However, before looking more closely at the supporting evidence, we should spend a bit more time on the precise nature of our "mental programs" and how they come to be written. Let us begin (for all the reservations held about calling our remarkably complex thinking apparatus "a machine") by doing just that, and assume, in the words of one of the most influential experimental psychologists in the field of man/machine studies, Kenneth Craik, that "the nervous system is...a calculating machine capable of modelling or paralleling external events." Craik saw the brain as the place in which the goings-on in the outside world were re-enacted on a small scale, like an exquisite miniature theatre in which every scene was faithfully reproduced down to each last sight, sound, touch, taste and smell. Through the senses comes the experience for this model representation of reality—the "input" to use the language of computers—and this in turn is woven into a script.

But scripts have rules or conventions. There are characters to be delineated, plots to be unfolded, climaxes to be reached. So, too, in reality we add to our internal representation according to certain rules—rules about what roles we play ourselves, or the roles borne by others; what our intentions or ambitions might be; how we seem to other people. The process is cumulative. Each day that passes adds a new layer to our mental image of the world and that image we are able to hold more or less intact through the action of memory. The new input arrives, is acted upon according to our internal "rules," is fed into the existing picture as stored in our memory and the end result is a revised view of the outside world. Say, for example, you happen to hold strong political views that have dictated your personal attitudes and voting habits over many years. You then benefit from an act of kindness by someone who, it turns out, has a totally conflicting ideology to yours. Suddenly your theoretical opponent has become in reality a friend. Immediately you revise your views on the quality of his opinions; slightly, perhaps, but appreciably. Now, you will see that this revision of your original opinion has effects on two timescales. In the short term you are well disposed towards one individual, but this *ad hominem* judgement turn has helped to modify the rules by which you tend to judge all others of a similar persuasion. From now on you will view them differently as well.

In the light of this sequence of experience, rules-memory-revision, that the human brain handles all the time, it is tempting to make comparison with the computer, in which the sequence runs input-program-output. The big difference, of course, is that the human brain is self-correcting where the computer is relatively inflexible. We can modify our rules or programs in the light of experience whereas it needs a human programmer to do as much for the computer. Take, for example, a huge military computer programmed to assess the strike capability of the Other Side in the event of conflict. It would quickly need reprogramming if intelligence sources revealed that the potential enemy had doubled its missile silos and quadrupled its submarine fleet. Only then could a computer simulation provide an accurate prediction of what would happen once the buttons were pressed.

The brain updates its programs automatically—and note that I say "updates" not "changes." As we gain in experience, as our input gets richer and more diverse, we modify our programs rather than replace them with a completely fresh set. In the language of the computer engineer this is what is called an "interlocking" set of programs in which procedures or instructions are never removed, but extra ones are added. That is why, incidentally, unlearning is more difficult than learning, because once we have modified the contents of our mental storage facilities the only way we can change things is by further modification. "Unlearning" is then a matter of a new program making our brains fork off in a different direction. Complex modern computer systems also have these interlocking programs which enable updating and refinement to be incorporated. Here too are many forking routines, branching off in the right directions and away from the wrong, including routines for editing out unnecessary material—an operation graphically called "garbage removal." In fact it is in this refuse-collection procedure that the actions of computers may closely resemble that of the brain. In a tightly-reasoned argument, Ted Newman points to the "cleaning up" that seems so necessary to both types of cerebral machine—the electronic and the human. Newman contends that mentally healthy people, as opposed to those suffering from psychiatric symptoms such as clinical depression, show a distinctive pattern of brain activity. They respond to events in the outside world in short bursts of brain cell activity, whereas depressed people take far longer to respond. It could be, says Newman, that the mentally healthy have better serviced brain programs which are freer from clogging refuse. It is that which makes them healthy.

If so, how and when might such a psychic clean-up take place? First the program is looked at in terms of its forking structure: the brain takes a random set of forks in a given direction and asks itself, "Does this seem right?" If it does, these forks or decision points are locked in to become an updated program while the rest are temporarily set to one side for later use. If they do not seem right another set of decision points is taken out for inspection until the right combination is found for the job in hand. Again the rest are locked out for the present but retrievable later if and when needed.

All this is analogous to what the computer scientist knows as "program clearance," which is constantly being carried out to meet changing circumstances. A program is scrutinized, checked, debugged and pruned so that it is appropriate for the task it has to perform and contains the minimum redundancy. No use a computer, for all its speed, having to slog through miles of useless instructions and act on them. Better to respond—like the mentally alert individual—in crisp, relevant bursts.

Both brain and computer then are or should be programmed to work at their most effective to meet their current needs; the computer needing an outside agency in the shape of a programmer; the brain being able spontaneously to do its own program husbandry. We now come to the big question of *when* this re-programming takes place.

Here, in essence, is the resulting computer-based theory of dreams and dreaming: A brain is a computer, a biological one, which must be controlled by a set of programs, and there are probably millions of them. Many of these programs are inherited and have to do with what we refer to as instinct: a creature is born able to suck, breathe and cry; a rabbit is born with a set of programs that make it behave like a rabbit and not a cat; a newly-hatched viper will strike, just like an adult does, at anything that threatens it. What there is at birth is the basic working model, and from then on programs are acquired, adapted and continually modified to meet the constantly shifting conditions in the world. Like a computer, the brain must be disengaged from the external world so that the programs can be run, up-dated and tested—and this is what I believe sleep to be. But what are dreams? Well, they are the programs being run: during Dream Type A (which was the term given to the process going on in all REM sleep and possibly, even, all sleep) the brain remains safely off-line; during Dream Type B (which was defined as that small portion of Type A we are actually aware of) the computer-brain comes on-line and our conscious mind has a glimpse of the programs being run. When this happens, an attempt is made by the conscious brain to "interpret" it as a kind of pseudo-event and a dream is remembered. The real core of dreams, of course, will be odd mixtures of stuff, almost all to do with recent events and experiences in the life of the dreamer, thoughts about recent or long past events, current ideas and obsessions, worries, desires, wishes and so on; in fact anything done in the course of the day which requires assimilating into the great mass of existing programs. The logic of the brain's program system, of course, need not follow the lines that we feel it ought to. This is important to help in understanding why the dream-program, when interrupted, often seems pretty crazy.

It's just as well, by the way, that our off-line mechanism is so potent and remorseless, for the experience of being fully conscious of a full night's dreaming would be, at worst, unthinkably horrific. Anyone who has had a bad fever and suffered a period in which sleep is persistently disturbed, and the raw hard stuff of dreams sampled intermittently throughout the night will understand what I mean.

The brain takes in information through the five senses: sight, hearing, touch, smell, taste. In every second of every waking hour, there is a veritable bombardment on each of the senses and the brain is taking in an almighty load of information—not all of it necessarily new—on thousands of different subjects to add to the body of knowledge (the millions of sets of programs) it already has. During REM sleep—and possibly at other times as well—the brain is scanning this new information, re-running and re-writing existing programs to see if they are relevant in the light of the day's experience. Dreams are, of course, visual —but visual programs are not the only ones we have. As we have seen, for example, time-lapse photography has revealed that there is a great deal of bodily activity going on during sleep. Perhaps we could say that this is a sign of muscle-movement programs being run, and that sleep-walking is the result of the brain going on-line during this. The same could well apply for sleep-talking.

According to Dr Edmond Dewan, a researcher at Air Force Cambridge Research Laboratories in Bedford, Massachusetts, it is "almost impossible" to explain the behaviour of the brain *unless* some reprogramming is taking place. Dewan, too, believes that REM sleep provides the ideal time for this process to take place and has carried out an important series of tests to support the notion. His thinking on the subject was influenced by two key observations, both readily verifiable by any sleep researcher worthy of the name. The first is that the sleep of many mammals contains a fairly uniform percentage of REM phases which does not differ all that significantly from the amount found in humans. However as one moves lower down the evolutionary ladder towards more primitive creatures whose behaviour is relatively inflexible (or "fixed programmed") in character the amount of REM decreases, sometimes disappearing altogether. It might be thought, then, that REM sleep and varied behaviour go hand in hand.

Secondly—and this is something that chimes very convincingly with Nick Humphrey's notion that dreams prepare us for social interactions during the day—the less mature an animal the more REM sleep it has. Human infants, we know, spend about half their sleeping hours in REM whereas in adults the average proportions of REM to non-REM (or, roughly, dream to non-dream sleep) are only 1 to 5. Going beyond babyhood, estimates have been made of the REM times of the human fetus, and here the percentage rises to a hundred per cent at around 24-30 weeks gestational age. "This could," argues Dewan, "be explained by saying that a large amount of programming takes place at the start of an animal's life." This seems to support the view that dreaming may—in humans at least—be concerned with running through and inspecting a social adaptation program, for it could be said that young children who have had little actual social experience in the outside world need to prepare for the interactions to come by staging their own nightly series of internal dramas. As we grow older the need begins to diminish because experience has taught us how to handle ourselves socially in a wide variety of situations. We become prepared to face the world through the lesson of real life, thereby relinquishing some of the fictions of our brain's own making.

That the young child needs a lot of time in which to dream may explain something that many parents and teachers observe when the youngster first begins school. He or she ends the day exhausted and ready for bed, often inordinately—if refreshingly—early. This will often happen even when the youngster in question has, as a preschooler, led a highly active life, physically speaking. In other words, it seems as if the desire to sleep, perchance to dream, is not simply a function (if at all) of an increased level of bodily activity. It could be that the crowdingly novel experience of mingling with lots of new friends, and all that this entails by way of social readjustment, necessitates more dream space in which to rerun, update and prime up the relevant "interaction" programs. No one to my knowledge has yet studied levels of REM in infants starting school, or nursery school, or playgroup, but the results of such an investigation would make fascinating reading.

Just why the brain of the baby should place such emphasis on social development is in part answerable by looking again at Michel Jouvet's cats, which, during sleep, seem to be obsessed with rehearsing their roles as predators. Every animal—including man—has been left by the process of evolution with just those attributes needed for survival. The remaining characteristics have been weakened or suppressed altogether over millions of years. A long time ago in our history the forerunners of *homo sapiens* were skilled in the tough crafts of hunting for food, which called for powerful muscles, a hardy constitution and a more rugged digestive system than we now possess. Increasingly, the mind has taken over from the muscle in ensuring our survival. It may well in fact be argued that "survival" for us, coddled as we are by the benefits of electricity, clean running water, adequate shelter and all manner of creature comforts both physical and recreational, has become a question of social survival. Having—for the most part—come to terms with and, indeed, to some extent tamed our physical environment, the problems we are left with are those produced by human beings with their attitudes, prejudices, failings and aspirations trying to get along with each other. This can be seen right the way up the scale, from the level of the family to that of the state, from the squabbles and affections of brother and sister to the power struggles and compromises of presidents and prime ministers. For us, other people are probably the most crucial environmental factor shaping our lives—or, rather, without other people our lives would have no imaginable shape. In Nicholas Humphrey's words: "No other class of environmental objects approaches in biological significance those living bodies which constitute for a social animal its companions, playmates, rivals, teachers, enemies. It depends on the bodies of other animals not merely for immediate sustenance in infancy and its sexual fulfilment as an adult but in one way or another for the success (or failure) of almost every enterprise it undertakes. In these circumstances the *ability to model the behaviour of others in the social group has paramount survival value*" (the italics are mine).

How then do we "model the behaviour of others?" Clearly we do it by what psychologists term the process of introspection — internal reconstructions, as it were—of external reality. And where else do we find such reconstructions but in dreams? If the ability to simulate social reality is crucial to survival and dreams are one vehicle—not the only vehicle no doubt—for doing this, then we can see how dreaming assumes such importance in evolutionary terms for *homo sapiens*. Likewise with the cat, dreaming of catching mice in case the need arises. Likewise, perhaps, with that cormorant perched motionless on a rock. It too may be dreaming dreams that re-run the programs for survival for cormorants, programs that have to be inspected even at the expense of the bird's immediate safety.

Thus we might, along with Edmond Dewan, be inclined to think that the fact that higher animals have more REM than lower "fixed pro-grammed" animals, and infants have more REM than adults, indicates that dream sleep is necessary for this programming function to take place. But "being inclined to think" is not good enough for the scientist. He wants and needs to find support for his hypothesis, which is precisely what Dewan set out to do, with the help of a psychiatrist from the Veterans Administration Hospital in Boston, Dr Ray Greenberg.

These two researchers approached the problem from an ingenious angle. If, they reasoned, dreaming involves some kind of program in-spection and some form of reprogramming or updating process within the brain, then there might be a way to monitor this in people whose brains are grossly malfunctioning. They went on to theorize that pa-tients with brain damage who are recovering well from their condition should have demonstrably more REM sleep than those who are not show-ing such signs of improvement because the former group are presumably "rewiring" their neurological circuits more rapidly. To test this idea they studied the sleep patterns of eighteen patients from the neurology wing of the Boston Veterans Hospital all of whom had had accidents that damaged their brains and left them unable to speak—a condition known as aphasia. Aphasic individuals, they reckoned, would provide a particularly good insight into this question of REM sleep and reprogramming because patients who are learning to produce or under-stand words are adding new information to their nervous system in the same way that a computer program feeds instructions to the central processor. They are having to reprogram from scratch, hence they should need more dreaming time in which to carry out the reprogramming function.

The eighteen aphasic patients were studied intensively by Dewan and Greenberg who followed their sleep patterns over several nights using, among other equipment, EEG apparatus. They then drew up a score card, showing how much REM sleep each had had. At the same time other researchers in the Aphasia Unit were also producing a score card for each patient, this time on their rates of improvement, which they assessed in relation to the severity of this initial injury. This information was kept away from Dewan and Greenberg until the latter had completed their sleep studies. Then, and only then, were the two score cards brought together—and the results immediately looked very promising indeed for the programming theory. The non-improving patients on average spent about 13 per cent of the night in REM sleep. The fast recoverers, on the other hand, spent more than 20 per cent of the time dreaming. The hypothesis that dreaming is linked with brain reprogramming had not been proved unequivocally; but in the cautious language of science the researchers were obviously satisfied with the results which they say are "consistent with the hypothesis that recovery of function after brain damage involves a process of reprogramming associated with sleep."

There are other experiments that relate to the question of sleep and programming. As we saw earlier young animals, including human children, seem to dream more than adults. There is one form of behaviour that many young animals adopt, especially chicks and ducklings, which is patently important to them, called "imprinting." Roughly twelve hours after hatching there is a critical period in the life of the duckling when it becomes "imprinted" with the image of its mother. Some curious process takes place by which the duckling, having seen its parent, becomes bound to it psychologically so that it will follow her around with an attachment that is uncanny. One of the most famous photographs in the field of animal behaviour depicts the celebrated ethologist Konrad Lorenz playing "mother" to a group of ducklings who had become imprinted with him and not their true parent, following their human leader around as if on some invisible string. Imprinting matters to the duckling. It is a bond which has to be made. Similar bonds are made right through the animal kingdom, including of course those between mother and baby which have effects on the capacity of the child to form strong and lasting relationships as an adult. No one tells the duckling that it is to become imprinted, nor when the process shall take place. It comes into being genetically ready-programmed for this important learning event.

Let us now speculate a little on what one might expect by way of dreaming patterns in animals around the time they are imprinted. If dreams are a form of program inspection one can predict two things about our duckling: first that REM amounts might be higher around the critical imprinting time, second that by administering a drug which suppresses REM phases one should effectively inhibit or at least impair imprinting. According to one researcher, E.H. Hess, this is almost precisely what is found in ducklings. He gave to ducklings a variety of drugs—both barbiturates and tranquillizers—known to decrease REM levels, and measured their reactions and imprinting times compared to those of a control group given no drugs. Sure enough, compared to the controls the animals given drugs showed signs of delayed imprinting. What is more, once these drugs were withdrawn there was the expected "REM rebound" effect, whereby an unusually high amount of dream sleep crowds in and this appeared to trigger off the imprinting process.

It would be reasonable, then, to assume, as does Edmond Dewan, the experimenter who looked at the relationship between REM sleep and recovery from brain damage, that dreaming is indeed a kind of cerebral rehearsal for important events to come—be this imprinting in the chick or the gradual return to normal speech in the aphasic patient. One way to picture this rehearsal or preparation is to see it as a time when the brain is spontaneously undergoing a process of re-organization—which I with Dewan am inclined to call "reprogramming"—to equip it for its current needs. In the case of lower animals these needs tend to be restricted to the day-to-day business of physical survival or to relatively straightforward social interactions. In humans we are talking about an immensely wide range of social, emotional, intellectual and creative needs that in their turn produce a rich diversity of thoughts and feelings within the context of our dreams.

There is, though, more to dreaming than simply producing nocturnal representations in the brain of events and circumstances that we are likely to encounter. There is, as we all know, a strong element of *up-dating* in that our dreams take in recent experiences—things we have seen, people we have met, places we have been—often coupling these with a scenario that is familiar. A common dream among women, for example, is one in which they suddenly find themselves naked or near-naked in a public place. The place may change and the people around her may change, according to the people and places she has encountered recently, but the basic plot remains the same. This element of new experience to modify the existing plot is paralleled in the work of the computer scientist who takes in new input—by way of revised data or changes in procedures—to update his program. Let us go back to that computer program designed to ensure that employees get their correct salary at the end of the month. There is the gross amount of pay from which various deductions are to be made—for tax, health insurance, membership of staff clubs or associations and so on—which will vary according to the circumstances of the individual. Income tax, for example, is scaled according to the number of children one has, so as soon as an employee becomes a parent (or a parent for a second or third time) the tax rate changes, the program needs updating and a new net salary total is produced. Taking in such new information—in this case on number of offspring—is very like feeding new experiences into our brain's programs. Both modify the basic pattern. Both produce a revamped form of a familiar story.

The brain-computer analogy thus seems a very tidy one. But is it tidy enough to resolve a number of questions about the nature of dreams that readily spring to mind? Here are just a few that will need a satisfactory answer if my computer theory is not to spring a few dangerous leaks.

What new input does the sleeping brain select for dreams? How is it selected?

Why do worry and anxiety often colour so many dreams?

What happens to material in our daily lives that doesn't find its way into dreams? Is this discarded?

Why do we vary in our ability to recall our dreams?

The sleeping brain demonstrably exercises considerable editorial sway over the material available for use in dreams. Watch a stirring movie late at night and next morning you may well remember re-running the film in a dream, modified of course, possibly incorporating yourself as a central character. In fact, a series of experiments carried out in a sleep laboratory showed just that. A stressful movie shown to some volunteers seemed to be incorporated within the first few minutes of their first REM stage of sleep. Yet during the daytime we will have experienced far more than this one film. Our lives are crammed with experience, a great deal of it of course, relatively low-key routine material, coming at us from all sides by way of the things we have seen, heard and felt. It is tempting, therefore, to conclude that the editorial brief of the brain is to "select only the highlights" for incorporation in dreams and "junk the rest." This would make the dream a kind of "memory filter"—a nightly examination of the vast mass of material collected in the course of the day, with a subsequent "rejection" of redundant or inapposite memories and responses.

Now this on the face of it would make the sleeping brain closely comparable to a computer. Computer scientists have now gained a good deal of experience in the adaptation and evolution of computer programs—particularly in cases where these are used for office routines. In such systems what tends to occur is that the programs keep up with new needs and improve their performance on old ones, by persistent minor modifications of programs. Inevitably, however, the computers get cluttered up with more and more unneeded instructions and it turns out that the increase in material tends to be exponential—doubling and redoubling over given intervals of time. In some ways this "junk gathering" does not matter much, but in other ways it is important for two reasons. First, computers are of finite size and speed and the unnecessary routines and instructions actually waste computer-time. Secondly, the increase in material interferes with the process of adaptation. All this can lead to functional breakdowns because of greatly reduced effective computer speed and general inflexibility.

There is, of course, a simple solution to this problem: programs must occasionally be run through and the unnecessary instructions cleaned off. A further obvious requirement is that the cleaning-up should be done at regular intervals and never unduly delayed, for the longer the delay, the more new program material will be affected (because programs in a finite system must interlace and share common paths) and the more difficult the tangle will be to unravel. This cleaning-up process is already essential to modern computers, and we will not need to stretch our imaginations too far to see that the same kind of argument should apply to the developing programs which exist in living creatures. These programs, too, should have periodic clean-ups, for brains, like computers are of finite size and speed of operation; furthermore, for the same reasons applying to the computer case, these clean-ups would have to occur in regular non-operating periods.

In the computer at any rate there is a simple but effective way of

cleaning-off a program. Certain "wanted" instructions, instead of leading
to the newly outmoded and unnecessary computing routines, must be
made to lead directly (or via a small number of extra instructions) to
those parts of the program appropriate to the latest method of working.
The necessary modifications can perhaps most readily be made at
"choice-points" in a program, where the computer is required to decide
what to do next on the basis of its previous calculations. Here, the
modification may simply be a matter of biasing the choice of different
ways. Once that has been done and a new route established, it is not
strictly necessary to remove the unwanted instructions, for since no part
of the pertinent program complex now leads to them, they are for all
practical purposes "forgotten". There might, it is true, be some slight
advantage to removing the unwanted instructions entirely, by erasing
them in some way, for new storage space would thus be made available.
As we saw earlier, however, storage space *per se* is not really a problem
either with computers or with the living brain, and there might indeed
be some value to retaining old routines which "may come in useful one
day" as new routines under new circumstances, when new links to them
could perhaps be forged. More importantly, the sub-complexes may often
continue to be required in completely different programs, to which access will remain via alternative sets of instructions.

The question of storage space reminds us that any theory involving
processes of memory and "forgetting" in man himself must take into
account the fact that apparently forgotten material may occasionally come
to light after years, even decades, of virtual dormancy. The sudden appearance of these distant memories, many of which may be entirely trivial
in content, may be precipitated by some abnormal physical or
psychological situation — a blow on the head, for example, or the
somewhat drastic action of ECT (electro-convulsive therapy). They may
even be induced experimentally, as Penfield and others have shown, by
direct electrical stimulation of micro-regions of the brain cortex during
surgery, producing "memories" — of sights, feelings, sounds or even
smells — which "haven't been thought of for years."

These facts seem to suggest (though they cannot show conclusively)
that all experiences which reach the level of consciousness have their
"niche" of representation in the brain, though the trivial and redundant are sealed off as we have proposed. The most obvious objection
to this view has always been that the brain is of finite size. However,
while estimates of the number of nerve cells in the brain and their possible ramifications and interconnections vary appreciably, all are agreed

that the brain is sufficiently large to accommodate several lifetimes of information sampled in day-to-day activity. The problem with the living brain is not one of storage space but rather of convenience and simplicity of access. In other words the human brain does not really "junk" any information at all. It merely discards it temporarily, holding it in store for some possible future use. What is more it does not discard all the routine trivia in dreams. A lot of the daytime experience—whether dull or exciting—is incorporated into our dreams. Where we have to make a careful distinction is between those dreams we remember and those we do not.

Ramon Greenberg, the sleep researcher who worked with Dewan to study brain-damaged patients, has also taken a considerable interest in what is remembered and what is forgotten. He, in common with other researchers, looks to the dream state as a time when problems are being worked on by the brain, but worked on in a particular way. "I wonder," he says, "whether the question of whether dreams are remembered or not, or when they are remembered can be looked at in terms of the kind of work the dream is doing and also whether or not it is successful." He then goes on to put forward a most intriguing idea—and one which appears to harmonize with what I was saying earlier about dreams as a rehearsal for potentially difficult social situations. "If you think about the times that people remember dreams I suspect you begin with those dreams that failed in their function, such that people wake up feeling anxious. In these dreams something hasn't been dealt with. The person wakes up and is aware of his dreams."

This is so. If you wake sleepers in the laboratory while they are in a REM phase (as shown on the EEG machine) you get good recall. If you wake them up outside REM phases you get poor recall, suggesting perhaps that forgetting is the normal state of affairs. Certainly many dreams have a definite element of anxiety and worry about them. Could it be that the problem to be ironed out still lingers, like a computer program which has not been completely "debugged" of inconsistencies, inaccuracies or illogicalities? If so one would expect people who are depressed, anxious or under stress perhaps to seek more dream sleep in order to work out their problems, to try to debug their programs.

Fortunately this is something one can investigate by looking at the sleep of so-called "variable sleepers," those people who have sleeping patterns that are so stable that it is easy for them to detect any changes in them. Dr Ernest Hartmann, for example, has carried out extensive studies on variable sleepers trying to relate increases or decreases in sleep time to what is going on in their lives during the daytime. His overall finding was that people seemed to notice decreases in their sleep when things were going well, when life and work seemed fairly agreeable. Increased sleep, on the other hand, came about with stress, change or depression, usually when people were tending to focus inwards on themselves. There was, for example, a number of young women who related their increased need for sleep to periods of loss of a boyfriend, a parent or some other important relationship. And among those reporting decreased sleep were people who had undergone successful psychoanalysis for their emotional problems, and a number of individuals who had taken up regular transcendental meditation.

Now these findings, though interesting, do not in themselves say anything about the relationship of anxiety to dreams, merely to sleep time. However Hartmann did not stop there. He went on to study dream sleep in a group of women who regularly were prone to depression and irritability just before menstruation, victims of pre-menstrual tension —(PMT)—during which time, incidentally, there are unusually high rates of suicide, homicide and admission to psychiatric hospitals. The PMT group of women all needed more sleep in total, but not very much more. What they did need, however, was considerably more time in dream sleep. They dreamed, it might seem, in response to, and perhaps to cope with, their depressions. Certainly Hartmann, taking this along with other evidence, concludes that certain lifestyles or emotional states produce changes in dream sleep requirements. He writes, "... worry, depression, certain kinds of stress... are associated with an increase in sleep requirement whereas happy, effortless 'preprogrammed' functioning with a lifestyle of keeping busy and not worrying about problems are associated with a reduced requirement." And he adds, "Dream sleep is the portion of sleep differentially involved, so that it is probably the requirement for D-(dream) sleep which changes under these different circumstances."

Dreams, then, are not all vivid or exciting. The vast majority are dull and repetitive routine affairs. The reason we may remember the more vivid ones is that they carry a strong emotional component, often highly coloured by feelings of anxiety, worry or frustration—such as trying to jump on a bus that keeps accelerating just out of range. There is an element of anxiety in the dream. Now this may be, as I suggested earlier, because off-line, the brain can inspect our daytime preoccupations without disrupting our waking lives. Or it may be that anxiety in a dream means a psychic conflict not yet resolved, an echo of Freud's theory.

The two ideas, in fact, are not incompatible. That is not to say that the computer theory of dreaming is nothing more than the Freudian theory dressed up in the language of modern data processing. Far from it. There are major, indeed irreconcilable, differences between the two ideas. But there is a sense in which re-running our mental program is akin to trying to resolve our emotional or intellectual conflicts.

To understand this idea, ask yourself what we really mean when we speak of "conflicts." We mean that we are worried about how our thoughts and feelings will stand up to exposure in the blinding revealing light of everyday life. Are we choosing the right job/car/marriage partner? Can we justifiably support Candidate A or Candidate B at the next election? Will conscience allow us to bend the truth slightly when we file our income tax papers—and if it does, what will be the outcome? Hartmann's research led him to conclude that the more of these unresolved preoccupations we have simmering away in our consciousness (or unconsciousness) the more dream sleep we are likely to need. Thus dreams seem to be necessary in some way to work on these conflicts.

Over the years I have received many thousands of letters from people about their dreams which follow a distinctive pattern. The place in which the dream is set is familiar, even expected. It is, say, the dreamer accompanied perhaps by his or her spouse standing in front of a house which bears a FOR SALE board outside. The couple are deciding whether or not to sell their present home and buy this one. Their discussions and deliberations range over the thousand and one pros and cons involved in the complicated business of changing houses. Suddenly their attention is caught by a crumbling brick at the base of the main wall. As they watch, the adjoining bricks too begin to crumble, until in the space of a few seconds the whole residence is toppling down before their eyes. Within a minute or two the FOR SALE board is sticking out of a heap of rubble. Then one of the couple remembers something. From a pocket or bag is produced a piece of legal-looking paper. The deeds to the house. The horrifying truth overwhelms them. They have just bought the house. The pile of rubble is their new home.

This is a common sort of dream, especially for people who are in their waking lives in the process of househunting or who have, indeed, just chosen their new dwelling. The crucial question, the nagging doubt, the conflict if you like is: have I made the right decision? Only by buying the house, moving in and living there, can this be answered satisfactorily. But in anticipation of the events in the real world, the sleeping brain appears to be putting forward one eventuality that could arise, namely some structural defect or the need for major repair work showing itself. In reality that can be a deeply vexing, not to say expensive, experience. So too in a dream, the crumbling masonry produces a cold shock, enough to remain as an unpleasant after-taste when we have woken up. But it is, we realize, not for real. It is by way of a rehearsal, a dramatized version produced by an essentially introspective creature to test, perhaps, his reactions to and ability to cope with a situation that may be encountered. The Freudian might talk in terms of a dream of this kind being an "ego-defensive mechanism," a method of strengthening one's personality by producing this profound degree of self-awareness. That is one way of putting it. However if we return to my idea of program inspection and clean-up, this dream may be looked at slightly differently.

Clearly this and any other dream is concerned in some way with *memory*. We remember in sleep that we are buying a house or going to vote or whatever. This in turn seems to stir up other, deeper memories. Buying a house is just a starting point. This may conjure up images of buying other things many years earlier, or memories of repairing a door lock last week, or bring to light an old school friend renowned for his caution. The list is endless. My point, however, is that memory is involved because a central theme seems to evoke associated images, the nature of the association being quite unpredictable. This fusing of images or thoughts, sometimes called by its technical name, *condensation*, could indicate that the brain is making new connections between previously unconnected material. The "dreamlike" quality comes from this condensation process, in which a new piece of input from our waking life (the decision to buy a house) gets linked to older inputs, already wired into the brain's memory circuits. Ernest Hartmann neatly compares this to the Freudian psychoanalyst's view that dreams derive from "a day's residue plus an old wish or fear it has aroused." But Hartmann prefers to describe this making of new connections between daytime memories, hitherto unconnected, and old pathways in terms of modern brain science or neurophysiology. Remember Penfield's remarkable experiments with stimulating the temporal cortex region of the brain which had the effect of producing in the subjects a whole story from memory which unfolded in perfect chronological order over the space of seconds or minutes. The new input or stimulus seems to act as a trigger for other related memories which are brought out for inspection. These fit together to produce a coherent—more or less—narrative but they are full of unexpected associations. As an example here is a vivid dream of my own.

I was conducting a fantastic experiment with some colleagues in the main cafeteria at the National Physical Laboratory, which had become filled from floor to ceiling with water in which a great range of fish of various shapes and sizes were swimming. By some device we quick-froze the water, thus locking the fish into a huge cube of ice, with the aim of studying the levels at which the fish had been swimming. The dream ended as we began to mark off levels on the icy wall of the cube. The plot of the dream was so far removed from anything I could begin to relate to reality that at first it resisted any kind of explanation. Trying to pin down the events within the dream and separate them out from the narrative, however, produced a few insights, some of which gave me a jolt of surprise. The first, and most trivial, was that I had the previous day eaten a fish lunch at the cafeteria, which happened to be unusual for me. Secondly, again on the previous day, I had finally got round to cleaning out the tank of a goldfish I had at the time. I had tried to siphon out the water with a short pipe, one end of which kept jerking out of the water. The result was a spasmodic lowering of the water level. I remembered distinctly thinking at the time, as the fish swam nervously around in its gradually diminishing world, that it was being forced to exist at different levels in the tank. Thirdly, on the same evening, I had watched, for the first time in some months, an evening's television. Out of an extremely dull session, one striking image, reiterated throughout the evening, had stuck in my mind. This was a commercial for fish fingers consisting of a shot of a lot of struggling fish in a net being hauled aboard a trawler, and then, by stop-action photography, being frozen into a block of ice to be transferred into a frying pan. However implausible the concept, my brain had evidently considered it to be a significant new image and it had been pulled into a special program which, on the face of it, would seem to have been dealing with fish. I have since amused myself with other examples, some equally bizarre, of this novel method of dream interpretation.

Let us go back now to our analogy with a computer program. In my dream, the program title is "Fish" and it is this concept that unifies the whole dream. There is a plot or scenario too, but this does not exist separately from the individual "fishy" parts. What may happen is this: by running through its fish program the brain presents itself with a collection of fish-centred data which it spontaneously lends shape to—the shape is the scene. But this picture—like a painting-by-numbers kit—is dictated by the quality of each of the parts. A Freudian would look at this from quite the opposite direction and reason that the plot or scene was already in my mind as some kind of unconscious anxiety or conflict. The fishy details were simply the most recent experiences summoned up in my dream to give this anxiety graphic form. That indeed is their "meaning." The fish data then—for the Freudian—enable one to re-enact an emotional preoccupation.

The computer theory takes "fish" as the operative word, the program access word if you like. The Freudian takes "anxiety" as its starting point with "fish" as a prop to colour a pre-existing plot. Why should the brain choose to look at its "fish" program and ignore its glass, or water or food programs? Well, most probably it does revise these programs also, ordering its inputs into organized patterns by way of a dream, possibly so that it might be able to slot in future new information more readily. That particular night was for me a "fish night," in that this was the sequence of operations that I recalled. That constituted my dream.

The most obvious question — and one that has probably already occurred to you—is: what is the function of this fish program? It is, you might think, all very well to describe a dream as a process of program clean-up if that program can be seen as useful in one's everyday life, such as the housebuying area, where some feeling of working out a real-life problem in the bizarre scenery of a dream might be said to be its "purpose." But fish? Surely not. What "function" is served by such a program? How does this esoteric assemblage of scaly images help me to resolve conflicts, or to socialize more freely, or indeed to do anything better after experiencing them as opposed to before the dream?

This is not any easy question to answer. Indeed it may be unanswerable in that it may reflect the fact that the brain's programming and storage system will follow its own internal rules and not necessarily correspond to the logic of the external world. Without appreciating this fully we cannot hope to understand the Alice-in-Wonderland pattern of our dream life. Programs might, for instance, deal with quite unexpected characteristics of the material stored in the brain—all events concerned with bicycles or spoked wheels might, to take a completely *ad hoc* idea, be the subject of a special program and *ipso facto* a dream.

Faced with many such weird assemblies of images or ideas the conscious mind would struggle to impose a meaningful "story" on the experience, and do the best it could with the material available. Try checking this idea by examining the content of your next major dream. The trick is to concentrate on the events within the dream and not be misled by the apparent fatuity of the story. Without too much effort the origin of these events will clock into place—this event was something from a magazine, that person from a conversation, the other from some television programme. All will be revealed as muddled or highly-coloured versions of recent experiences.

It is just possible that what these versions represent, however, is not a whole program but a tiny fraction of one, perhaps a sub-program or sub-sub-program concerned not so much with helping us to come to terms with great issues and anxieties but with brushing up on more technical functions of the brain such as logical thinking, the ability to memorize or recall information, the ability to make deductions or associations from existing evidence. These are all cerebral activities in which we indulge all the time: putting a name to a face or *vice versa*; remembering a holiday from a postcard found in a drawer; finding one's way along a route first travelled twenty years ago. Could the strange gymnastics in time and space contained in our dream be a way of practising this kind of daytime behaviour? Descartes' famous proposition, "I think therefore I am," might be reworked as, "I dream therefore I think."

I realize that my computer theory of dreaming has raised at least as many questions as it has answered, and for that I can make no apology since the workings of the human brain are never likely to be comprehensible to us—least of all during sleep when communication with the dreamer is practically impossible (perhaps not totally though, as we shall see) so we are very limited in the sorts of investigations we can make during the course of the dream itself.

Nevertheless I offer the theory as a means of explaining the characteristic flavour of dreams, their undoubted importance, and perhaps their various functions. You may like to assess for yourself the value of the theory in the chapters that follow when we move from the theoretical to the practical and investigate just what it is that people dream about.

Chapter 17

THE STUFF OF DREAMS

AS THE IDEA began to form in my mind that dreaming might be our biological equivalent to the computer's process of program inspection, it quickly became apparent that sooner or later I would be confronted with the awkward task of setting this attractive, if novel, theory within the very broad context of other people's dreams as well as my own. After all, I reasoned, there is enough raw material around in the dreams of one's friends and acquaintances alone to provide a rough yardstick by which to measure the theory—and perhaps to suggest that it was some way adrift.

The first step was to accumulate basic information on what people actually dream about: the themes, plots, characters, props of their dreams; the feelings these evoke; the recurring vivid dreams; the times when they dream more than others. From this one might be able to put some flesh on the rather spare frame of a theory, looking at such fascinating areas as the nature of the brain's programs and how they vary from one individual to another, or within one person over a number of nights; whether these programs are indeed, as I suggested earlier, often concerned with social interactions; how much anxiety and conflict they tend to represent; to what extent dreams might tell us something about the basic mechanisms of the human mind, with its own inner and so far virtually unexplored logic and conclusions. (Why, in other words, did my fish program dream take the form it did?)

Collecting the raw data took various forms, the most productive in terms of sheer volume of dream content being a series of surveys carried out in association with several British magazines. The response to the questionnaires on which these surveys were based was quite staggering. If ever one needed proof both of the magnetic fascination of dreams for people and of the perennial importance attached to them, these media-based research projects provided it in superabundance. Thousand upon thousand of completed questionnaires have reached me over the years, together with even more letters describing dreams in detail, sometimes with a remarkable precision. The very weight of paper activated by my enquiries tended to back up what I had long felt intuitively and what my computer theory tended to reinforce: namely that here, within the raw material of the dream, could lie keys to open at least a few doors into those unimaginably vast interiors of the mind. Surely no activity that was so prevalent and so powerful in its appeal could be just gratuitous? There had to be more there, if only one could pick through the "noise" to home in on the signal.

I was not, of course, the first psychologist to have become hooked on the subject of other people's dreams. Freud, as we saw earlier, used them to try to understand the nature of personality problems and conflicts. As well as Freud and the psychoanalysts, there have been others who have attempted to catalogue the events and feeling contained in dreams and tried, like me, to find common denominators—clues to the function of our nocturnal representations. In 1920 C.W. Kimmins published his classic studies of dreams, in the wake of the Great War 1914–1918 where dreams, argues Kimmins, came into their own, as Freud had suggested, as "a most valuable instrument in the successful diagnosis of certain forms of mental disability caused by the stress and strain and the abnormal conditions imposed by the severe struggle of long-continued warfare." Fortunately, however, Kimmins chose *not* to follow the Freudian path and study mainly the dreams of people suffering from various neurotic disorders, brought on by the "stress and strain" of the trenches of the Somme or the Marne. Instead he decided to concentrate on normal, healthy subjects and, being Chief Inspector in various London schools, used his professional niche to secure thousands of descriptions of dreams from children, their ages ranging from five to sixteen years.

Kimmins, influenced strongly by Freudian ideas, was remarkably sure of the "meaning" of many of these accounts. One five-year-old boy, for example, recalled, "I dreamt that a robber came to our house and broke all the cups." (Robbers incidentally play a large part in young children's dreams.) Kimmins then says that this dream had an interesting sequel because further investigation showed that the boy in question had broken a cup and was in constant fear that his mother would find out about his misdemeanour. If a robber broke all the cups, therefore, it would never be known that the boy had broken just one. "So," concludes Kimmins, "the boy's dream was clearly wish-fulfilment." In fact wish-fulfilment is the interpretation Kimmins repeatedly places on many of these dreams. Girls, he reckons, dream about the return of their father and relatives from the War, about receiving presents of various kinds, about eating and, above all, about visits to the country, travelling and entertainment. Boys, on the other hand, have six times as many dreams about bravery and adventure as girls—again, argues Kimmins, enacting in their dreams the hopes and wishes they cherish in their waking life, coloured by the all-pervading Great War. Thus dreamers see themselves receiving the Victoria Cross or returning home from the battle front to the cheers of a grateful crowd.

It should be clear by now that I am deeply suspicious of this method of interpreting dreams, but there is a great deal in Kimmins' work that is valuable, insofar as it begins to provide a factual catalogue of the stuff of everyday dreams of normal people—especially since his subjects were children whose dream life, as we have seen, is generally more extensive than that of adults. As well as the expression of "wishes" in dreams, Kimmins also found a great deal of fear: fear of strange adults, animals (larger ones such as lions and tigers for boys, rats and snakes and so on for girls), ghosts, houses on fire and so on. Bizarre movements, loss of muscular control and dreams of falling were also common, as was the converse in which dreamers were able to float, glide and swim with considerable ease. Recently-read books (and, not surprisingly, visits to the cinema) also found their way into dreams, usually producing an agreeable situation such as a transmuted fairy story. Rarely does school life figure in the children's dreams, although their teachers do quite often in some out-of-school context, a remarkable fact perhaps since half a child's waking life is spent in the classroom.

Many of these themes are echoed in my own research more than half a century later, though there is of course a parting of the ways over how they are to be interpreted. Even so, Kimmins may perhaps have been foreshadowing my computer theory, unwittingly, when he commented on the vivid dream of a nine-year-old boy, who was crippled. The account contains many of the common elements catalogued by Kimmins. "Last night," wrote the boy, "I dreamt that I was a brave knight. A great big monster came running after the most beautiful lady I ever saw. I drew my sword and hit the monster on his back. He roared so loud that the lady screamed. I said, 'I will soon slay this monster,' and hit him again and then I cut off its head, and he fell dead on the ground. The lady said 'You are a hero.' Then I awoke."

In his comments on this adventure Kimmins seems to me to come close to articulating the idea of the brain coming on-line for its own apparently inscrutable purposes. "The conditions of the dream, with the complete absence of anything in the nature of critical reasoning, are obviously favourable to freedom for an extended use of absurd combinations in the bringing together of a great variety of previous experiences, not in their original connections, but in a new orientation, to meet the purpose of the dream. Many of these amusing combinations found in a dream would have been impossible in the waking condition without the very rare gift of an imagination capable of freeing itself from the chains of conventional methods of grouping experiences." And it is precisely this unconventional grouping of experiences that, in the computer theory of dreams, constitutes the steps of a complex program. The sequence of steps is determined not by the logic of everyday but by another cryptic logic necessary to the proper functioning of the dreamer which Kimmins and others are forced to call "absurd," so remote is the nature of the dream from that of the waking world.

Another piece of research that also seemed to echo my own was much more recent; in fact it was taking place roughly at about the time I was developing the early versions of my computer theory. This was carried out by David Foulkes, James Larson, Ethel Swanson and Max Rardin who, like Kimmins, decided to concentrate on children's dreams. Foulkes and his associates were able, by this time, to take advantage of Dement's finding that, if you wake people during REM phases, in the majority of cases you find that their ability to recall dreams is very marked. In Foulkes' research project the subjects were 32 boys aged from six to twelve years who were studied in the sleep laboratory for two nights each. Altogether the boys were woken up for a total of 249 times during REM phases, and their recall rates were practically as high as in adults, 72 per cent. A second study was carried out with a small number of boys from a slightly older age group, thirteen to fifteen, but the interesting point here was that they were all residents in an institution for emotionally disturbed adolescents, all the victims of parental abandonment or neglect. As it turned out, this last group showed the higher incidence of bizarre and disturbing dreams, seeming to indicate that the more likely the child was to have some kind of psychological or personality problems during the day, the more prone he was to have unpleasant dreams.

These two studies enabled Foulkes and his associates to come to some conclusions about the content of childhood dreaming that are consistent with the computer program idea. First, they emphasize that the dreams of normal children are predominantly centred on play and recreational activities. They do not see them—as does the Freudian, such as Kimmins—as being instigated by unconsummated wishes from the daytime, but rather as extensions of the child's waking impulse towards exploring and manipulating his environment. Play for the child, as any parent, teacher or educational psychologist will tell you, is as decidedly serious as it is all-pervasive, being nothing less than a medium through which the developing individual learns about the world and the people in it. A game of "Mothers and Fathers" is a rich formative experience for the four-year-old, learning about communication, about compromise, about exploring creative possibilities, about competitiveness. Adults too, of course, feel the need to take part in or watch games. The child enacts and anticipates reality: the adult perhaps, from time to time, needs to escape from it.

Would it not then be reasonable to assume that "play programs" figure very prominently in the brain's store? Indeed, play can be regarded as a whole class of main programs, analogous to the predatory programs of the cat, while my "fish" program is one of innumerable sub- or sub-sub-programs, less essential to survival and therefore less likely to figure so regularly in the nightly repertoire. In other words, it is possible, from research such as that carried out by the Foulkes team and other sleep investigators, to think of the content of dreams as a kind of hierarchy of programs. At the top may come the principal programs, essential to survival, programs concerned with fundamental aspects of life (these varying according to whether you are a bird or a person and so on). These may be succeeded by a subsidiary set of less essential programs, followed by a lesser set, then a lesser set and so on down.

Armed then with this sort of speculation, I set out to discover for myself what normal, healthy adults are regularly dreaming about. If my theory were valid it should be possible to look at a number of dreams and arrange them in the sort of "program hierarchy" I have tentatively proposed. And if the sub-programs eluded me, I stuck to the hope that I might at least be able to clarify the main programs—the basic survival instructions that the brain needs to keep on revisiting by way of dreams. In the event, that hope was not altogether a vain one. And in some respects it has even been exceeded.

My sources of information over the years have been fourfold. Four magazines, each aimed at different sections of the population, have carried questionnaires on dreaming which I have devised, providing me in total with what must surely be the most comprehensive body of information on the raw material of mid-twentieth-century dreams yet assembled. The papers involved were: *Destiny*, a popular magazine dealing with psychic phenomena and the more curious byways of our mental life; the *TV Times*, the programme guide to British commercial television; *Honey*, a sophisticated, late-teenage magazine with a substantial readership; and the Magazine section of the London *Sunday Times*. Taken as a whole, here were four channels of information fitted to give the researcher insights into the dreams of individuals especially interested in psychological oddities: men and women of all ages, backgrounds and interests; youngsters, including those in their early twenties; middle-class and working-class individuals; intellectuals and the less cerebrally inclined; introverts and extroverts...the whole gamut of personality. types. In short, a representative as well as voluminous sample of the population at large.

Some additional dream types were added to the *Honey* and *Destiny* questionnaire, as the written responses to previously published surveys had indicated they too were commonly experienced. Not surprisingly, as many of the replies came from youngish women, 70 per cent and 67 per cent of them had dreams about their husbands and boyfriends. Thirty-one per cent (34 per cent) had dreams about parties and social gatherings. Empty houses figured in the dreams of 31 per cent (43 per cent), and although I have not obtained quantitative data on this, I have noticed that many dreams are set in the dreamer's childhood home or the home of an important person in their lives, like a beloved grandparent. Often several houses are blended together and strangely altered, though still recognizable. Teeth breaking or falling out featured in the dreams of 22 per cent (30 per cent) of the replies, and 11 per cent (10 per cent) had dreamed about aeroplane crashes.

From the many thousands of data sources, one obvious bias emerged from the outset. There were far more completed questionnaires from women than men. One obvious reason for this was the magazines in which my surveys appeared, for with the exception of the *Sunday Times* Magazine, all had a predominantly female readership. On the other hand, there is some evidence to suggest that women are basically more interested in—or more loquacious about—their dreams than men. So bias to some extent was inevitable. Nevertheless I was able to use the male/female breakdowns to try to answer two questions: (1) do men and women differ significantly in the routine of their sleep habits and in the amount of dreaming which they believe they do; and (2) do they differ in the content of the dreams they report? The answers were fairly clear-cut. The sleep habits are remarkably similar, and so, to a certain extent, are the amounts of dreaming reported. But in their attitude to dreaming and, most specifically, in the content of the dreams themselves, there are some striking and intriguing differences. There is a difference in age distribution, with a noticeable, though not particularly radical, bias towards middle age in the women, but the peak response in both men and women lies in the age-group 22 – 31, and the second peak in the age group 17 – 21, so the skew is not very important and unlikely, on the whole, to account for the differences in reported dream content.

The questions asking for general details of sleep habits produced rather predictable results—most people (61 per cent) slept for between six and eight hours a night, about 36 per cent over eight hours, and less than 4 per cent for under six hours on average. Here the male/female breakdown is remarkably similar, suggesting that the somewhat different age distributions introduce little, if any, bias into the results. In fact, considering the large size of my sample over the years and the two-to-one preponderance of women over men, the very similar percentage figures (61.5 per cent of men sleep between six and eight hours, 61.6 per cent of women) suggest a high reliability in the response and in the scoring methods. No one, incidentally, has reported that they never sleep at all—suggesting either that such people have no interest in dream questionnaires, or, more likely, that there is no such animal.

Fifty-seven per cent of the people said that they awake refreshed after a night's sleep, and the figure is almost identical for men and for women. When, however, I have tried to ascertain how many people use a drug to help them get to sleep, the first important difference between men and women appears. Only 9.5 per cent of men as opposed to 17.2 per cent of the women—nearly twice as many—use some hypnotic drug. Surprisingly, the use of these drugs seems not to increase noticeably with age—women just find it a bit harder to get to sleep than men. On the other hand, there is probably some ambiguity over what constitutes a drug. Alcohol is a fairly efficient short-term central nervous system depressant, and men who tend to "have a nightcap" may not have realized that this really places them in the category of drug takers.

Bearing in mind the research showing a decrease in REM sleep with age I have usually asked in my questionnaires whether people felt that they sleep less now than they did when they were younger. Over 65 per cent of men and 60 per cent of women felt that they did. But on the matter of complete insomnia, a highly significant difference between men and women emerged: in all, many thousands of people have reported to me at least one totally sleepless night, but of this total, two thirds were women and only one third men. This finding ties in with the feminine preference for sleeping pills, and could indicate that women have "more to worry about" than men, or are more likely to carry their worries to bed with them.

Clearly, men and women differ in their estimation of the frequency of their dreaming. While under 1 per cent of both men and women report never dreaming at all, 11 per cent of men feel they dreamt only once a month as compared to 8 per cent of women. Other comparable figures follow: dreaming once a week, 13.1 per cent men, 8.7 per cent women; two or three times a week 26.8 per cent men, 22.3 per cent women; once a night, 14.6 per cent men as compared to 15.4 per cent women; dreaming several times a night, 34.4 per cent men and 44.9 per cent women. A number of interesting points are raised by this breakdown. Firstly, well over half the sample believe that they dream at least once a night and probably more. Secondly, the fact that women seem to remember their dreams, or be more aware of them, than men, ties in once more with their slightly poorer sleep habits.

Easily the majority of men (79.6 per cent) state that they enjoy their dreams on the whole, while rather fewer (72.4 per cent) women make this claim. This difference, if it is significant, may be partly explained later when we examine the breakdown of the kinds of dreams which people remember experiencing. Certainly, nightmares are more common with women, 8.6 per cent of them having them often, 72.3 per cent occasionally and only 13.3 per cent never. For men the comparable values are 4.2 per cent often, 72 per cent occasionally and 22.8 per cent never.

One common reported psychological oddity which I myself had hitherto believed to be universally experienced is the curious phenomenon known as *déjà vu*. This generally takes the form of a rather sharp sensation best described as "I have done this before" or "I have been here before." My questionnaires have contained a question about this phenomenon producing rather surprising results. All in all, 80.5 per cent of all my respondents are familiar with the experience, 81.7 per cent women and 78.3 per cent men. To many people the surprising fact will be that about one in five individuals have *not* had *déjà vu*, and it would be interesting indeed to see if this finding applied to a random sample of the population.

The content of dreams reveals the widest gulfs between men and women. At the outset 38.9 per cent of men felt that most of their dreams were pleasant and only 12 per cent felt that most of them were unpleasant, as against 31.5 per cent and 17.1 per cent for women. A detailed analysis of the frequency with which various common type dreams were experienced produced these results: anxiety dreams, perhaps predictably, are more common with women (78 per cent against 66 per cent for men), as are those great psychoanalytic standbys, dreams about the sea (40 per cent as against 27 per cent). This latter finding is a particularly fascinating one, for the difference between male and female here is highly signifi-cant, and one is left desperately intrigued about the origins and sym-bolic values of this dream. Sea dreams are often reputed to represent the stirrings of the unconscious—a poetic notion which is really no more than a piece of inspired guesswork on the part of dream interpreters. Dreams in colour are common—rather more women (59 per cent) ex-periencing them than men (53 per cent); but to make up for this men have more sexual dreams (85.7 per cent) than women (72.1 per cent). This is not too surprising, but what is, to anyone who remembers the spectacular nocturnal emissions or "wet dreams" of male adolescence, is that 15 per cent of men appear never to have had them!

Women are also more likely to have had dreams about the future which came true (31.6 per cent), though as many as 26.4 per cent of men were similarly inclined. Dreams about smoking were rare in both sexes, and dreams about nuclear explosions—one of the archetypal images you might think of the twentieth century—are reported by only about 10 per cent of the total sample. Recurring dreams—type unspecified—are reported by 75 per cent of women but only 67 per cent of men, and dreams about reading by rather more women (13 per cent) than men (10 per cent). One relatively common dream, often experienced by people when their finances are tight, is of finding coins showering from a telephone call box, or lying in great profusion on the ground. Here, as many as 24 per cent of men recall this dream as opposed to only 17 per cent of women, which makes sense in view of the fact that men traditionally bear the principal financial burdens in a family.

When the psychologist William James (brother of the more famous Henry) had his famous "anaesthetic revelation"—Higamus Hogamus, women are monogamous, Hogamus Higamus, men are polygamous— he believed that this little doggerel revealed the secret of the universe (which it may well do). My research tried to assess the frequency of revelatory dreams of this kind in normal sleep, and found them to be high and, surprisingly, more common with men (19 per cent) than with women (14 per cent). It could be that women are simply less interested in the secret of the universe—or at any rate less inclined to think they have found it.

In the remaining four categories of dreams listed in my questionnaires women (38 per cent) are far more likely to dream about famous people such as politicians or movie stars than men (27 per cent), whereas men spend more time having dreams of violence (49 per cent against 44 per cent for women). The "falling" dream—one of the most often quoted—comes up in only 71 per cent of men and 76 per cent of women, while dreams in which the individual is being chased trouble only 69 per cent of men but 75 per cent of women.

Most people claim to have heard voices or talking in their dreams, but when asked whether they hear music less than half of all dreamers appear to do so—38.9 per cent of men and 43.4 per cent of women had had auditory dreams of this kind. However, auditory dreams are probably more common altogether than is generally realized, visual experiences being more easily remembered and more readily described and therefore more frequently reported. Roughly an equal percentage of both sexes, incidentally, claim to have had some form of hallucination while they were awake, the rather high figure of 25 per cent being recorded altogether. If these figures are correct, what price the objectivity of flying saucers or the general reliability of human witnesses anyway?

After collecting the results of one survey it transpired that 6.3 per cent of male respondents and 6.6 per cent of women (not a significant difference) had undergone psychoanalysis (figures which some will find surprisingly high and some surprisingly low). In answer to a sub-question, about half of these had felt that the analysis subsequently influenced the latent content of their dreams. Talking in one's sleep was, as one might expect, exceedingly common (70.9 per cent of men and 74.9 per cent of women), but rather more alarming are the figures given for sleep-walking (25 per cent for women, 20 per cent for men).

Are dreams felt to be beneficial? When asked this, most people (57 per cent) felt that "dreams are helpful and beneficial to us in some way;" only 3 per cent (again equally so for men and women) felt they were definitely not beneficial. Roughly 11 per cent of both sexes subscribe to the idea that "a good night's sleep is a dreamless sleep," and about 30 per cent felt that "dreams just happen and are neither good nor bad."

It is exceedingly difficult to imagine the pictorial quality of someone else's dreams. One can catch the feel of one's own dreams quite easily, but the big question remains as to whether other people employ the same kind of visual currency. In an off-hand shot at tackling this question, I have asked people if they had ever seen a film which seemed to recreate, particularly well, the special feeling of a dream. They had indeed. In fact many replied to this by sending in their own particular dream movies and this allowed me to compile a list of those films in which the visual content evidently matched, to some degree at any rate, the visual content of readers' dreams.

A huge anthology emerged (including some very peculiar films indeed like *Lassie Come Home* and *Meet Me in St Louis*) and with certain titles coming up so frequently that a Top Twenty for both men and women could easily be compiled. They make marvellous reading—and perhaps the first compilation of this kind that has ever been put together.

Top of the list was, perhaps predictably, *Last Year in Marienbad*, Resnais' cinematic breakthrough, in which the conventions of decades of film-making were triumphantly overthrown. With its out-of-phase chronology and its subtle distortion of the framework of space and time, *Marienbad* expresses the interior logic of the dream perhaps more completely than any other earlier film and it is no surprise to see it at the top of the list. Incidentally, women decisively voted it as their number one choice—men were less certain, giving pride of place to Kubrick's *2001*, presumably because of its psychedelic light show at the end. In over-all third place was Fellini's *Juliet of the Spirits* (second for women, third for men) with Jonathan Miller's *Alice in Wonderland*, made for BBC television, in fourth place. Miller has since explained, incidentally, that he based his version of Carroll's *Alice* very firmly on the grammar of his own dream life. One of the most famous deliberately simulated dream sequences of all, the opening shots of Bergman's *Wild Strawberries* with its handless clocks and ritual funerals, pushed it into over-all fifth place, while sixth place was taken by the pop-art cartoon, the Beatles' film *Yellow Submarine*—an interesting insight into the night adventure of some people. In seventh place came Fellini again, with *8½*, with Welles's sombre treatment of Kafka's *The Trial* eighth. Interestingly, this is the highest placing accorded to a paranoid dream-film (a healthy sign, some might think). *Blow-Up* came ninth (much preferred by men), with Cocteau's magnificent *Orphée* in tenth place. Another Cocteau, *La Belle et La Bête*, just made the Top Twenty, which seems to be a striking tribute to the potent imagination of the French poet of the cinema.

One of the more puzzling highly placed candidates was *Dr Zhivago* (over-all eleventh), but this seems to have appealed most particularly to women, who placed it seventh, as opposed to men, who rated it nineteenth. Why should women have found this straightforward narrative film so singularly dreamlike? *Incident at Owl Creek*, based on Bierce's superb short story about the dying split-second of a Civil War soldier, came twelfth and the Gothic horror comic *Repulsion* followed it. The explicit sexual fantasies of a woman pushed *Belle de Jour* into an over-all fourteenth place (thirteenth for women, seventeenth for men). After *The Seventh Seal,* another Bergman candidate (fifteenth) and *A Man and a Woman* (sixteenth), men had their own special choice of sexual fantasy in *Barbarella,* seventeenth over-all but tenth for men and twenty-first for women, who evidently fail to respond so patently to that kind of dream language.

So much then for the raw material of the dream. The definite finding that the content of the dreams of men and women can differ so extensively, as measured by surveys, of course raises more questions than it answers. But after many years of purest guess-work it is useful to have some facts on which to work, which is what we shall be doing in the next chapter

Chapter 18

IN SEARCH OF PATTERNS

FOR ME AND for the purposes of trying to justify my computer hypothesis, the most important questions in the various surveys concerned dream "types," the recurrent themes commonly reported by dreamers of both sexes. If dreaming were the equivalent of program inspection, you might surmise that the commonest dreams were not only the most vivid (which is why we remember them so clearly) but also the most "important" to our physical, social, emotional and intellectual well-being, or, to put it another way, they should come higher up the program hierarchy.

To begin with one could hazard an informed guess at what these dream-types might be, basing any selection on the voluminous literature on dreams that has accumulated over many centuries, some contained in the closely documented pages of the history books, others in the fantasy world of creative fiction. From this initial list it was possible, using the various survey results, to add, subtract, refine and arrive at a master list that appears to be broadly representative of our principal dream themes. It is not of course a series of categories into which *every* dream will fit, but it is highly indicative of our nocturnal preoccupations as recorded in our dreams.

The list of dream-types looks like this:

Dreams of: flying or floating in the air
anxiety
the sea or lakes
sex
the future—which comes true
smoking
recurring events
reading
finding money
discovering the "secret of the universe" (forgotten
though on waking)
famous personalities, politicians

    violence
    falling
    being chased
    parties, social gatherings
    dead friends, relatives
    shoplifting
    films or TV programmes seen that evening
    historical scenes
    nakedness

This bald catalogue, of course, is merely a statistical exercise in summarizing dream content, uncoloured by the bizarre quality with which scenes link up, characters emerge and fade away, time and space are crossed with ease and alacrity. As we saw in my "fish program" dream, this linking process—the means by which the sleeping brain melds recent events to those that took place a long time ago, or links events that did occur to those that did not and could not in the real world—is of crucial importance. These are what make the dream hang together as a separate, discrete program or sub-program. So before we come to any conclusions about the nature of these dreams, whether they are indeed recognizably important "programs," we ought to dwell a little on the myriad ways in which dream sequences are strung together.

The diffuse iconography of our dream-life takes place in a world where imagery varies from the gaudy to the formally staid, where emotions may be those of the ecstasy of happiness or of petrifying and unspeakable terror. The adventures may be the purest Cinemascope: "I find myself standing on the deck of a great ship. In front of me I see rows of bearded, sunburned men—slaves I assume—rowing at a steady pace to the thud of a drum that marks the time. The ship is passing through heavy weather and occasionally I am drenched in spray, but the sky is a brilliant blue." Or scenes which are presumably taken from an Accountant's Hell: "I am seated in a drab room and before me is a desk with stacks of ledger notebooks, heavily bound. I open one. It is full of columns of numbers written in a neat hand. The other books are similarly filled. I somehow realize that it is my job to add these numbers with the maximum precision, and that I will not be free until I have added them. I notice suddenly that the walls of the room are lined with similar ledgers—all to be counted. As I start to count I now notice a door leading out of the room. Putting down the book I go towards it thinking it may be an escape exit. I open it, and to my horror and dismay I see it to be a vast library, silent as the grave but with row upon row of shelves stacked with the ledger books which I am doomed to work on for eternity."

The nakedness dream, which will be familiar to many, takes place in a public setting, producing strong feelings of shame and "indecency." Indeed so powerful are these emotions that they swamp any sense of logic and proportion in the dreamer: "I am out in a busy street with many people about and much traffic. I am clad only in a shrunken vest, much too short for me. I am full of shame and try to pull it down in front. This has the effect of causing it to ride up sharply at the back exposing all my backside. I hastily pull it down at the back and, in covering my rear, my even more vital front is exposed. This goes on for a long time and I can find no shelter to hide myself. All the passers-by stare at me with great disapproval and hostility, even those in passing vehicles. I am utterly wretched and burning shame sears me like a mortal wound. This is the most hateful dream of my life and one I cannot forget."

If we need to urinate while asleep the bladder sends warning signals to the brain which will interfere with or, if sleep is deep, become incorporated into the ongoing program of dreaming, which in computer terms is being revised or updated at the time. As the distress signals mount, the conscious mind will stir and will attempt to interpret the raw material of the dream. For most of us this will consist of quest for public lavatories which, when found, tend to be either closed or mysteriously transformed. Normally, fortunately, the signals become so strong that we wake in time to find a real lavatory. One dreamer produced an amusing variant on this theme: "The only other major types of dream I can recollect is what I may call 'exposure' dreams, where one is urgently seeking a lavatory, and when, after a long Odyssey, one finds one it turns out to be entirely of clear glass, open to the view of all and sundry! One occasion I arrived at a vast place about the size of Paddington Station, with hundreds of lavatory seats in a light oak finish, in row upon row —and no screening or privacy whatever!"

Broadly speaking, we dream about what we experience (and that includes thoughts as well as action), the main difference between our internal and our external realities being in the logic of the association of events and their chronology. Hence strange people are blended together in unlikely places, and the time sequences may be chaotic. We must dream therefore about our thoughts, and at a deeper level about our worries and our obsessions.

Dreams of violence, blood and pain are common, as might be expected.

In the two extracts given below, the first vividly recaptures the quality of some of the nightmare creatures we occasionally meet in our sleep. The second, from a young secretary, has heavy psychoanalytic overtones with its apparent equation of sex, blood and pain:

"I dreamed that I was back at school and in the playground. There were a lot of other kids standing with me and we were all peering over a wooden gate at a big brown dog with a huge mouth. He was chained to a wall. A master came along and said: 'It's all right, he won't hurt you' and let him off the leash. As soon as he did so, the dog turned into a sort of moth (only it wasn't a moth, it was like a worm with wings) and a very evil-looking one at that. The other kids didn't seem bothered by it at all, but I was terrified, especially when the master said that it would be perfectly all right so long as we didn't let it get at our throats, as it had a tendency to bite a nice juicy throat. Ugh. So, while everyone else was preoccupied with the master and talking and playing I was determined to get the darned thing and did so, squashing it with my heel. It might be worth mentioning that it had a straight row of iron teeth, which were very vivid."

"Another recurrent dream is where I am at a dance with my fiancé when someone stabs me in the stomach. I look down and can see all red blood oozing so vividly that I feel sick. In a blind panic I race out through a door. Outside it is raining very heavily. I see a field with a fence and over the other side is a small wooden hut with a luminous doctor's sign above it. I stumble over the fence heading for the hut almost bent double, holding my stomach, leaving a trail of blood. The rain has turned to snow this side of the fence and it is about waist deep. Every step I take I seem to get further and further away and the action of my arms is likened to the front crawl in swimming. After what seems hours I reach the other side of the field and struggle over the fence. I reach the wooden hut and bang on the door to find a sign saying 'Gone for Lunch.' Here I wake up."

Another common type of dream is the one in which some abstruse or delicate operation is performed with total ease:

"I once dreamt that I was Picasso, painting a life-size picture of a medieval woman—as I thought the picture should alter, so it did, without my laying hand or brush on it. This was so vivid that I could not rest till I had consciously painted my dream picture. It was a compulsion so strong that I ended up painting it, life-size, on the wall of the flat we rented at the time. We called her Muriel and hung a coat over her every time the landlord called."

"A few years ago I had aspirations to be a pianist and often dreamt of myself being a concert pianist giving a dazzling performance. I could always see my fingers moving over the keys and knew what sound or piece I was playing, but in recalling these dreams afterwards could never consciously remember hearing the music, especially of the orchestra. (I have always found this with my dreams—I am sure, for instance, of a gun being fired but not of the sound of it being fired.)"

We undoubtedly retain our sense of humour in our dream-life though it may take exceedingly bizarre forms. One woman reported an apparently premonitory dream which came true—but in a humorously twisted form:

"A day or two before the start of a cruise round the world in 1959 I dreamt I saw a large black car draw up to the gate, from which two men removed a long box like a coffin, covered with a sheet. This car was followed by another large black car, apparently part of the funeral procession. I began to have horrid ideas of one of us dying suddenly on the eve of the cruise. Then on the afternoon of Thursday May 14, about eighteen hours before we were due to start, a large black car drew up at the gate; two men got out and lifted out a large box-like object, covered with a cloth—our new radiogram which had been on order for weeks and which we had given up hope of seeing before we started. While they were installing it, the second big black car arrived and drew up behind—our chauffeur for the drive to Southampton next day, come to report arrival and take instructions as to time of start, route etc."

Strange words or phrases sometimes feature in dreams, and one reader sent us two dream proverbs with a delightful *Alice in Wonderland* flavour. He writes:

"One is rather dependent on information supplied by others, but at one time I was apparently liable, in the state between sleeping and waking, to give vent with an air of profound solemnity to some great, hitherto unrealized truth. Two only have survived:
A happy marriage is second only to a raspberry tart.
Too many hares (?hairs) in a rabbit pie spoil the pie."

The comic may merge into the zany in a characteristically frenetic way:

"Then there was a splendid Keystone Cops sequence. The hero was Sydney Tafler but it was actually happening, it was not a film. The police were after him for some minor fraud. Four or five of them ran him to earth in a field on the edge of a wood. He was very nervous, but to every one except him the thing was exceptionally comic. One of the policemen had a motor cycle and was parking it. As they moved in on him he ran in a panic to the motor cycle, jumped on and roared off erratically—I don't think he'd ever ridden one before—bumbling about like made over the grass. The police gave chase and eventually caught him. They didn't seem to mind that he had taken the motor bike. As he was being led away he dropped a pound note, picked it up, examined it, dusted it and put it away carefully. It seemed terribly funny because I knew that he wouldn't need money in prison. Then he produced a map of London Airport as if in his defence and began babbling wildly about it. It was all so funny even the police were laughing."

Nightmares are frequently described, and few are more evocative than the following:

"My husband and I, also two other friends of ours, a husband and his wife, seemed to be in America. We enjoyed all we saw and visited. I pointed out the black children playing with white children happily together, running in and out of the sea. We all walked on sightseeing. I felt that four other people we knew in England were in front of us all the time but they were my enemies. We all seemed to be lying down in the sun on some concrete. I saw a black polony with the end of its skin tied to a red polony. All of a sudden it started to writhe and twist and became a hideous cobra. It wriggled and reared itself to me and I could not move. It got inside me as I lay on the concrete floor and I squeezed and squeezed its head tightly as it tried to crawl up inside my body. In can remember the insanity of my begging and crying for help to my husband. I was desperately trying to move to wake him, but they all seemed unconscious and I couldn't reach them to help me. All the time I was squeezing this horrible thing to prevent it killing me. Finally I woke up crying and sweating to discover it was a nightmare."

In this case the dreamer was a woman who had been successfully operated on years before for stomach cancer. She had recovered, but her memories of the event seem to have taken on the evil form of the serpent, a common, perhaps even universal, symbol of evil of some kind. In chronic pain, a common form of the dream may involve an animal inflicting a wound. In one rather grim case-history, a man with developing throat cancer dreamt night after night that a cat was gnawing at his throat.

In our dreams, happiness may take a multitude of forms. Sexual ecstasy is one of the most common, and it may vary from the most straightforward lust to the poetry of eroticism, as in the following examples, of which the first comes from a lady who had to, as she put it "play at Monks and Nuns" for medical reasons during a pregnancy. Her husband was a member of the local cricket team.

"I was the only female in an all-night sex orgy with the aforesaid team. I partook of promiscuous delights with all the players except my husband! In the mornings I would wake absolutely exhausted....mind you, it was fun while it lasted but I couldn't have stood the pace indefinitely."

"The most entrancing dream I had was very short and it paralleled developments between myself and a woman I loved. At the start of the dream we were both in murky water, full of sediment, swimming side by side in full daylight. Next instant it was a very dark night. We were on an island composed of glowing (with light only) frosted glass of soft gold colour like the early moon. The sea was ebony black and the starless sky was navy blue in colour. The only light came from the golden glow at our feet. I was conscious that I had to leave, but the decision rested not with me. We were both naked and I knelt in front of her. With an infinite tenderness and sadness, I kissed her erotically and turning, without looking back, entered the black sea. There in the distance was passing, felt rather than seen, a raft with a small light, the sort that an ancient oil-wick Grecian lamp would provide. There was no one on it and I sailed into the darkness away from the island."

Occasionally, however, sexual feelings are less easily gratified, and may be inappropriately attached:

"I was in church—sitting naked in all the pews were rows of people, in fact, we were all naked except the priest. He asked us to come and take the bread and wine but instead of lining up in an orderly and civilized manner we rushed to the altar in a sort of stampede— holding out our hands and opening our mouths. Eventually the priest got to me (he was very tall and dignified, wearing a long white robe); he gave me the bread and wine and then took me to one side, suggesting that we meet afterwards for sexual intercourse. I was outraged to think that the vicar, who seemed to stand out among us as being so pure and undefiled, should suggest this and I was profoundly disappointed."

In some dreams happiness and exhilaration may appear unpredictably —for example this dreamer's relish in his supernormal bouncing powers:

"Experience of bouncing is quite common. Control of the ability to bounce is completely within my power. Great exhilaration is felt in realizing this ability. Power to bounce up and down and also to travel by bouncing is experienced. If I want to examine something higher than six foot I can bounce up and with great facility alter my bodily position in whatever way I choose. Speed of bounce varies. Small bounces are always quick. As bounces become bigger they also become slower. The bigger and slower the bounce, the more enjoyable it is. Too big a bounce causes the experience to terminate and I awake. The vividness is so clear that even after waking up a great feeling of freshness and well-being continues. In travelling by bounce I seem to have to be more aware of what I am actually doing. It is not very familiar to me, as though I was learning to ride a bicycle. The result is that I am not as free to observe things as I would like to be."

Perhaps this is merely another form of the flying or floating dream which is reported by most people as exhilarating, but by others as terrifying. Another frequent dream of this kind is of rushing down a ski slope or hurtling over Niagara Falls. The origin of such dreams is obscure but it is possible that they are triggered off by objective internal sensations —such as minor gastric upsets or indigestion which, while not strong enough to wake the sleeper, convey feelings to the brain which are incorporated into the ongoing program and woven into the fabric of the dream.

The strange choreography and imagery of dreams, vividly expressed by ordinary men and women relating their own experiences, have a unique quality that has inspired many creative artists. Tired of a form of expression rooted in the mundane, logical world of concrete reality, they have looked inwards in search of originality and surprise. Sometimes the search has taken them to extremes. The painter Hieronymus Bosch, for example, delighted in the fantastic grotesqueries of the nightmare to people his canvases with disturbing and often monstrous creatures. In the early part of this century the Surrealists tried to recapture the quality of everyday dreams using subtle images, suggestion, symbols—basing their art on the psychoanalytic ideas of Freud and Jung. The movement spread. From poetry, to painting, to novels, to cinema, to advertising and even fashion photography, giving us, as the science fiction writer J.G. Ballard puts it: "evidence for a positive logic other than that provided by reason."

That "positive logic," quite distinct from the everyday form of "reason," is, in a sense, the grammar of the dream narrative, producing a heightened language quite different in flavour from conventional forms of expression. So one can understand its attraction for innovative imaginative artists. Yet although dreams have often been exploited by poets and painters, they are not simply fleeting, illusory states where weird images and circumstances parade themselves. They do, as Ballard says, have a degree of internal logic and structure, even though the juxtapositions and toings and froings in space and time are, by waking criteria, absurd. Where does this inner pattern come from?

It could stem from the fact that our remembered dreams are not in themselves literally the whole story narrated by the brain, but just a section of it glimpsed if for some reason our sleep is disturbed or when we wake in the morning. As the conscious mind "comes to" it catches the brain in the middle of its vast job of program updating and clearance (and, as my "fish program" shows, the brain applies its own logic in the sorting and filing process). Existing programs are being inspected, outdated ones revised in the light of recent experiences, useless ones or the remnants of modified ones are being shunted to one side perhaps for future use. As all this is taking place, the conscious mind intrudes. For a moment it has no way of knowing whether the events are internal or external in origin. It sets to work, therefore, to try to make sense of the program or fragments thereof that are being run through, and the result is what we call a dream—though presumably we should call it an *interrupted* dream.

Here, then, might be found that deep "positive logic" that drives so many dreams, and colours so much dream-inspired art. Here too may lie the keys to some of those territories of the brain where unusual degrees of creativity are to be found, if only we could exploit them.

How do dream-types tie in with the notion of a hierarchy of brain programs? This ground is not far removed from that explored by Jung who, as we saw earlier, treated dreams as if they were archaeological vestiges of the mind. Jung went on to set these images within a mystical framework, making them occult manifestations or the language of the supernatural, a conclusion unsupported by scientific evidence. There is, however, no need to veer off into the tenuous reaches of mysticism to explain the major themes revisited by the collective unconscious. Instead we can set them within the more scientific context of modern psychology and neurophysiology and regard them as vital programs to which all human beings feel the need—unconsciously—to return.

The point of establishing a set of dream patterns, or main programs if we can call them that for the moment, is that these—if they are as important as I have suggested—should persist whatever our daytime experience. We saw how a cat, well fed from balanced cans of food, still apparently dreams of chasing mice. Do our main programs persist even when our everyday lives are such that there is no apparent reason for them to do so? My guess is that they do, and another dream of my own may serve to clarify the point.

Some years ago, after my cigarette consumption had edged up to the fifty-a-day mark and I was beginning to be troubled by an early morning cough, I suddenly stopped smoking one cheerless morning. Three weeks later the worst of the withdrawal symptoms had subsided, my palate had improved noticeably, the cough was fading and I began to congratulate myself. And then came the first of the dreams: I dreamed I was at a party, submerged in a sea of smoke and chatter. Then in my hand I noticed—horror!—a lighted cigarette which I had evidently just been smoking. Rage at my own foolishness boiled up. To go back so stupidly after suffering so much! Throwing the cigarette on the floor in a dramatic gesture I stamped on it. And at that point I woke up.

As a psychologist I was immensely intrigued by the dream. It seemed to contain all the elements of anxiety, guilt and desire which, though I was not consciously aware of them, must be battling still at some point in my brain. Obligingly the dream recurred, always the same, at approximately fortnightly intervals for at least a year. In the second year the dream shifted its form. Gone was the anxiety: in its place was a sheer wish-fulfilment sequence in which I would be sitting in an armchair inhaling deeply and luxuriously. This dream in turn metamorphosed into a wickedly insidious one: I smoked coolly and casually in my dreams, telling myself that this is quite all right as I have the habit under complete control. The appalling picture of the sheer depth of addiction revealed by these recurring dreams made me wonder if anyone else suffered in this way, and so I included a question on smoking in my surveys. Smoking dreams tend to fall into one of three or four categories. Among smokers, there is a typical dream of puffing away in some crowded place—at parties in particular—and this seems to confirm the heavy social overtones associated with smoking which cigarette advertisers have not failed to notice. Of the non-smokers, more than half are young people, aged under twenty, whose dreams show evidence of considerable anxiety. One reported looking at a cigarette which suddenly sprouted hairs in a nightmarish way, others were caught by their parents or smoked guiltily in some secret place. Others reported a dream about smoking in bed and feeling anxious in case it caught fire. Most interesting of all, however, are the dreams of those who have successfully given up cigarettes, almost all of whom notice that their dreams began after they had broken the habit. Nearly half the ex-smokers describe dreams which are exceedingly similar to—in one or two cases almost identical to mine. This one is from a doctor:

"I successfully gave up smoking in 1947 after a six-week struggle. From that time I began to get my smoking dreams but with a decreasing frequency. At first they appeared once per month but fell off until I have only had one or two in the past ten years or so. The dream itself does not vary very much. Usually I am with a group of people and my attention is diminished because I am arguing or in a relaxed social mood. Suddenly I realize that I have smoked about one quarter of a cigarette which I have unwittingly accepted or picked up. I think, Blast! Here I am smoking again without thought—after all the effort I put into giving up!"

In terms of the computer analogy, one would say that heavy smokers lay down important programs to do with smoking which are not easily erased when the habit is physiologically broken. Giving up cigarettes would involve even more significant programs, strongly allied to the conflicting emotions involved, and hence would feature boldly in one's dream-life. All in all this serves as a dire reminder that the smoking habit can become far more deeply ingrained than any of us might care to admit. Perhaps this is not too surprising for one is, after all, grafting the habit on to one of the most basic of human drives—the need for oral stimulation. No wonder that, once hooked, people find it hard to give up, and even when they do, they continue smoking in their dreams!

It is not, then, too big a jump to suggest that all most commonly experienced dreams elicited from my surveys are indeed linked to fundamental drives, needs, aspirations, fears and anxieties. The main programs are reinspected more regularly than sub-programs because they are literally central to the business of being human. "Fish" or "chair" or "nail" sub-programs recur less frequently because it is less important to us to ensure that they are brought up for inspection and updating quite so frequently. There are probably hundreds of thousands, if not millions, of these lesser programs, but significantly no more than a couple of dozen primary sets of instructions. Dreaming, then, is a reminder—or perhaps reaffirmation—of what it is to be human.

If a certain dream is just a particularly vivid and remembered fragment of a larger process of program inspection, it could well be that every night we run through the main programs *in toto* and that the parts we recall—the dreams—are little sub-routines contributing to the whole. Here then is a way for our programs to "interlock," to use the jargon of the computer scientist, that is to dovetail into the main programs by taking over subsidiary functions.

Before we leave the question of dream-types it should be pointed out that my own researches into the stuff of dreams are not the only investigations to point in this direction. A British psychologist, John Radford, some time after the death of his father had an extraordinarily vivid dream in which his late parent returned from the dead: "He walked, spoke, and ate; yet he was unmistakably dead. He was lifeless; an animated corpse. The dream had strong emotional force, both during it and afterwards. The image was a vivid and unforgettable one."

Musing on the experience, and versed in the writings of Freud and Jung on archetypal images that are the residue of basic human experience, Radford appealed in the *Mensa Journal* for readers' accounts of dreams of the dead. What had impressed him about his own dream was the fact that his father had appeared and acted in such a bizarre form. A living corpse. Was this an image shared by others? In fact, there were three categories of dream to emerge from Radford's mini-survey:

1 In which a "dead" person appears as in life, not known to be dead in the dream.

2 As a corpse.

3 As a "revenant," either normal or in the form of a ghost, but essentially known to be dead in the dream.

The dreams in the first category nearly all seemed to be accompanied by mild and pleasant emotions, as if, says Radford, they were part of the process of adjusting to the death. Where the dead person was known to be dead in the dream and perfectly normal in appearance, a number of dreamers felt what one called "a good sense of meaningful communication"—as if, you might say, the adjustment had been made. However, this was not always the case. Sometimes when the dead person returned in the form of a ghost, the dream would arouse unpleasant, even terrifying, sensations in the dreamer. One in particular reported having dreamed of ghosts a hundred times, another that her late grandmother sat up in her coffin, crawled out and began to chase her.

Not only do these dream reports confirm the prevalence of dreams about dead friends and relatives which I had found, but they also show how a main theme is represented in a variety of forms and engenders a range of emotions, some negative, some positive, some powerful, some vague according to circumstances. On one occasion such a dream may serve as a means of allowing the dreamer to come to terms with bereavement, to make it emotionally less distressing. On another the purpose is less clear. Recurrent terrifying ghostly visitations are not on the face of it particularly "useful" to us, except perhaps to remind us of our ultimate mortality in advance of its occurring. Is this one way we prepare ourselves mentally to die? One can only speculate, but such an apparently far-fetched notion as this may be valid. If our brain's programs allow us to rehearse for day-to-day living, why should they not also make it possible for us to glimpse in advance the period when it is all coming to an end? As a child we think of our own demise with a sudden chill shiver. Yet the older we get and the nearer we approach our death, oddly enough, the less terrifying it seems. Has dreaming over many years gradually enabled us to meet the inevitable with equanimity?

Strange though this idea may seem, it is not outside the bounds of the possible. Indeed it may well be among the least surprising features to be discovered among the landscapes of the mind, the world of inner space that we shall be exploring in the next few chapters.

Chapter 19

THE FACTS OF SLEEP

THEORIES IN SCIENCE have been described by an eminent researcher and writer as "stories" made up about the world. After creating the story the scientist then goes on—by observation and experiment—to collect as many facts as possible to see to what extent they fit with the narrative.

One of the problems that besets the sleep researcher is the rapidly growing volume of facts about his subject, so much so that any theory, unless it be hopelessly vague or ambiguous, is constantly being subjected to the discomfitting light of fresh evidence. There are, indeed, some people whose own investigations may lead them to question my computer theory, offering hard-won experimental data that do not appear to fit with my scheme. This is understandable; and may well be inevitable. The theory outlined in the preceding chapters will probably undergo a number of modifications in the future, as it has in the past, to accommodate new findings, just as theories about elementary matter concocted by physicists and mathematicians such as Einstein and Bohr have been refined by successive generations of experimenters and theorists in order to accommodate discoveries about the bizarre nature of those enigmatic fundamental particles such as quarks, leptons, muons and pi-mesons. In short, the more one studies any subject in the natural world the more complicated it appears to become—paradoxically even as it seems to appear more "simple."

However, it is a good time to assess the merits of the computer theory alongside the seven major facts I pointed to in Chapter One which would have to be taken into account for the notion to satisfy the objective inquirer. To take them in turn:

1 *Sleep is widespread in the animal kingdom, with "higher animals" needing it, some in large amounts. The higher the animal on the phylogenetic scale, the more REM it seems to have.*

This was graphically illustrated by an experiment carried out by two biologists at the University of Houston in Texas, Warner and Huggins, who decided to study the sleep patterns of the common ancestors of birds and mammals (both REM sleepers), namely the reptiles. To do this they kitted out some cayman crocodiles in the latest thing in EEG detection outfits and lulled their unlikely subjects off to sleep in a warm tank. As the caymans sank into unconsciousness, with a slowed heartbeat and breathing and reduced muscle tone, the EEG picked up slow wave, or quiet sleep, quite distinctly. However there was no sign of REM or active sleep or any other features of mammalian-style snoozing. So one is forced to conclude that there is a strong correlation between an animal's place on the evolutionary tree and its requirements for dreaming.

The computer theory chimes very well with this observation. The lower animals—that is those with less REM requirement—have in general, compared to say primates or man, a relatively restricted range of behaviour programs. This means that, although they need to rerun them and do so presumably during dream phases, they need appreciably less time for this activity. They rely to a much greater extent upon instinct, and from a much earlier age. The lower down the animal kingdom one goes, in general, the better the creature is equipped at birth to perceive its environment. Look at it another way and say that the simpler the creature and the less well-equipped its cerebral cortex, the more wiring and circuitry there is built into it and carried over to every member of the species. This of course is what is meant by instinct—an inherited behaviour pattern or function of some kind which appears in every member of a species at birth. Instincts born with a creature mean it doesn't have to learn the instinctive task. On the debit side, however, is the fact that one can't unlearn the instinct either, so that the more of them one has, the more likely they are to get one into trouble if one is a creature likely to change its environment in a radical way. Instincts are good for creatures with limited cerebral capacity, but a big handicap for those who want to respond in a flexible way to the world around them.

The fact that cayman crocodiles and, indeed, many other animals spend a considerable proportion of their time in a quiescent state is not significant in a discussion of dreams: keeping still and well hidden is safer; it uses up less energy and, therefore, keeps down the food requirement. An animal needs to find food, find a mate and reproduce itself; to spend the rest of its time wandering around and admiring the view would be, quite simply, a waste of energy.

2 *Sleep is not universal in all biological systems. Plants, so far as we know, do not sleep, nor do the very simplest living organisms.*

Again this is not surprising in view of the computer theory which treats dreaming as a means of rerunning daytime experiences, taking out from the brain's enormous store the appropriate program and running this through while inserting any useful or appropriate experiences within it, thus bringing it up to date. In humans this procedure reflects such experiences as social interaction, anxieties, and ambitions—all totally alien to any plant and therefore inessential to its survival.

3 *Sleep deprivation produces disorientation and bizarre behaviour.*
Because dreaming is so prevalent, it would seem to be an evolutionary necessity, in particular for the brain. As the brain controls all our behaviour, the computer theory suggests that dreams keep this control mechanism working properly by a process of nocturnal cerebral housekeeping, sorting out what is and isn't needed, organizing, shaping, honing the instructions that run the machine—the brain. You can imagine bizarre behaviour resulting from several sorts of disruptions. The brain's cells could become damaged—like a computer's components developing serious faults—or they could continue to function properly but receive the wrong sets of instructions for so doing—a program failure. The parallels seem to be practically irresistible.

4 *Sleep requirements alter with the age of the animal.*
The computer theory, as we have seen, ties in very nicely indeed with this observation. If animals are born with sets of programs and dreaming is a way of refining these by way of experience, then you would expect the young animal to devote a lot of sleep time to assimilating new experiences. *Everything* the infant animal sees and encounters while awake is novel so it has to be taken in at a well-paced rate if the creature is not to run into an internal traffic-jam. Hence, the younger the animal the more REM sleep it appears to take.

5 *There are two types of sleep as measured by electrical activity in the brain.*
Perhaps the best description of the intense electrical activity observed during REM phases is that favoured by the French psychologist Michel Jouvet, who worked with the sleeping cats we encountered earlier. He calls it *paradoxical* sleep, during which phase the brain is working overtime to prepare itself for the waking periods. Actually, although most researchers tend to equate REM (paradoxical) sleep with dreaming and the rest of sleep (slow wave) with no dreams, it is not altogether clear that this is the case. Dreams may well spill over into non-REM phases. However, this does not substantially affect my theory (it is an example

of the sort of fresh evidence I mentioned a moment ago), because the main point is this: sleep has a distinctive "architecture" in which the brain runs through various patterns of electrical activity, and the aim of this structure is to serve the needs of the brain for getting itself into good shape for the daytime world. Why it cannot simply lapse into intense REM activity, fulfil its reprogramming needs and slide back into consciousness again is not known. But it may reasonably be thought that the non-REM states are themselves "rest" periods or buffer zones or transitional states or whatever, serving both to space dreaming over the night and allow the brain to take a breather between its frenetic paradoxical bursts. Or again, these states may involve some kind of non-visual dreaming.

6 *The so-called "rebound phenomenon" is well-established. Deprived of any particular kind of sleep—REM or non-REM—an animal selectively makes up on that kind when next allowed to drop off.*

This again fits with my computer theory, and follows from 3, 4 and 5 above. Experiences must be assimilated for the mental/emotional well-being of an animal, so it is not difficult to understand why a loss of REM would be followed by an above average amount of dream sleep to make good the deficit. Non-REM phases, too, seem necessary to complement REM periods, so again one might expect some sort of proportional replenishment.

7 *There is the striking psychological nature of dreams with structured thought patterns—often strange—and a strong narrative form.*

We come here to the most difficult point of all. My theory suggests that the brain's programs are many and various. Some will probably be concerned with recognizable "situations," such as meeting people at social gatherings or sitting examinations, so if a dream were to be centred on one of these, it could be said that we were recalling one of those programs or experiencing parts of them being run. However, it is highly likely that the overwhelming majority of programs are not discrete, coherent stories or adventures but "key word" programs: programs relating to a particular linking theme (such as my "fish" program). There could be as many—if not more—of these programs as there are words in the largest dictionaries and we could run through thousands of these during every REM phase. Why, then, do we recall only one or two of these and why do they hang together with a unifying plot?

The answer could be that what often determines whether or not we recall a given dream is its vividness. So many programs will be routine and dull that the highspots are more likely to stand out. This is one possible interpretation. Another is that we tend to impose both the vividness *and* story on the dream as we recall it. A dream is a fragment of the brain's activity during an unconscious period called up during consciousness. The conscious mind could have the agility required to string a list of scenes, objects and people together to make an instant story. Let us imagine that the program being inspected is concerned with "metal": keys; furnaces; knife-grinder; motor cars. The conscious brain, coming to, could in a flash impose on this assemblage of images a coherent (if quaintly logical) story about losing car keys, vainly asking a passing knife-grinder if he can cut some more, returning forlornly to the locked automobile to see it being towed away by the police to a local furnace for melting down. The next time you have a dream, see whether the story-board logic is the only one it contains. Could there be a "key word" interpretation in as well?

To a large extent, then, the computer theory is compatible with these seven key observations about the nature of sleep and dreaming—and as such it offers a "story" about natural phenomena that is well supported (notice I do not say "proved") by at least some of the facts.

In the course of compiling and analysing questionnaires over many years, it has been possible to learn from dreamers of all ages, backgrounds and persuasions about the aspects of dreaming that most fascinate them, and at the top of the list comes that oft-repeated, purely quantitative enquiry: *how much sleep do we need?* Although apparently innocuous enough, this whole issue of how long we sleep is, on close inspection, fairly complicated. The bald facts can be quickly stated. The average adult—according to recent surveys taken in France and elsewhere—sleeps for seven hours and twenty minutes; while the baby, for reasons we have already discussed, sleeps on and off around the clock. The elderly—who often take short naps during the day—rarely sleep for more than six hours a night, possibly revealing the other side of the coin to that shown by the baby: that the amount of time in sleep is roughly related to the amount of time needed for dreaming, which in turn relates to the amount of fresh information needed to be processed by the brain.

The range of variation in sleeping patterns, though, is considerable. One person in twenty-five sleeps naturally less than 5½ hours a day, while another needs more than ten hours. A few lucky (or perhaps they are unlucky) individuals have practically no sleep requirement at all, getting by quite happily (not counting any cat-naps they may take) with only two or three hours a day. Interestingly, these people also seem to need very little REM sleep—only about fifteen minutes altogether, which is just 12 per cent of their total sleep time. Compare this to the seven-hours-a-night sleeper who spends 22 per cent of the time (about ninety minutes) in REM phases and this tiny vigilant minority seems to be breaking with the norms in more ways than one. (There is no evidence, by the way, that these natural short sleepers differ from the rest of the population in terms of their mental health, stability, intellectual competence and the like, so it seems doubly odd that they should not, if my computer theory is valid, indulge in proportionately the same amount of REM as anyone else.) A British sleep researcher, Dr Jim Horne, noticed this anomaly and the fact that these short sleepers have, in minutes per night, just as much slow wave sleep as the 7½-hour sleepers. From this he is inclined to deduce that slow wave sleep (SWS) is an "obligatory" form of sleep while the REM phases come under the heading of "optional." He divided sleep into two halves: the first half of the night, containing mostly SWS and proportionately little REM, and the second half, where the ratios are the other way round. Dr Horne found that subjects in his sleep laboratory at Loughborough University tended to be able to dispense with this second half of the night more readily than the first. In other words, the REM phases seem to contain an element of "redundancy" while slow wave sleep is more necessary if the sleeper is to wake refreshed. Now this is an interesting finding for two reasons: firstly it raises provocative questions about the nature of the brain's program inspection process (if indeed that is what is going on) during REM by suggesting that it does quite a bit more cerebral housekeeping than is strictly necessary, hence the redundant component. I have already said that I believe we sleep in order to dream. But perhaps it is not unreasonable now to add the corollary that, vital though dreaming is (indeed we simply cannot do without it as dream deprivation experiments have shown), the brain may well, like an over-zealous nightwatchman, do more than is necessary for the immediate present. It may also, as Dr Horne suggests, use dreaming as a form of self-indulgence, a recreational activity whose purpose in part at least is to give its owner some fun.

The second interesting point to emerge from this research is that its findings appear to be the modern, scientific justification for well-worn adages such as "early to bed, early to rise," and "the hour before midnight does most good." Most people establish a sleep pattern that suits them as they grow up. In the past, when candles were expensive and not very efficient, people tended to relate their sleeping habits to the hours of light and darkness, but it would not be very practical to do so today. However, 70 per cent of all the deepest sleep occurs in the first third of the night and the reverse is true of dreaming: only 15 per cent of the total occurs in the first third of the night and over 50 per cent in the last third. This may be why the first part, "the hour before midnight," seems the most beneficial. People used to think that deep, dreamless sleep was "good" sleep, and dreaming a sign of disturbed or "poor" sleep. Both are now known to be indispensable. Attempts have been made to change the twenty-four-hour awake/sleep pattern completely. In 1938 two American scientists went down into a cave and tried to change their sleeping pattern, first to a twenty-one-hour day, then to a twenty-eight-hour day. The latter proved extremely difficult. Yet the architect Buckminster Fuller once trained himself to have half an hour's sleep every three hours, totalling four hours out of twenty-four, and kept it up for a year.

A study of 240 adult people, all pursuing their usual occupations, made over a two-month period, indicated how wide the range of sleep of ordinary people is. The number of hours of sleep recorded varied from less than five to more than nine, though by far the largest proportion of the group slept from 6½ to 8½ hours. This variation shows that it is impossible to lay down how much sleep any particular person ought to have—most people learn by experience what suits them and take that amount regardless of anyone else's habits.

At the other end of the spectrum are those people who find themselves sleeping what seem to be excessive amounts every night. Normally when one has had enough sleep one wakes up, without necessarily being prompted by any external clues such as the sun streaming in through the window or the sound of an alarm clock. In a healthy person, too much sleep should be impossible. If a person does suddenly begin sleeping abnormal amounts it might be a sign of a rare disease such as narcolepsy (uncontrollable bouts of sleep), or of some mental disorders. A survey of 800,000 people sponsored by the American Cancer Society showed that those who said they slept more than ten hours had up to twice as many heart attacks and up to three and a half times as many deaths from strokes as did those who reported sleeping only seven hours a night. It is not possible to say if the excessive amounts of sleep cause the disease or are a symptom of it.

Generally, however, the reasons why there is such variety in people's sleeping patterns are gradually becoming clearer, and they are worth dwelling on for a moment or two. Some psychologists have tried to investigate the question from the point of view of the personality of the individual concerned. They reason that major personality traits, such as the degree of extroversion or introversion, seem to link in with so many aspects of behaviour—from the tendency to smoke to the propensity to commit crimes—that there could also be a correlation between personality and sleeping behaviour. Unfortunately the results of such studies, while fascinating, are not wholly convincing. Dr Ernest Hartmann, the psychiatrist at Boston State Hospital's Sleep and Dream Laboratory whose work on variable sleepers and lifestyles we looked at in Chapter 16, has been highly active in this area, finding what he considers strong links between personality types (as determined by psychological testing) and the length and nature of sleep. He divided his twenty-nine subjects into "long" (more than nine hours a night) and "short" (less than six hours) sleepers after observing them for eight nights in the laboratory, and identified each group as follows:

> The short sleepers as a group were efficient, energetic, ambitious persons who tended to work hard and to keep busy. They were relatively sure of themselves, socially adept, decisive.... Their social and political views were somewhat conformist...and "All American." They were extroverted and were definitely not "worriers."

Compare this personality profile with that of the long sleepers—who were, by the way, less easily definable as a group.

> ...they tended to be nonconformist and critical in their social and political views.... They appeared in general not very sure of themselves, their career choices or their lifestyles; however several appeared to be artistic and creative persons....Over-all they were definitely "worriers."

Although I have abbreviated Dr Hartmann's descriptions, the distinctive character of each group does emerge quite readily: long sleepers are creative, introverted, fairly eccentric individuals while short sleepers are thrusting, confident extroverts. This rather simplistic dichotomy, however, Hartmann himself admits has not been universally supported by other researchers. Indeed one can immediately call to mind celebrated short sleepers such as Thomas Edison or Barnes Wallis, who surely deserve to be placed in the "creative" group. In fact when Dr Wilse Webb at the University of Florida carried out a survey similar to Hartmann's, he failed to find the same personality correlates. His 54 volunteers were all college freshmen, again long and short sleepers, whose personality profiles showed no greater link with their sleeping patterns than one would have expected from chance. Hartmann accounts for this discrepancy by pointing out that his own volunteers were all over twenty years of age—that is, their sleeping patterns were stabilized—while Webb's group consisted of seventeen to eighteen-year-olds whose sleep tended to be less regular in pattern. Indeed, Hartmann had disqualified young students from his own study because, among those who claimed to have a low sleep requirement, were some who were prone to make good the deficits by "napping in the class."

Another study of personality and sleep behaviour was carried out in Britain at the Medical Research Council's Unit for Research on Occupational Aspects of Ageing, housed in the University of Liverpool. Here the help of several hundreds of Liverpudlians ranging in age from twenty to seventy-four years was sought, each person being asked to keep a sleep chart record for a period of two months. There was an equal number of men and women. Again a personality questionnaire was completed but this time the breakdown was simply between introverts and extroverts—the most basic psychological yardstick of all. What emerged most strikingly was that the extroverts as a group slept for an average of twenty-five minutes longer each day than the introverts, this difference increasing with age so that by the time they reached their seventies the gap had widened to over an hour. So long sleepers in Boston tended to be introverts while in Liverpool they were extroverts—a disparity that might well be indicative of something about the way these two studies were conducted rather than the influence of the Atlantic Ocean that separated them. In truth, it is simply very difficult to measure "personality" properly, and there remains a lot more work to be done in this field.

Other findings tend, as I have said, to complicate the issue rather than simplify it. It has been discovered, for example, that people who practise transcendental meditation—alleged to be a surefire route to peace of mind—appear to have significantly less REM sleep than those who do not. Eliminating some of the need to use the brain's program inspection time to work out anxieties and other difficulties, it might be argued, enables the sleeper to dream less. But this neat if esoteric re-affirmation of the merits of the computer theory is complicated somewhat by another curious snippet of information gleaned by some researchers at the Royal Edinburgh Hospital in Scotland. They monitored the sleep patterns of sixteen people and found that REM sleep time was directly related to the body weight of the individual. The fatter they were, the more they dreamed. This tied in with two observations: that people suffering from acute starvation had much less dreaming sleep than normal people, and that patients with anorexia nervosa (that distressing condition of self-inflicted starvation) started to dream more as soon as they put on weight. Could dreaming times be more a function of the rate at which the body converts food into fat and other substances than the personality of the sleeper? Is our physical metabolism the key to sleep and dream variability and not levels of anxiety, extroversion or ambition? Most probably the truth lies somewhere between the physiological and the psychological in that mind and body are interacting, not independent, entities. So it would not be surprising if variations in our metabolic state were reflected in our brain's activity, nor would it be outlandish to suggest that temperament, character or personality may be projected into sleeping behaviour.

There are, however, other factors that certainly affect sleep patterns. The environment undoubtedly plays an important part, as researchers Lewis and Masterton discovered when they became the first scientists, nearly thirty years ago now, to measure the effects on the human sleep/wakefulness cycle in the rigorous conditions of the North Pole. They based their work on the day-by-day sleep charts completed by men on the British North Greenland Expedition, based about eight hundred miles from the Pole where the usual daily light/dark cycle was absent for six months of the year. The men, living in extreme cold, were subjected to continuous darkness during the winter months, and three months' unbroken daylight in the summer. Incidentally, a similar study was carried out by Dr Helen Ross on a group of ornithologists camped on the borders of Finland and the USSR, again living in harsh conditions. In both cases, despite the unusual environment, the average daily duration of sleep was the usual eight hours or so, the majority taken in one consolidated period, but with a liberal sprinkling of naps at various times during the day. In fact it was this distribution of sleep, with more frequent naps appearing on the chart during the winter months, that constituted the major break with normality. Yet a further study made on climbers in the Himalayas showed that particular environmental circumstances in high mountains produced a similar tendency for sleep to be distributed more widely over the twenty-four hours, but curiously, the study also showed a tendency to sleep longer every day the higher the climbers ventured.

Whatever changes environmental conditions produce—be they extreme, such as one finds in the Arctic, or moderate, such as short-term modifications to one's working hours—there is a tendency for the sleeper to make good a "sleep debt" as soon as possible, either by sleeping longer or by changing the pattern of sleeping over the course of every day. Different people accumulate different types of sleep debts and make up the loss in different ways, and, incidentally, with varying degrees of success. Detailed investigation of the kind of sleep taken by people paying off a sleep debt has produced some intriguing findings about their dream-life. For example, when Dr George Tune studied the sleep and wakefulness patterns of a group of fifty-two male shift workers working in the engineering industry, he found that over a ten-week period they took a higher than average amount of sleep every twenty-four hours as well as more and longer naps outside the major sleep period than people who did not work in shifts. Clearly the stresses of the job built up a sleep deficit which needed to be made good, just as it does with Polar explorers — and, incidentally, with hospital physicians who have a tendency to catch up during holiday periods. Shift workers, too, show this same tendency during rest days. That in itself is not surprising, but when the EEG characteristics of the daytime sleep of shift workers are compared to those of men working normal hours, it transpires that the former spend significantly less time in REM sleep. Poor sleepers generally also show this lack of dream sleep. Yet another curiosity concerns normal individuals trying to catch up on two or three restless nights. When an ordinary sleep debt is made up by an extra-long night's sleep, the usual Stage 4 (deep sleep) cycle occurs before any dreaming takes place, though the sleeper will dream more than usual that night to make up for what he has lost. Shift workers and poor sleepers do not appear anxious to repay an REM debt by taking unusually large amounts of this form of sleep, a fact which led one researcher to describe their sleep as more "awake like." Indeed it is a complaint often voiced by shift workers that they find their sleep "unrefreshing" or "shallow;" it is certainly not especially rich in dreams. On the other hand there are some people whose patterns of sleeping illustrate quite a different sort of accumulated sleep debt: patients suffering from depression, it has been observed, appear to be deficient in Stage 4 or deep sleep. Just why this particular pattern should appear is something of a mystery.

Some normal, healthy individuals whose main sleep period is for the most part perfectly ordinary make good sleep deficits in the form of cat-naps. President Kennedy used to call a break if a conference got dead-locked and take a five-minute sleep with his head on the table while others smoked or drank coffee. It is not certain whether these cat-naps are refreshing because they allow a little bit of dreaming to go on, or whether they simply allow a release of psychic tension. Certainly, people under constant intellectual and physical stress are especially prone to take cat-naps. Churchill and Lloyd George both took afternoon snoozes, though they lasted for an hour or so, while the explorer Thor Heyerdahl was able, even while aboard a flimsy reed boat in the middle of the ocean, to enjoy a brief sleep and wake refreshed. Even sleeping on your feet is possible for short periods, as is sleeping with your eyes open. Tiny seizures of sleep known as microsleeps and lasting two or three seconds have occurred in people deprived of sleep. Mark Twain recorded a microsleep in his *Mental Telegraphy*. He recalled watching a stranger approach a house and then vanish. Twain hurried to the house, went inside and found the man standing in the hall, although he had not seen him go in. Twain concluded that he had fallen asleep for the few seconds it had taken for the man to ring the bell and enter the house. If he had not followed it up and found the man, Twain admits he would have been convinced that "I was one of the favoured ones of the earth and had seen a vision—while wide awake."

Very short sleeps are also taken by certain animals, usually those which live in particularly hazardous circumstances. Think, for example, of the giraffe whose sleep occupies only a total of about two hours a day. During REM periods the giraffe rotates its head and lowers it on to the thigh in a "sleeping swan" position, putting it in a highly vulnerable state, given the added disadvantages of the giraffe's anatomy that makes this gangling creature need about ten seconds to stand upright in order to flee a marauding predator. Something of a record for bizarre sleeping habits must, however, go to two species of dolphins. The blind Indus dolphin, which lives in fast flowing water, has a continuous problem of survival: if it stops swimming for more than a very short time it runs the risk of being dashed on to the rocks. Clearly long sleep periods would be out of the question, so during the day it takes many short naps, only about ninety seconds at a time, thus managing to keep a watchful eye on possible hazards. Another dolphin, the bottlenose, goes one better. According to researchers at the Severtsov Institute in Moscow, this species has evolved a fantastic brain mechanism which allows it to sleep and stay awake at the same time. The paradox is explained when one learns that the bottlenose sleeps with one half, or hemisphere, of the brain for about an hour or so, and keeps the other hemisphere in a state of vigilance (when fully "awake" it keeps both hemispheres conscious). Moreover, during sleep, one eye remains open, the other shut!

In all these cases evolution has contrived to produce adaptations that enable the animals in question regularly to get their quota of sleep in the face of external hazards, be these predators or changing environmental conditions—proof, surely, that sleeping is no mere self-indulgence, nor a means of restoring a tired body, but a cerebral activity of pressing importance in the business of survival.

Another striking example of the need to dream, whatever the circumstances, was recorded in 1964 when a satellite was launched from Cape Kennedy for a thirty-day orbiting flight around the earth carrying what newspapermen were quick to call an "astromonkey," Bonny. Bonny was wired up to all kinds of equipment to monitor the heart, brain and muscles and its reaction to long-term weightlessness. Bonny, as you might expect, went to sleep and 250 miles over Santiago in Chile there came back evidence that the animal, despite its unnatural setting in a high-technology space exploration package, was slipping into REM sleep. In spite of—or perhaps it was because of—her role as an involuntary astromonkey she felt the need to dream.

We can only speculate, of course, on what dolphins and monkeys dream about during their hard-won sleep phases, but I have attempted to probe a little into the dream life of domestic pets with the help of readers of the popular zoology magazine *Wildlife*. The questionnaire I devised (later revised and used with equal success in an American magazine) attempted to collect data on some of the issues discussed already in a human context, namely:

Does a household pet sleep more or less now than when young or newly-born?
What is its sleeping pattern and total sleep time?
Is some sleep "deeper" than at other times?

As well as these fairly straightforward general questions, there were also some directed more specifically at possible dream experiences in the sleeping pet:

Does the animal perform any ritual before going to sleep?
Does anything make you suspect your animal dreams?
Have you noticed anything strange about your animal's sleep habits?

When the results came in they revealed readers to be predominantly dog and cat owners, with dogs outnumbering cats almost exactly in the ratio three to two. The next most popular animal, perhaps a little surprisingly, was the gerbil, followed closely by the rabbit. Next, approximately equivalent in popularity, were budgies, hamsters and guinea pigs. In all, twenty-seven different types of animals were referred in the questionnaires, including pigs, roebucks, mynah birds, rats, tortoises, parakeets, horses, foxes, sticklebacks, frogs, newts, cows, ducks and hens. Among the more unusual animals were monkeys, badgers, slow-worms and racoons. Evidence of dreaming—at least in the form of twitches—was reported from all the mammals featured in the answers, and evidence of sleep was noted even in the birds, fish, reptiles and amphibians. Twitchings and squeakings were the most common of the "dream symptoms," though easily my favourite was the finding—reported by a number of budgie and mynah owners—that their birds talked in their sleep! Apparently their conversation, like human sleep-talking, tends to be garbled and nonsensical.

Taken as a whole, it emerged that the more complicated the animal is in terms of its brains, the greater time it devotes to sleep—presumably because the more "adaptive" the nervous system the greater the number of programs involved in driving it. There was also a lot of fascinating data on favourite places for sleeping: periods of apparent "deep" sleep were reported, accompanied by snoring, heavy slow breathing and sometimes strange noises in the throat. Many people noticed that their pets managed to sleep through the most terrific din, and cat owners pointed out that their animals seemed to adopt very characteristic postures during deep sleep periods. But it was the questions related to dreams that produced the really intriguing responses, particularly when pet owners themselves assessed the evidence for their animals' dreaming. Few owners had failed to observe behaviour which suggested to them that the animals dreamed. The most common behaviour cited as likely evidence of dreaming was a twitching of the paws, whiskers or tail; making strange noises (such as howling or mewing) was also very common, particularly in dogs (92 per cent) but markedly less in cats

(52 per cent). The howl made by some dogs in their sleep is apparently an unpleasant and eerie sound, and when the animals were woken up they would appear frightened and disturbed, as though the howl had been relating to some unpleasant dream. Many people also commented that sleep with many obvious signs of dreams often came after their animal had had a "stressful" or "exciting" day—after fighting with another animal, for example, or moving home.

The next most common symptoms of dreaming were forms of eye movement, described as twitching or rolling of the eyes. In those animals which tended to sleep with their eyes open or partially open, this was a peculiar but very characteristic and easily observed phenomenon. Some 30 per cent of dog owners and 20 per cent of cat owners had seen REMs in their pets. Another interesting symptom apparently associated with dreams involved periods of rapid or irregular breathing which were noticed in dogs and cats, though more in the former than in the latter. Incidentally, such evidence as is available from laboratory studies also suggests that animals' dream states are accompanied by the various types of phenomenon mentioned above.

The question on pre-sleep rituals also provoked some interesting responses and once again the bulk of the data comes from the dogs and cats. All kinds of strange rituals were mentioned: some animals could only go to sleep holding something in their mouths, while others did not seem able to rest unless the TV set had been switched on! Summarizing the major conclusions, one can say that pre-sleep rituals are quite significantly more common among dogs than cats, that the favourite dog ritual involves circling the bed, while the most usual cat ritual involves grooming. Cats in fact were twice as likely to groom as dogs.

My final question dealt with animals' strange sleep habits, and most of the observations here seemed to refer to dream-type behaviour. Other observations were confined to the peculiar posture that their animals adopted, sleeping in uncomfortable places, or lying with their heads raised, or on their backs with their legs in the air. Clearly animals are just as idiosyncratic about their sleep habits as are humans.

Of course none of this gives any index of *what* the creature is dreaming about or whether it has any conscious experience of its dream in the way that humans do. One frequently reported phenomenon, however, seems to suggest that conscious dream experience may be present in dogs and cats. This is the observation that many animals, if disturbed in the middle of what appears to be a dream period, would wake, jump to their feet and look around, either angrily, in fear or, as some owners commented, "looking surprised" at their surroundings. Often the animals would wake apparently spontaneously from the dream state and again show evidence of surprise or alarm. There are of course a number of interpretations that can be put on this, but one perfectly reasonable one is that the animal was "surprised" as it made the transition from the dream world to the waking world—in much the same way as humans are. But what are they dreaming about? All the evidence points to support for the computer-based theory, particularly when we remember Jouvet's experiments with the cats which, during REM sleep, exhibited every sign of stalking and catching some kind of prey. In my survey, nose, eye and paw movement in sleeping dogs was widely reported, and the dog like the cat is a hunter which uses scent and speed to catch its food. Apart from this, if there is any basis of truth in the computer theory, one might surmise that the animal is dreaming about the things that have happened to it during the day. As I have said, many people commented that their dogs and cats showed most obvious signs of dreaming after a successful or exciting day. Supposing (to take a specific domestic example) that you have a cat and you move house. This agitates the cat no end, for it has to learn all over again where everything is in a completely new world which involves an enormous amount of reprogramming. When the cat is sleeping, the programs that originally related to where to find its food, which is the warmest part of the house, how to get in through the back door etc. have all got to be updated, so perhaps we could say that this is what the cat is going to be dreaming about. Of course, moving house is just an example, for a dog or cat is continually dealing with new information every day of its life, but not in quite such a dramatic way. By this token it would be interesting to know if a sedentary town-dwelling dog records less REM sleep than, say, a working sheepdog.

Before we leave the sleeping behaviour of domestic pets, there is just one more item of information that may or may not come as a surprise to those of you with an animal around the house. It was gleaned by two researchers at Harvard, Alan Hobson and Ted Spagna, whose speciality is the use of time-lapse photography to analyse the amount of tossing and turning we do in the course of the night. They found that the bodily movement patterns of the pet owner seem to be reflected in the animal, in this case a cat. Both man and beast slept in synchronized cycles.

In an experiment at the University of Pittsburgh, Dr C. J. Vaughan trained rhesus monkeys to press a bar every time an image was flashed on to the screen in front of them. At the rapid eye movement stage in sleep, they suddenly began pressing the bar as they did if they saw an image when they were awake. The following day they continued to press the bar only when they saw an image on the screen. The work seems to suggest that monkeys see visual images in sleep.

Some animals also (those, of course, that are colour-conscious) appear to dream in colour, and probably for the same reasons that humans do. The extent to which colourful as opposed to vague, colourless images figure in our dreams appears to vary with the individual concerned. If you asked a group of engineers to put up their hands if they dream in colour, you may perhaps get a one in five response. But put the same question to people who are professionally involved in using colour, such as graphic designers, and the chances are that every hand will shoot up. Similarly the animals that have colour vision will probably also have colour dreams because they make use of colour in their everyday lives, so the programs that feature colour are going to have to be updated accordingly. In fact, some animals might have glorious technicolor dreams compared to ours because colour may be used more intensively by them on a regular basis. As far as humans are concerned it is known that something like 60 per cent of women regularly dream in colour and 50 per cent of men, but why half of all dreamers do not have colourful dreams, one can only speculate. It may simply be that these are people who have little colour "sense" or sensitivity during their waking hours —the difference between the engineer and the artist. Or it may be that achromatic dreams take place because the areas of the brain's visual cortex that need to be stimulated to produce colourful images are for some as yet unknown reason not brought into play. Certainly the evidence from people with brain tumours producing visual field defects is that they lose their colour perception before black and white and regain it more slowly, suggesting that the nerve fibres transmitting colour signals to and from the brain are more readily blocked than those handling achromatic information. But it remains a mystery as to what produces this blockage—if this is in fact the case—during some people's dreams.

It is just possible that the dreamer may be influenced by external circumstances, such as noises or movements or lights, during sleep which in some way shut down the colour-sensitive brain cells. This is not quite as improbable as it might first appear when you think of those dreams you have almost certainly had when you are, say, watching a fire engine screaming along the street ringing its bell, and you wake up to find the alarm clock ringing. Although, during sleep, dreams are not monitored by the conscious mind, outside sensations are received by the brain though they may not at first be sufficient to wake the sleeper. It then attempts to make sense of this material by incorporating it into the dream in the kind of "story" we associate with dreams. In the initial stages of waking, the conscious mind cannot clearly separate internal and external events and makes an amalgam. As consciousness returns, the mind is able to distinguish between the dream sound and the reality. Experiments in influencing the content of dreams have shown that if you apply heat or cold to a volunteer, or sprinkle water gently on the face, these sensations may be included in dreams. So too can other kinds of physical experiences. Take for instance an old wives' tale, with a grain of truth in it, that eating cheese around bedtime brings on nightmares. Eating cheese would not induce a special kind of dream, but if the late snack led to a minor digestive upset this could cause disturbed sleep so that one woke and remembered one's dreams, some of which might very well be unpleasant.

Finally, to close this review of some of the facts of sleep, there is another long-standing piece of folklore concerning the length of time that each dream lasts. There used to be a lot of misconception about this, of which the most striking was the belief that they were over and done with in a fraction of a second. A famous example which seemed to justify the old belief was the dream of a Frenchman, Alfred Maury, who dreamt that he was a victim of the French Revolution, was tried and sent to the guillotine. He felt the knife fall—and awoke to find the bedrail had fallen on his neck. It seemed that the whole dream must have taken place in the fraction of a second between the rail hitting his neck and his waking up. When Freud, however, began to study the dream because of the fame it had acquired, he suggested that it "represents a fantasy which has been stored up in his memory for many years and which was aroused...at the moment he became aware of the stimulus which woke him." Maury's book on dreams was published in 1861; any Frenchman of his age could have imagined, or had told to him, such a tale and have it ready for discharge as soon as the right stimulus occurred. Now, although my computer theory takes issue with the Freudian approach, on this point there is no disagreement. Whether Maury's tale was a repressed fantasy or a story told to him by someone else, there it was stored in his brain's memory banks ready to be activated by the agency of the falling bedrail. Here was the stimulus the conscious mind needed to impose on the dream that had just preceded it (which may well have been a rerun of a program on knives, Revolutions or some other subject) a coherent structure, in the form of a story.

PART FOUR

The Quest for Inner Space

Chapter 20

A KEY TO CREATIVITY

SO FAR OUR journey across the ever-surprising landscapes of our dream-life has, for all its speculative nature, been helped by the findings of sleep researchers trying to piece together a few bits of hard evidence in the face of an implacably difficult phenomenon. It has, I hope, resulted in a fairly coherent, though admittedly incomplete, theory about the function of dreams that is consistent both with the objective data as well as with the more subjective feelings that many people have had over the centuries—that the sleeping brain is actively engaged in performing functions of relevance in our waking lives. Jung went a lot further than this, suggesting that it was hopelessly misleading to think of dreaming as an "interruption" of waking. "It is," he wrote, "on the whole probable that we continually dream, but consciousness makes while waking such a noise that we do not hear it." There is, for the reasons discussed in detail earlier in this book, no need to go to these lengths to justify the importance of dreams. My computer theory, in which the brain is continually updating its vast library of programs during the off-line sleep phase, has one crucial element in common with the approaches of Jung and Freud, namely that dreams are not just gratuitous, purposeless, meaningless exercises performed by a brain with so much spare capacity that it chooses to wallow in episodic acts of self-indulgence, unconnected to its duties and behaviour when the organism it directs is awake. Indeed, the more one penetrates the experience of dreaming (one is tempted to say "use" of dreaming here) the more widespread this realization seems. The American Indians, for example, have often exploited the possibilities that dreams are a rerun of, or rehearsal for, wakefulness. The children of the Winnebago tribe would hope to dream, sometimes after a period of fasting, of a guardian spirit who would help them through life's crises, while in Malaysia the Servoi tribe make dreams a focal point of daily life, influencing activities ranging from the choice of friends to the best spot in which to build a future village.

This relationship between dreams and wakefulness is what we shall be exploring in this chapter and in particular the deliberate use—even manipulation—of our dream life to enhance our emotional or intellectual performance during the day. There seems to be little doubt that the two are related, and not only according to the folklore of certain Indian or Malaysian tribes. A number of studies, for instance, suggest that people who are going to be faced with a tricky or demanding situation in life, such as a job interview or driving test, register a demonstrable increase in dream time. Conversely people who have already been confronted with emotional stress or trauma may use dreams to accelerate their readjustment. This has been demonstrated by a psychologist at the University of Texas, David B. Cohen, who carried out an experiment in the sleep laboratory whereby subjects were subjected to what he calls an "ego-threatening presleep experience" before turning in. During the night they were woken up and asked to recount their dreams, which produced a clear-cut division: those who had dreamed about the bad experience were less anxious and tense the next morning than those who had not. Perhaps, argues Cohen, dreams are a way of resolving problems. Similarly a Chicago researcher, Dr Rosalind D. Cartwright, investigating the dream behaviour of a group of recently divorced women, found that those who were "significantly depressed" seemed to need much more dreaming time. They dreamed, like young babies, practically all the time they were asleep (including, incidentally, during non-REM phases) as if, according to Dr Cartwright, they needed to do a lot of "emotional reprogramming" while in the throes of a major life change. The other side of the coin is seen in a group of happily married women whose dream patterns conformed to the norm. The parallel between these findings and my computer theory will not have escaped you. Indeed, Dr Cartwright herself makes the connection when she describes sleep as the time for sifting through odd fragments of feelings and emotions recorded in one's short term memory but unexamined during the day: "This sort of processing of information is our regular night-shift work. We reconcile new information to our old self and put it all together so we can get up and fight another day."

The use of dreams to face the waking day is not just confined to our emotional life. In fact Dr Cartwright did a further experiment on the possible role of dreaming in maintaining intellectual performance. She woke up a group of subjects who had been asleep for a few hours and showed them a series of pictures of everyday objects; having made sure that they had remembered the objects, she allowed them to go back to bed. The next morning she retested their memory and found that those who had recorded the most REM sleep remembered as much as, or even more than, they had during the night. The group with little REM—

and therefore one assumes fewer dreams—remembered less than they had earlier, suggesting that dreams have an information processing and storage function, as well as an emotionally stabilizing role.

Given, then, that dreaming does seem to have a bearing on our thoughts and feelings during waking hours, we can now move one step further and ask to what extent this relationship can become a profitable partnership—not just in the sleep laboratory and not just in the restricted circumstances of an experiment, but in a wider context. If sleep, and in particular dreams, perform necessary psychological functions, can we exploit this nocturnal processing to improve our creativity, our memory, our capacity for solving problems or any other intellectual skills? To begin to answer this enticing question it may pay us to spend a little time with some conspicuous examples of creativity where there was most definitely a carry-over from night to day of ideas, inspiration or insights stirred up by dreams.

In science, where dreams have frequently had a concrete pay-off, perhaps the best documented example of the use of dreaming took place one cold winter afternoon in 1865 when the professor of chemistry at Ghent, Friedrich August von Kekule, sat dozing before a roaring fire. Kekule had for some years been baffled by a problem: that of the molecular structure of trimethyl benzene, and was, like many other scientists, unable to visualize how the atoms of benzene might lock together. Tucked warmly in his armchair on that particular afternoon he nodded off facing the fire and began, not for the first time, to see atoms dancing before his eyes. His account of what happened on that particular afternoon is one of the most graphic to emerge from the history of scientific discovery:

> This time the smaller groups (of atoms) kept modestly in the background. My mental eye, rendered more acute by repeated visions of this kind, could now distinguish larger structures, of manifold conformation; long rows, sometimes more closely fitted together; all twining and twisting in snakelike motion. But look! What was that? One of the snakes had seized hold of its own tail and the form whirled mockingly before my eyes. As if by a flash of lightning, I awake...

At that moment the problem was resolved. Carbon compounds such as benzene, Kekule saw, were not open structures but closed chains or rings—a snake biting its own tail in molecular form. And with this revelation came something of a revolution in the field of carbon-based (or organic) chemistry. Later Kekule acknowledged his debt to the mind-expanding properties of dreams by advising a group of colleagues to try to cultivate them. "Let us learn how to dream, gentlemen," he declared, "and then perhaps we will discover the truth."

Other cases where the clarity of a dream helped to dispel the fog of intellectual uncertainty hanging over a scientific problem are not difficult to find. A dream was reckoned by the Nobel prizewinner Otto Loewi to have helped him make the immeasurably important discovery that the nervous system uses chemical messengers or transmitters to shuttle information to and from the brain. Similarly a dream provided Hermann Hilprecht of the University of Pennsylvania with the key to an archaeological find. It happened in 1893. Hilprecht went to bed, pondering on some inscriptions made on two small fragments unearthed in the ruins of a Babylonian temple, the problem being that these broken relics of the distant past did not make any sense. The puzzled scientist had a dream in which a "tall, thin priest" proclaimed that these two fragments, which were housed in separate cases in a museum in Istanbul, in fact belonged together. When Hilprecht went to the museum to verify this he was able to see that the two pieces did indeed fit together to form a single decipherable inscription.

On occasions dreams which later proved to be productive had, initially, a nightmarish quality. Perhaps the most familiar case here is the nocturnal vision that ultimately led to the invention of a device that did for the clothing industry what the internal combustion engine did for transport—the sewing machine. The inventor was Elias Howe, who had been struggling for some time to find a way of mechanizing the sewing process. One night he had a terrifying dream in which he was taken captive by a very hostile tribe who presented him with an ultimatum: produce a machine that can sew, or die at the end of a spear in the next twenty-four hours. In his dream, Howe was unable to deliver the goods so his assembled captors made ready to plunge their spears into his trembling body. As they descended, however, Howe noticed something peculiar. In the tips of the spears were eye-shaped holes. Howe awoke, carrying the memory of those oddly-placed holes, and realized that his sewing machine might just work if the needle carried the thread at its tip and not where he had been experimenting with it. Dreams, then, for scientists and inventors have been useful avenues to heightened or creative thinking, presenting a technical or theoretical problem in a vivid form that the brain has been unable to conjure up during the day. Leonardo da Vinci, a fertile genius in both science and art, clearly recognized this when he asked, "Why does the eye see a thing more clearly in dreams than the imagination when awake?"

Nothing illustrates this enhancement of daytime faculties more than the fascinating circumstances surrounding the composition of Samuel Taylor Coleridge's superb narrative poem "Kubla Khan" which begins:

> In Xanadu did Kubla Khan
> A stately pleasure-dome decree:
> Where Alph, the sacred river, ran
> Through caverns measureless to man
> Down to a sunless sea.

This, too, was written after a deep sleep in which Coleridge "composed" several hundred lines after reading the following account in a history book: "Here the Khan Kubla commanded a palace to be built, and a stately garden thereunto. And thus ten miles of fertile ground were enclosed within a wall."

Dozing off, Coleridge wrote later, he began to see sharp images rising up with a clarity that gave them an uncanny realism, all interlocking "without any sensation or consciousness of effort" to form a coherent story. Immediately on waking, he took up his pen and dashed off the lines of his great poem, only to be tragically interrupted by the famous —or rather infamous—"person on business from Porlock." When he returned to the task of completing his narrative, although the memory of the dream persisted faintly and the general outlines could still be recalled, the detailed imagery, with a few scattered exceptions, had evaporated like, as he poignantly recorded, "the images on the surface of a stream into which a stone has been cast."

Another writer who profited from his dreams was the great storyteller Robert Louis Stevenson who was able to dream complete narratives in their proper sequences on a regular basis, even being able to pick them up on subsequent nights where they had finished the night before. In fact, Stevenson used these dreams-by-instalments to write exciting episodes with a lot of suspense for his adventure books. But his most famous dream of all, as he related in his book *Across the Plains*, was that which led to the magnetically attractive story of Jekyll and Hyde. Stevenson's dream was also inspired by a daytime preoccupation which manifested itself in the persistent feeling, brought on no doubt by the constant interplay of dreaming and waking in his writing career, that he was leading a double life:

I had long been trying to write a story on this subject, to find a body, a vehicle, for that strong sense of man's double being which must at times come in upon and overwhelm the mind of every thinking creature.... Then came one of those financial fluctuations.... For two days I went about racking my brains for a plot of any sort; and on the second night I dreamed the scene at the window, and a scene afterwards split in two, in which Hyde, pursued for some crime, took the powder and underwent the change in the presence of his pursuers.

Musicians as well as writers have exploited dreams to further their act. The Italian composer Giuseppe Tartini once dreamt that the devil appeared to him and offered him a Faustian pact. In return for Tartini's soul, he would teach him to compose even more beautiful music. Tartini, still dreaming of course, agreed and handed over his violin to this creative Lucifer, who began to play with consummate skill which Tartini thought of such exquisite beauty that it transcended by far anything his own imagination had been able to aspire to. He told a friend afterwards:

> I was delighted, transported, enchanted, I was breathless and I woke up. Seizing my violin, I tried to reproduce the sound I had heard. But in vain. The piece I composed, "The Devil's Trill," was the best I had written, but how remote it was from the one in my dream!

Inspiration from dreaming of a rather different sort came to a statesman whose personal vision shaped the destiny of the whole of Europe: Bismarck. In 1863 Prussia was confronted with considerable opposition to its expansionist plans, so much so that even Bismarck, renowned for his determination and singleness of purpose, was beginning to lose some of his seemingly inexhaustible self-confidence. His policies looked inappropriate and impractical, until one night in the grimmest days of his struggle when "no human eye," as he put it, "could see any possible escape," he had a dream:

> I dreamt that I was riding on a narrow Alpine path, precipice on the right, rocks on the left. The path grew narrower, so that the horse refused to proceed and it was impossible to turn round or dismount, owing to lack of space. Then, with my whip in my left hand, I struck the smooth rock and called on God. The whip grew to an endless length, the rocky wall dropped like a piece of stage scenery and opened

out in a broad path, with a view over hills and forests, like a land-
scape in Bohemia; there were Prussian troops with banners....This
dream was fulfilled, and I woke up rejoiced and strengthened.

What lessons can we learn from the experience of writers, poets, painters,
inventors, scientists, statesmen and all the others who have drawn on
dreams as a source of inspiration, of heightened vision, of original ways
of thinking? If we look closely at the tiny selection of creative dreams
described above, a few interesting common threads can be discerned.
First, whatever one thinks dreams to be—either an updating of the brain's
programs or even a visitation from the world of the supernatural—there
is little doubt that they are not random events, disconnected from the
thoughts, feelings and preoccupations of the day. Indeed they are all
very obviously extensions of an obsessive train of thought, both artistic
and scientific. The psychologist Patricia Garfield believes that if a person is consciously working on a problem "it is very likely that his or
her unconscious will continue working in the dream state, drawing on
all inner resources to put together new combinations and present them."
Much as the Freudian ring of the "unconscious" worries me in this
assumption, its general thesis seems to be irrefutable: dreams continue
work begun during consciousness. Of course it does not always happen
that they complete this work satisfactorily. For example, in my surveys
people often say that they dream that some secret of the universe is
revealed to them but when, in the morning, this is written down, instead of having a powerful message it reads like gibberish or fatuity such
as "Piston rings need vitamins," or some such neo-Jabberwockiana. Such
a dream can well be said to have failed.

This brings me to my second observation about the "successful"
dream, namely that they are unusually coherent and well-formed narratives, fanciful but shaped in such a way as to be acted on, either as
stories or poems to be transcribed or courses of action to be followed.
I have already suggested that the coherence of dreams may well be
imposed by the awaking mind, which means that to be useful a dream
has to be "shaped" by the dreamer. How is this to be done? A sleep
researcher once studied this shaping process with a group of subjects
who were awakened during REM phases and asked to write down their
dreams. They were then asked to record them again a few hours later,
and the two accounts were compared. The later versions were patently
more logical and coherent than the immediate ones, suggesting that
wakeful time is of the utmost importance in how we use our dreams.

Coleridge, inspired by his dream images of "Kubla Khan," imposed order and sequences on them with the skill of a magnificent poet. He was not being guided in every syllable by some invisible psychic hand; it was his conscious brain that produced his unfinished masterpiece.

Some artists have revelled in the ambiguities of the situation produced by dreaming, and especially on the way in which, by practising their art, they seem to move back into a quasi-dreamlike state, something like that peculiar hypnagogic phase I looked at earlier, when the sleeping brain is just coming to; or its converse, the hypnopompic state. The painter Yves Tanguy devoted his whole career to producing delicate, bizarre canvases dotted with curiously illuminated objects that lie on an empty beach—the interface, it seems, of the real world of concrete reality and the inner reaches of the dream. Another artist, Jeffrey Schrier, was seized with the impulse to draw a dream image upon awakening in order to give pictorial form to those pieces of himself that remain elusive during the daytime, again a bridge between consciousness and unconsciousness. Interestingly, Schrier claims that while making his drawings he practically moves back into the dream state, and certainly the end product, as represented by his intriguing collages, produces a strong sensation of this having happened.

To use the conscious mind to transmute the imagery of dreams into art, and to move back from wakefulness into a dream-like state, might seem quite a long way to go in exploiting one's dreams. However, perhaps the process might go even further: could one consciously transport oneself into and out of a dream itself, move from the familiar landscapes of the mind to the uncharted territory and back again? This sounds, admittedly, like pure wishful thinking, but it may be less of a fantasy than it at first sight appears. It may be possible for us to learn to take some kind of command of our dreams. This suggestion emerged very recently with research in Britain and America on a particular type of experience which most of us have from time to time (I certainly have myself) known as *lucid dreams*.

A lucid dream has a character all of its own. The dreamer becomes aware that he or she is asleep and dreaming but can to some extent "control" the content of the dream and how it unfolds. There are a few people who regularly have such dreams, some practically every night, but the rest of us have to wait for them to come along before we can experience the fairly rare sensation of manipulating events that normally take their own unpredictable course. The leading British researcher into lucid dreams, Dr Keith Hearne, describes them as dreams in which objects seem to be, and feel, solid, and the lucid dreamer is able to hold intelligent conversations with the characters that people them. The quality of the dream's imagery, moreover, is sometimes very intense and detailed because the dreamer is able to perceive it through all the senses, so that not only the colour and taste of a wine may impinge on his awareness but also its bouquet. One of the most important characteristics of the lucid dream in the context of its use as a creative tool is the capacity the dreamer has for controlling the action, often in superhuman ways. He can, say, transport himself from one continent to the other to talk to a relative who has emigrated. This suggested to Dr Hearne that, if it were possible for a person to begin to dream lucidly by design, he or she might be able to take into such a dream some ideas, exercises, problems or ambitions which could then be carried through. If so, then—quite apart from the mind-boggling possibilities this opens up —it would mean that sleep research had moved into a totally different phase. Hitherto the traffic had all been in one direction, from the dreamer to the researcher. Here, with lucid dreams, might be a way for the sleep researcher to "talk" to his subject while he is actually in the process of lucid dreaming. Dr Hearne asked his subjects to signal as soon as they reached a lucid dream state by making a series of left/right eye movements which he could pick up on the electro-oculogram. He devised a system whereby a lucid dreamer could indicate by the movements the various stages of a dream. If, for example, flying figured in a lucid dream, the sleeper was to perform a certain number of eye movements to indicate the start of flying and another number to show that it had finished. One subject did this with some success, it is claimed, and his account of his dream on waking corresponded closely to the record of the electro-oculogram. Incidentally, one by-product of this phase of the research was further confirmation that dreams do not happen in a flash but take some time to unroll.

Having established criteria for knowing when lucid dreams were taking place, Dr Hearne then gave his subjects tasks or "experiments" to perform in the lucid condition. Here is his account of some of these as recorded in the magazine *New Scientist*:

I noticed that in some accounts of both ordinary and lucid dreams, the subject referred to an inability to "switch on a light" in the dream scenery—that is, the light would not work. I followed up this observation with a further eight lucid dreamers. I instructed them to look around for a light switch in the next lucid dream that they had, and they reported back in isolation, not knowing the purpose behind the request. Six subjects reported that the light would not work properly, one "could not find the light switch," and one subject stated that she *could* perform the task but it was after she had "closed her eyes" in the dream and so abolished the imagery. That and other evidence points to the possibility that there is a ceiling-limit on "brightness" in the dream imagery at a given point, and any attempt to violate that level, by manipulating the dream, results in rationalized avoidance of the intended situation. If so, it would suggest that an autonomous dream-producing process operates, which has to manoeuvre the dream within such limitations of imagery.

Thus, lucid dreams can be manipulated, but only within certain limits. They are, moreover, to some degree controllable by the dreamer in collaboration with the sleep researcher, who together decide on some of the activities that are to take place. And the researcher can monitor progress, or at least some of it, while the dreamer is still asleep. The next step was to try to produce lucidity on demand. After all, if the content of dreams could be in some measure predetermined, this would open up magnificent opportunities for recreation—dreams of sex, money, power or status could be called up whenever required, enabling us to wallow in experiences which could not be readily available in real life. Moreover, controlled lucid dreams could even have a medical application by providing realistic settings for people with, say, a phobia to try to conquer their fear in the non-threatening context of a dream. Then, finally, there are the possibilities for taking into a lucid dream a problem to be solved and using the experience to try to reach an answer. Kekule had to wait for the licking flames of the fire to stimulate his vision of the snake swallowing its own tail. Could some future scientist take into a lucid dream a current preoccupation and carry on doing so until a range of solutions, perhaps *the* solution, had been found?

All these exciting possibilities depend on the dreamer being able to induce lucidity when needed, and, as we have seen, lucid dreams only seem to come to the majority of us on a very sporadic basis. Dr Hearne claims to have got round this by building a "dream machine" to trigger lucidity. The device detects REM sleep and then gives the sleeper a tiny electric shock to a nerve at the wrist. Before going to sleep the subjects have been told how to recognize these impulses and, when they do, to consider whether or not they are dreaming. They then signal by their eye movements that they have reached lucidity. Dr Hearne claims that this machine has been successful in a few cases, but that the subjects vary in their ability to control their dreams. The secret, it seems, is to "look around" the dream to find an appropriate setting for the dream you want.

At the Stanford University Sleep Center in California another researcher, Stephen La Berge, without the benefit of any hardware, reckons that he can use such dreams for a variety of purposes. By training himself to remain aware he contends that he can ask characters in his dreams for advice, conquer his enemies and engineer the happy endings of his own choosing, thus making himself more self-confident during the day. By responding with courage or creativity to dream situations he believes he can face waking life better, because lucidity involves balancing involvement and detachment in a way that can be of considerable use in the real world. As well as using lucid dreams for solving emotional problems, La Berge is also trying to exploit them for medical purposes, testing the power of lucidity to speed the healing of small lesions on his arms. It is not at present clear how far this line of research has advanced, but there is no doubt that the strange phenomenon of lucidity does have some potential usefulness, if only to tell us more about the nature of unconsciousness itself as it suddenly seems to switch on within the unconscious state. From this paradoxical situation might stem some insights into what it means to be a "conscious" organism as opposed to a non-sentient entity. Another benefit could be in the study of such perennially enigmatic areas as the nature of human personality, as researchers compare dream reports in the lucid condition with those filed later after waking. The field of lucid dreaming is an odd and relatively neglected one, but it may prove to be an exceedingly fertile terrain for approaching some of the basic conundrums of the workings of the brain.

While on the topic of dreams as a window into our personality or, as Thoreau put it, dreams as "the touchstones of our character," there does appear to be some evidence that we can, in some measure, use our dreams to tell us something about the sort of people we are. According to the British psychologist Professor Liam Hudson, there are surprising links with dreams and our cast of mind as expressed in our styles of thinking. Hudson divides people into two classes, based on thinking styles. On the one hand are what he calls the "convergers." These are individuals with the sort of analytical intelligence measured by conventional IQ tests, tending—if they pursue higher education—to specialize in the physical sciences and inclined to have a more authoritarian personality than the second group, known as "divergers." Divergers have a bias towards open-ended, freer sorts of reasoning processes and tend to gravitate away from the rationalization of science as a career or university course choice, preferring the humanities.

Underlying these two very different frames of mind, Hudson reckoned, could well be two different psychological mechanisms. He thought that convergers might be the sort of people who drew a sharp dividing line between rational and non-rational aspects of experience while the divergers might be "intellectualisers" revelling in the traffic between the two realms but weak, perhaps, in the skills of impersonal argument. Hudson went on to speculate that this difference, if it existed, could show itself in the ways in which convergers and divergers coped with an apparently non-rational aspect of existence, namely dreams. He hypothesized that convergers would be more likely than divergers to forget their dreams. And, after testing in the EEG sleep laboratory in Edinburgh University, this is indeed what emerged. Wake a converger in mid REM sleep and unlike a diverger he or she often fails to recall a dream. Divergers, on the other hand, have excellent recall.

On closer inspection, however, an even more interesting picture emerged. Rapid eye movements are not continuous. The movement phases are interspersed with quiescent periods known as REM-Q (as opposed to REM-M during movements), the punctuation points between bursts of intermittent activity. It transpires that although convergers have comparatively poorer recall during active REM—that is, REM-M—periods, their performance is if anything slightly superior during REM-Q. In fact it is more or less perfect. What is important about this observation, argues Professor Hudson, is that there is some evidence that REM-M and REM-Q are associated with different kinds of thought. He writes:

REM-M is associated with what has been called "primary visual experience": with the eruption into consciousness of images that seem arbitrary and "ego alien."

REM-Q is associated with "secondary cognitive elaborations," with the individual's attempts to make sense of the images that he has just experienced.

Thus the convergent, rational type of thinker seems to be skilled at making sense of images experienced in the dream, of rationalizing them into a coherent story, whereas the diverger, while recalling strings of vivid, arbitrary-seeming images, has trouble in imposing order and logic on them. From this one can see several interesting implications. Clearly the "dreamer" type of personality, the person who is happier reading poetry than a car maintenance handbook, reflects his or her liking for subjective experiences, for symbolism, for apparent illogicality, chaos, and the breaking of the rules of rationalization in the sort of dream content recalled. Conversely the scientifically-orientated, analytical individual—whatever the nature of the images in his dreams—remembers them as more or less conventional narrative structures, having quickly subjected them to the constraints of common sense.

I have already discussed how "dreams" should properly be described as "remembered dreams" in that they are the products of a conscious mind rapidly imposing order on disorder, narrative on disconnectedness. Convergent thinkers seem, as it were, to anticipate this remembering process by consolidating their dream stories at various points during REM, namely the REM-Q periods. For the waking diverger, however, the images are recalled in a more raw state, unprocessed into sequences, and so it is more difficult suddenly to impose order on them. If many of your dreams, then, are characterized by arbitrariness whereas other people's seem better "structured" the difference may be explained by a fundamental dissimilarity in your thinking styles. And, of course, if the diverger has a more direct channel into the richly associative, figurative world of dreams than the converger, one can easily see how this provides sustenance for artistic expression or appreciation, while the converger's analytical frame of mind in turn is well served by *his* dream-life.

It may well be that both types of thinkers—all of us, that is—have more or less the same range of dream imagery. It is what our brains subsequently do with this material that differs, which may have repercussions in another area of our inner life—the ability to use dreams to solve problems.

Chapter 21

DREAMING TO LEARN: LEARNING TO DREAM

THE SUGGESTION THAT dreams can, and do, act as a doorway into the processes of creative inspiration, both scientific and artistic, coupled with the possibility of our being able deliberately to insinuate ourselves across the threshold, is undeniably intriguing. But not all of us are gifted poets and painters or eminent scientists capable of formulating problems to carry into dreams or acting subsequently on the stimulus they provide. So what is there in dreams for us? In this chapter we shall be examining the possibilities of using dreams to solve problems (not necessarily on the scale of those encountered by Kekule or the archaeologist Hilprecht whom we met in the last chapter), and to improve learning. Then, afterwards, we shall look again at the dangers of interfering with our natural dream-sleep cycles, for the sake of the smooth functioning of our intellect as well as our emotional stability: a true cautionary tale if ever there was one.

The term "problem-solving" covers an enormously wide spectrum of activities, from trying to figure out how to make ends meet every week on a low income to choosing between two equally sumptuous outfits to impress an eminent dinner guest. It ranges from making precise calculations of the loading to be imposed on a bridge one is designing to weighing up nebulous, subjective variables such as the likely outcome of an incipient love affair, yours or someone else's. Often there are many factors to be put into these mental equations and it can be frustratingly difficult to hold them all in concert to reach a measured conclusion. Sometimes no solution at all presents itself, as we are all too well aware. Another complication is that we tend to approach problem-solving in rather stereotyped ways, whereas solutions are more likely to be teased out by offbeat, "lateral" thinking—the sort of approach that the celebrated Barnes Wallis applied when he came up with his ingenious, dambusting "bouncing bomb." Can any or all of these difficulties be resolved in the free-wheeling, almost gymnastic thought processes common in dreams?

At Stanford University the distinguished sleep researcher William Dement carried out a revealing series of experiments, involving five hundred students who were given a few brain-teasing problems to solve. There was a strict protocol governing the procedure to be adopted by the students. As well as the problem, they were handed an accompanying questionnaire and given instructions not to look at the problem until fifteen minutes before going to bed; then they were to spend fifteen minutes trying to solve it. The next morning they were to record any dreams remembered from the night; then, if the problem had not been solved the previous evening, to work on it for another fifteen minutes. Their answers and dream reports were then handed to Dr Dement for assessment. Before we look at the solutions and over-all results you may care to try your hand at the three problems used in the experiment.

Problem One: The letters O,T,T,F,F...form the start of an infinite sequence. What is the rule for determining any or all successive letters? According to your rule what are the next two letters of the sequence?

Solution: The rule is that the letters are the first letters of the words one, two, three, four, five...so the next two letters are S (six) and S (seven)!

Problem Two: Consider these letters: H,I,J,K,L,M,N,O. The solution to this problem is one word. Find that word.

Solution: The word is "water." The sequence is "H to O," or as a chemical formula H_2O, that of water!

Problem Three: Another sequence: 8,5,4,9,1,7,6,3,2. What is the rule governing their order?

Solution: If spelled out as words these numbers are arranged alphabetically!

If you were less than successful in cracking these puzzles it could well be that you are unfamiliar with this type of problem. Actually, when one has been given the solutions to a few such exercises, it is surprising how one approaches new, unseen problems with more competence. They have a characteristic style to which one can get accustomed, rather like a familiar crossword puzzle. Anyway, for Dr Dement's purposes the interesting thing was whether any of the students seemed to benefit from a dream to reach a solution. The over-all finding was that some did. But only a few.

The complete questionnaires recorded 1148 attempts to solve the problems, of which 87 seemed to be linked to relevant dreams, 53 directly, 34 indirectly. The correct solution however, only appeared a total of nine times, and of these two had to be ruled out because the students concerned had managed to arrive at the right answer during the fifteen minutes before turning in. There were, too, by Dr Dement's own admission, one or two shortcomings in the design of this particular experiment. Unlike those cases, such as that of Kekule, where an individual had been desperately trying to reach an answer for many years, Dement's students, even the most diligent among them, had no such incentive to find the solution. And, of course, it was also possible that some of the participants might have discussed the problems among themselves, or attempted to crack them before the allotted fifteen minutes to bedtime.

Setting aside these considerations for the moment, the handful of relevant dreams do merit close attention. Take this account used to solve Problem One:

> I was standing in an art gallery looking at the paintings on the wall. As I walked down the hall, I began to count the paintings—one, two, three, four, five. But as I came to the sixth and seventh, the paintings had been ripped from their frames! I stared at the empty frames with a peculiar feeling that some mystery was about to be solved. Suddenly I realized that the sixth and seventh spaces were the solution to the problem.

Here the student, by means of a vivid series of images in a picture gallery, arrived at the answer by the sort of tangential mental process that is difficult to reach by a deliberate, conscious act of will—a process common, of course, to dreams. On other occasions the solution may be presented similarly but not recognized as such by the dreamer. Here, for example, is a record of dreaming after a student had pondered on Problem Two, the "water" question.

> I had several dreams, all of which had *water* in them somewhere. In one dream I was hunting for sharks. In another I was riding waves at the ocean. In another I was confronted by a barracuda while skin diving. In another dream it was raining quite heavily. In another I was sailing into the wind.

It does seem as if this dream was part of some "water" program which, one might speculate, the brain had pulled out for inspection after being faced with a problem in which it had already recognized "water" as the solution, albeit unconsciously. However the student in question had, before going to bed, already solved the problem to his own satisfaction, offering the (incorrect) answer "alphabet." So he had not, on waking after a veritable cascade of water images, made the connection that one guesses he might have done had he still been looking for a solution.

Thus, although dreams can provide the solutions to problems and perhaps do so quite regularly, it could be, as Dr Dement points out, that "only the most perceptive dreamers possess the ability to recognize a solution that is presented in a disguised or symbolic fashion." In short we must, if we are to profit from our dreams, think about them carefully, paying particular attention to thematic or keyword elements, however foolish, illogical, embarrassing or surreal a narrative line they take. This is certainly true of problem-solving of the conventional kind. It may also, according to Dr Dement, be applicable to anticipating problems before they arise as this dream, narrated in his book *Some Must Watch While Some Must Sleep*, suggests:

Some years ago I was a heavy cigarette smoker—up to two packs a day. Then one night I had an exceptionally vivid and realistic dream in which I had inoperable cancer of the lung. I remember as though it were yesterday looking at the ominous shadow in my chest X-ray and realizing that the entire right lung was infiltrated. The subsequent physical examination in which a colleague detected widespread metastases in my axillary and inguinal lymph nodes was equally vivid. Finally, I experienced the incredible anguish of knowing my life was soon to end, that I would never see my children grow up, and that none of this would have happened if I had quit cigarettes when I first learned of their carcinogenic potential. I will never forget the surprise, joy and exquisite relief of waking up. I felt I was reborn. Needless to say, the experience was sufficient to induce an immediate cessation of my cigarette habit. This dream had both anticipated the problem, and had solved it in a way that may be a dream's privilege.

Only the dream can allow us to experience a future alternative as if it were real, and thereby to provide a supremely enlightened motivation to act upon this knowledge.

We can summarize then the prospects for using dreams for problem-solving thus: Analysis of key features of a dream experienced during a period in which one is working on a problem may yield a solution. The computer theory provides a method of analysis which can be applicable here, in that it encourages one to look beyond a dream's surface "plot" to pick out its consistent, underlying theme, namely the program. To benefit from a dream requires, therefore, a certain amount of conscious effort, so obviously it would pay to write down all dreams in as much detail as possible and try various "program" interpretations to see whether any might give the solution, or at least a clue to it. Do not discard any program as impossible, however improbable it may at first sight appear. The solution, if you are fortunate, may leap at you in a sudden flash of insight but more likely you may need to work at it to tease it out.

Given that the brain, particularly during the dream periods, shows signs of considerable activity and that this may (as I have suggested with my computer theory) relate to some kind of updating of material stored in the brain, it seems logical to consider that sleep, and in particular REM sleep, may enhance memory. There has been evidence to suggest that a good night's sleep before, say, an examination will make for a good performance the next day. Students who sleep badly or not at all certainly tend to be less efficient at answering questions than sound sleepers.

To test the relationship of REM sleep to memory rather more closely, a psychiatrist at the Royal Edinburgh Hospital in Scotland, Dr Chris Idzikowsky, devised a fascinating experiment. It involved getting university students to learn lists of nonsense syllables—triplets of letters such as QOH which are fairly hard to learn because they cannot be related to everyday objects as reference points. This material was learned at different times of the day, and the students' recall of it tested at other times of the day. In this way Dr Idzikowsky was able to compare the performance of those who had slept in the meanwhile to those who had not. When the results were analysed, the sleepers did demonstrably better than the non-sleepers. Interestingly it was also found that if one "sleeper" group were deprived of sleep for a second night they still seemed to recall the material as well as a group of sleepers allowed to sleep for a second night. Thus, whatever the beneficial effects of sleeping as regards memory, these are all loaded into the sleep period directly after the learning takes place, an observation, one is tempted to conclude, that is consistent with the program clean-up theory.

If sleep can be important in enhancing memory for material acquired during the daytime, what about learning during the sleep period itself? The prospect of being able to tap the "wasted" night-time hours to cram into one's head facts, ideas or any other kind of useful matter for long periods that are normally "unused" in any overt, deliberate manner has attracted a few astute, commercially-minded people who have marketed so-called "sleep learning" equipment. On the face of it there might seem to be a point: think, for example, of a mother recently delivered of a baby, asleep in the maternity ward of a busy, urban hospital, her off-spring sleeping in a separate room with a dozen other new arrivals. Suddenly her baby wakes up and, above the clatter of hospital trollies, the rumble of traffic outside and the general hubbub going on all around, the mother instantly wakes up too, immediately recognizing her own child's cry. Clearly the brain of the sleeping mother is not only open to incoming information in the form of a cry but also able to discriminate finely by interpreting the source of the cry as emanating from her off-spring and not someone else's. If the channels of receptivity are open to this degree, there could well be a chance that a tape-recording played at the right volume during the night will likewise transfer its information to the sensitive brain.

Experiments in sleep learning or "*hypnopaedia*," to give it the technical label, have been going on for decades. In 1942 the American investigator Le Shan tried to use the "waste periods" of sleep to deflect a number of children from nail-biting during a stay at a summer camp just outside New York. His method was as follows: two and half hours after the nail-biters had apparently fallen asleep, a recording was played to them containing one "conditioning" spoken sentence, repeated time after time: "My finger-nails taste horribly bitter." In all, the children heard this unequivocal comment 16,200 times, the volume being lowered (not turned off) if they showed signs of restlessness. After this barrage of repetitions, Le Shan claimed that 40 per cent of the group had given up their nail-biting. He also claimed that another experiment, in which a recording was used to teach a string of nonsense syllables, produced a similarly dramatic result. Subsequently other researchers set up comparable experiments, including one designed to speed up the learning of letters by mentally-retarded and speech-defective children, with varying degrees of success.

Unfortunately these early attempts were not altogether satisfactory from a scientific point of view, especially since it was not sure whether the subjects were actually asleep at all times during the playing of the recording. Many tests were carried out without the subjects being connected up to an EEG machine, so it is perfectly possible that if "learning" took place at all it was at the conscious rather than the unconscious level. Even when EEG monitoring was used it still was not clear whether the subjects were sleeping, because experiments were not always performed in the closely-controlled environment of the sleep laboratory but in volunteers' own homes.

A series of studies in the 1950s by Charles Simon and William Emmons, however, did show a considerable degree of care in ensuring that the subjects were asleep. They gave them a general knowledge test to begin with, then, having marked their papers, eliminated all the questions with the correct answers. The incorrect responses were used as the basis for sleep learning material. The researchers played these questions (with their correct answers this time) over and over during their subjects' sleep periods, monitoring this carefully on the EEG. Then they re-tested their subjects the next day, when they found little evidence of learning taking place at any level of sleep. But this experiment, too, had its design faults. Because the recall tests were carried out next day —and not immediately after the learning tapes were played—it was not possible to contend that the sleepers learned nothing. They may well have learned something but this could have been dissipated by events between the recordings being played and the tests being administered.

Since these various experiments seemed inconclusive I decided to carry out my own investigations, along with colleagues at the Department of Education at Cambridge University, the Maudsley Hospital in London and Watford College of Technology. Again we used the familiar set-up of a taped message being repeated to the sleeper by way of a small loudspeaker fitted in a pillow. The message was, in fact, fifteen pairs of nonsense syllables, the sort of material that is equally difficult to learn whatever one's background or experience, and these were repeated twenty times for each individual. There was also a tape of computer-generated random musical noise played for about the same length of time, about thirty minutes, to a "control" group. The idea was that sleepers who had heard the syllables repeated during sleep should—if they were "learning"—have been able to memorize these more quickly while awake than the control group. They did not. Once again an experiment on sleep learning carried out in such a way as to eliminate misleading results failed to provide positive evidence.

The significance of the failure of the sleep-learning experiments will not have escaped the reader who has understood all the ramifications of the computer-based theory of sleep and dreams. You will remember, for instance, that when a computer's programs are being rewritten, debugged, updated etc.—those activities which I believe take place in the sleeping brain-computer—it is absolutely essential that the system is taken off-line, that it is uncoupled from the outside world. It has also been shown that suppressing the dream process, or interfering with it, can lead to a variety of behavioural and psychological problems. It might, then, be argued that attempting to inject new material while the brain is performing its nightly housekeeping tasks should at best be ineffectual and at worst actually dangerous to an individual's mental well-being. The following account of an experiment done in the Soviet Union is, therefore, particularly interesting.

Psychologists in the USSR have for some time held curiously strong beliefs about some of the offbeat aspects of human behaviour. There has, for example, been quite a lot of research into areas such as telepathy and extrasensory perception (ESP) which are definitely on the fringes of scientific orthodoxy, if not respectability. Sleep learning, too, has exerted a fascination for a number of scientists, some of whom appear to believe in its usefulness and have endeavoured to demonstrate this experimentally. Unfortunately the picture that emerges from Russian laboratories is too blurred for us to share their confidence: again, some of the experiments "demonstrating" sleep learning are, scientifically speaking, less than rigorous. There is a tendency to make it quite plain to the volunteers in the experiments what the purpose of the exercise is rather than adopt a "blind" technique in order to try to eliminate any bias from the results.

Even if the Russian experiments are inconclusive, they are not altogether without value. In the course of his experiments, a 27-year-old physician, Balkhashov, found that prolonged attempts to make use of sleep time for learning had some disturbing effects on his mental and emotional health. Balkhashov set out with the intention of learning Italian during sleep so that he could read the Italian medical literature. He had thirty language instruction lessons tape-recorded and these were played, an hour at a time, to him during sleep over a period of seven months. The Czech researcher Hoskovec described the results as follows:

> At the beginning and in the process of this course, feelings of heaviness in the head, intensive headaches, decreased appetite, hyperesthesia in the fingertips [itching], and greater fatigue during subsequent waking mental and physical work temporarily resulted. Sometime awakening appeared after the automatic onset of the recorder once with hypnagogic hallucinations and anxiety. Nightmares occurred during the whole course. Some night sessions failed. It is mentioned

that all of the symptoms disappeared spontaneously, without any medication. The author reported success in translating a series of Italian medical articles after completing the course.

Balkhashov, then, enjoyed some success in learning the basics of Italian but, it seems, at a price. In fact, other Soviet researchers have come to a similar conclusion, finding that, after some weeks of long periods of attempted sleep learning (say forty-five to sixty minutes at a stretch), subjects experience various forms of physical discomfort and mental d·stress. Is it possible that this is the result of interfering with their natural sleep patterns in general, and with their dreams experience in particular?

The realization that one of the main functions of sleep is to allow us to dream makes one think again about the various ways in which we might disrupt a vital process. Sleep learning is one way in which we could delay or prevent dreaming, especially if it is used over long periods. Rather more widespread a danger, though, is the use of drugs as hypnotic agents. Central nervous system depressants, such as barbiturates or alcohol in large doses, might well not only act as soporifics, but also push the sleeper down too deeply for him to dream properly—with unpleasant long-term effects as a backlog of outdated programs builds up. If this effect were pushed too far, the dream mechanism might well switch desperately into action when the brain was "on-line" (awake), and the result would be hallucinations of an unpleasantly real kind—such as those which prevail in the delirium tremens of alcoholism. Given all this, it seems ironic that "dream suppressants" such as barbiturates and tranquillizers are regularly prescribed for people with mental problems.

On the other side of the coin is the thought that hallucinogenic drugs such as LSD might produce their spectacular effects by kicking the dream mechanism into action, again when the brain-computer is "on-line." This would be contrary to the fundamental rules of cerebral mechanics, and while the inner world of the mind would indeed be revealed to the drug-taker awful risks would be involved. Firstly one would predict a steady deterioration in the ability to distinguish between "inner" and "outer" reality—a condition reminiscent of the schizophrenic state. Secondly, and no less horrifying, is the possibility that "on-line" dreaming would make one hyper-programmable and any stimuli fed in during this time might be incorporated into a major program, so trivial events could assume massive significance to the individual concerned. This feeling of having had a revelation out of trivia is commonly reported by LSD-takers. The real risks, it seems, of LSD and similar drugs may not be in the arguable matter of chromosome damage, but rather in the sledge-hammer assaults on one of the brain's most important functions—the dream.

Epilogue

THE DREAMS OF COMPUTERS

THE JOURNEY INTO the *terra incognita* of our dreamscapes has been long and painstaking, one circumspect pace following another. To attempt the expedition at all has involved ridding ourselves of a certain weight of intellectual baggage, namely the physical, paranormal and psychological (especially Freudian) theories that have, in one combination or another, persisted for many centuries. This should have enabled us to penetrate the enigmatic nature of sleep and dreams more readily, even though the overall result of this attempt has surely been an enhancement rather than a diminution of the mystery. Sleep, and especially dream sleep, remains largely an undiscovered country. What the computer theory and some of the recent ideas discussed in this book provide are a few basic navigational aids for pushing deeper into the hinterland.

Several obvious lines of further investigation present themselves. Many researchers contend that depriving an individual of sleep and, more critically, of the opportunity to dream will of necessity have detrimental effects of one kind or another: on mental and physical health; on intellectual performance; on mood, and so on. Given the functions of dreaming inherent in the computer theory, one can readily appreciate why this should be so. One development we can hope to see emerge from the sleep laboratories in the future concerns the ways in which we might be able to engineer dreams for specific purposes by understanding the subtle, brain-creative expression suggested within the situations generated by dreaming. Clearly there are two sides to this enticing notion. We first have to know more about the nuts and bolts of our creative and intellectual life before we can go on to construct ideas to order; then we have to know how to perform the construction work, which means learning how to use a dream once dreamed. On this second point, the computer theory, with its program hypothesis, can be valuable as a means of analysing the content of dreams, though it may take a certain amount of self-training to view dreams in this novel way.

So far as understanding the mechanisms of the brain that are activated during our higher intellectual or creative moments are concerned, progress sometimes appears slow. But there is progress nonetheless. In the 1930s the father of modern neuroscience, Sir Charles Sherrington, spoke of the brain as an "enchanted loom," an imaginative evocation of the vastly complex menage-flashing action of billions of inter-communicating brain cells. Yet, however attractive such an image may be, it does not really tell us very much about the operational nature of the brain—not because it is generally wrong but because it is particularly vague. Like many other analogies, Sherrington's cerebral switchboard notion does not take into account the sheer variety of operations of the brain which the brilliant and influential biologist Professor J.Z. Young calls its "outstanding characteristic." Young is attracted by the idea that this diversity of operations may be explicable in terms of programs or rather sets of programs written into the genes and brains:

> Some of these programs may be called "practical" or physiological and they ensure that we breathe, eat, drink and sleep. Others are social, and regulate our speaking and other forms of communication, our agreeing, and our loving or hating. We also have long-term programs, those that ensure continuing not of ourselves but of the race, programs for sexual activity and mating, programs for growth, adolescence, and, indeed, for senescence (growing old) and dying. Perhaps the most important programs of all are those used for the activities that we call mental, such as thinking, imagining, dreaming, believing and worshipping.

It needs no further comment to draw parallels between Young's view of the brain programs and the computer theory of dreams. The two concepts interlock quite readily on their own. If dreaming — itself a "programmed activity"—is concerned with keeping vital programs in good order, we have a reasonable explanation for some of the striking phenomena associated with sleep, from the oddly unprotected cormorant dozing in the sun, to the recollection of the name of a watch unremembered during the day, to a dream about fish that fuses images collected from a variety of sources. If the computer theory is *not* applicable and dreaming serves some other function, then these are just a handful of experiences that any alternative theory will have to accommodate. As this book has shown, there are also very many more aspects of dreams that would have to be taken account of in any comprehensive counter-theory. No one idea can be "proved" in any conclusive way, but the computer-based theory accords best with the facts as we know them now. It is my belief that as more facts emerge from the sleep laboratories, as more is learned about the working of the brain, and as computers develop in sophistication, this basic theory will stand. Very recently Professor Francis Crick, Nobel Laureate for his work on determining the structure of the DNA molecule and a biologist who has been compared in stature to Charles Darwin, put forward a notion on the function of dream sleep which also has overtones of computer program "tidying up." Crick's idea is that dreams during REM sleep are necessary to rid the brain of unwanted or "parasitic" modes of behaviour. We dream, he argues, not so much to reinforce what we need to keep updated so much as to "unlearn" undesirable information. In a paper in the journal *Nature* (14 July 1983) Crick advances an interesting though admittedly speculative biological mechanism by which the brain might carry out this unlearning, and his point is helped by another paper in the same issue from a team at various American universities who have modelled the natural neural mechanism proposed by Crick on a computer. Whether or not Crick's view is accurate it does show a pre-eminent scientist regarding the brain during sleep as performing a necessary "housekeeping" function that cannot be done during the waking state and that this function can be simulated on a computer. One intriguing feature about the brain-computer analogy—and thus any attempt to draw conclusions about the two systems and make theories on that basis—is that we know exactly how one system works and remarkably little about the other—that which, paradoxically, we carry around with us every waking (and sleeping) moment of our lives. As computers move towards the Ultra-Intelligent Machine, it is not unreasonable to suppose that we can only learn more about the way our own brain-computers work. It might be argued that computers will be developed upon different lines, but on the whole that is unlikely: man will want his servant to have the same thought-processes he himself has. Anything else would, at best, be inconvenient.

Now, finally, imagine if you will a computer operator at the end of his day's work. Throughout the day he has been feeding information into the computer about such intriguing things as sales, orders, invoices, customers' accounts and so on. His last task is to switch the computer off-line and instruct it to run its routine end-of-day program. It now goes about its nightly task of updating programs and incorporating into them all the new information it has been given that day.

Leaving the computer asleep and dreaming, the operator goes home.

POSTSCRIPT

The central theme of this book—the computer theory of dreams—began to take shape in the mid-1960s when the late Christopher Evans, a psychologist alert to the potential of computing science, first published a couple of brief articles sketching the broad outlines of his intriguing notion. At the time these were received by sleep researchers as an interesting contribution to their growing stock of knowledge. The computer hypothesis seemed an eminently useful way of looking at sleep and dreams which had the added merit of being compatible with a good deal of current research into the hitherto largely inscrutable nature of our regular excursions across the landscapes of the night.

For Dr Evans himself, as friends and colleagues were aware, the next phase had to be the arduous slog to accumulate data against which to measure the computer analogy. Being duly scientifically cautious he was reluctant to rush into print in book form without a lot more research of the most circumspect kind. So more than ten years of work on and off had produced a draft of little more than half this book. His untimely death in 1979 cut short the endeavour.

When approached by his publishers and literary agent to complete the unfinished manuscript, my prevailing emotion was trepidation. How far is it possible to think oneself into the mind of another person, however well you know him (and we knew each other only as occasional professional acquaintances)? Then, how can one possibly predict how that person would have gone on to shape his thoughts? Although I had free access to his papers, notes and library, I saw no ready solution. There were a number of routes I might have justifiably taken. There was no map to guide me through the unfinished half of the book—the half in which the computer theory was to be delineated—beyond a skeletal synopsis of the most generalized kind. So I decided to abandon the obviously vain hope of thinking myself into Chris as it were, in favour of thinking through the theory and its ramifications for myself; an equally demanding task given the mighty weight of sleep research that had piled up in that intervening decade.

What has emerged is, I hope, true at least to the spirit of Chris Evans' intentions if, inevitably, removed from the letter of their expression had he been here to complete the project himself.

ACKNOWLEDGEMENTS: To Times Newspapers Ltd for permission to use material by Christopher Evans and Brenda Jones from *The Sunday Times* Magazine of 16th February and 30th November 1969; *New Scientist* and Keith Hearne for permission to quote from an article by Keith Hearne on Lucid Dreams; Yale University Press for extracts from *ESP: A Scientific Evaluation* by C. E. M. Hansel, and W. H. Freeman Ltd for extracts from *Some Must Watch While Some Must Sleep*. Extensive quotations are also taken from Christopher Evans' Oration "Dreams of Computers," delivered in 1974 to the Royal Society of Arts; his various surveys investigating dreaming have been published in *Destiny*, *Honey*, *TV Times*, *Wildlife* and *The Sunday Times* Magazine.

Grateful acknowledgement is made to Ted Newman for his contribution to the origination of the computer-based theory of sleep and dreams.

Finally, grateful thanks to Miss Stephanie Burton for her assiduously careful typing of the final manuscript.

PETER EVANS
London 1983

SELECT BIBLIOGRAPHY

The literature on sleep research and dreams is vast and ever-expanding. Below is listed a brief selection of some useful titles, some concerned specifically with dreams, others treating related topics such as ESP. Yet others are general introductions to an even broader topic, the workings of the human brain.

Blakemore, Colin, *Mechanics of the Mind*. Cambridge, New York: Cambridge University Press, 1977.

Chase, Michael (editor), *Proceedings of the Symposia of the First International Congress of the Association for the Psychophysiological Study of Sleep*. Los Angeles: Brain Research Institute, University of California, 1972.

Dement, William C., *Some Must Watch While Some Must Sleep*. San Francisco, Oxford: W.H. Freeman, 1974.

Diamond, Edwin, *The Science of Dreams*. London: Eyre and Spottiswoode, 1962.

Rene Drucker, Colin; McGaugh, James (editors), *Neurobiology of Sleep and Memory*. New York, London: Academic Press, 1977.

Faraday, Ann, *Dream Power*. London: Hodder and Stoughton, 1972.

Fisher, Richard B., *Brain Games*. London: Fontana, 1981.

Freud, Sigmund, (translated by A. Strachey), *The Interpretation of Dreams*. London: George Allen and Unwin, 1955 (3rd imp. 1967).

Hadfield, J.A., *Dreams and Nightmares*. London: Penguin, 1954 (1973 edition).

Hansel, C.E.M., *ESP: A Scientific Evaluation*. New York: Scribners, 1966.

Hartmann, Ernest L., *The Functions of Sleep*. New Haven, London: Yale University Press, 1974.

Hartmann, Ernest L., *The Sleeping Pill*. New Haven, London: Yale University Press, 1978.

Hill, Brian (compiled by), *Such Stuff As Dreams*. London: Rupert Hart-Davis, 1967.

Holroyd, Stuart, *Dream Worlds*. The Darsbury Press, 1976.

Hoskisson, Jack Bradley, *What Is This Thing Called Sleep?* London: Davis-Poynter, 1976.

Jones, Ernest, *The Life And Work of Sigmund Freud*. London: Penguin, 1974.

Kleitman, Nathaniel, *Sleep And Wakefulness*. Chicago, London: University of Chicago Press, revised edition 1963.

Lee, S.G.M.; Mayer, A.R. (editors), *Dreams and Dreaming*. London: Penguin Education, 1973.

Luce, Gay Gaer; Segal, Dr Julius, *Current Research On Sleep And Dreams*. US Dept of Health, Education and Welfare, NIH, Bethesda, Maryland.

Luce, Gay Gaer; Segal, Dr Julius, *Sleep*. London: Heinemann, 1967.

Meddis, Ray, *The Sleep Instinct*. London: Routledge and Kegan Paul, 1977.

Oswald, Ian, *Sleep*. London: Penguin, 1970.

Oswald, Ian, *Sleeping And Waking*. Elsevier Publishing Co., 1962.

Roche Products Ltd., *Medieval to 19th Century Interpretation of Sleep and Dreams*. 1966.

Roche Products Ltd., *Classical Interpretation of Sleep and Dreams*. 1966.

Rubin, F. (editor), *Current Research in Hypnopaedia*. London: Macdonald, 1968.

Rubin, F., *Learning And Sleep*. Bristol: John Wright and Sons, 1971.

Ullman, Montague; Krippter, Stanley; Vaughan, Alan, *Dream Telepathy*. New York: Macmillan, London: Turnstone Press, 1973.

Vernon, Jack, *Inside the Black Room*. London: Penguin, 1966.

Young J.Z., *Programs of the Brain*. Oxford, New York: Oxford University Press, 1978.

INDEX

by Richard Raper
of Indexing Specialists, Hove